Pedagogical Desire

Pedagogical Desire

Authority, Seduction, Transference, and the Question of Ethics

edited by
jan jagodzinski

BERGIN & GARVEY
Westport, Connecticut • London

KH

Library of Congress Cataloging-in-Publication Data

Pedagogical desire : authority, seduction, transference, and the question of ethics /
   [edited by] jan jagodzinski.
      p.   cm.
   Includes bibliographical references and index.
   ISBN 0–89789–765–X (alk. paper)
      1. Teaching—Psychological aspects.   2. Teacher–student relationships.
   3. Psychoanalysis and education.   4.   Lacan, Jacques, 1901–   I. Jagodzinski,
   Jan, 1948–
   LB1027.P3862   2002
   371.102'3—dc21   2001043010

British Library Cataloguing in Publication Data is available.

Library of Congress Catalog Card Number: 2001043010
ISBN: 0–89789–765–X

First published in 2002

Bergin & Garvey, 88 Post Road West, Westport, CT 06881
An imprint of Greenwood Publishing Group, Inc.
www.greenwood.com

Printed in the United States of America

∞

The paper used in this book complies with the
Permanent Paper Standard issued by the National
Information Standards Organization (Z39.48–1984).

10 9 8 7 6 5 4 3 2 1

10/25/04

To make oneself understood is not the same as teaching—it is the opposite. One only understands what one thinks one already knows. More precisely, one never understands anything but a meaning whose satisfaction or comfort one has already felt. I'll say it to you in a way you won't understand: one never understands anything but one's fantasies. And one is never taught by anything other than what one doesn't understand, i.e., by nonsense.

—Jacques Lacan, *Television*, xxvi

Contents

Acknowledgments

I wish to thank my colleagues who have contributed original essays to this collection to help advance a psychoanalytic understanding of pedagogy. In order of appearance I wish to thank: Gustavo for his energy and passion; Derek for his insightful political analysis; Douglas for his splendid role as provocateur; Robert for his always brilliant and succinct analysis; Marshall for his deep respect and empathy toward others; Kirstin for her patience and feminist insights; Mark for his generosity and openness; Betty-Anne for her deep commitment to the classroom; J. C. for his biting wit and political nerve; John for his critical stance toward technology; and Harry, who has never given up the "good" fight. Without you this statement could not have been made. My thoughts go out as well to those who wanted, but were unable to contribute to this collection due to the constant derailing that "life" brings. Their good intentions and support are duly noted and missed.

A Strange Introduction:
My Apple Thing

jan jagodzinski

Savoir

Not the ego **but** its lack
Not behavior **but** *jouissance*
Not imagination **but** fantasy
Not knowledge **but** ignorance
Not regurgitation **but** transformation
Not motivation **but** *objet a* as cause of desire
Not the exam **but** the subject in process and on trail

... so I cut the apple in half and discover the paradox of Nature staring at me in my face: seeds hidden in a vulva-like cavity waiting to be born! ... I am trying to draw an impossible *picture* (see above) to give a would-be reader of this book on pedagogy a sense of the Lacanian Real which, by definition, defies all description and representation. The Real is perhaps one of the more perplexing and difficult terms to grasp in the Lacanian lexicon, capitalized here to distinguish it from the "real" which already denies a Lacanian pun to play on their difference and sameness. I know already that the *picture* I am trying to present will be a failure, but I try anyway. Obviously, I have somehow "always-already" been "touched" by choosing an apple as a trope for this introduction. I have chosen it, and it, too, has chosen me. An apple supports a constellation of thematic meanings that might be usefully exploited to grasp pedagogical desire—a symbol for the transference of knowledge between teacher and student for one; a Biblical reference to forbidden fruit (knowledge and its accompanying *jouissance*) and Eve's "hysterical transgression" for another. The apple as Eve's gift—as blessing or curse—can be a location of deconstruction as the feminine Other works itself through masculine pedagogy; or even a marvelous dehiscence can be made between Cézanne's caressable apples and Apple's computer symbol as a way to explore postmodernism's embrace of digitalization. But what was *I* touched by? . . . And touched yet again after an intrusive, violent cut had been made to see what was inside?

Despite my cut, the mystery of the apple's embryogenesis—its reproduction and development—remains intact. The motive force, or primary cause behind its development—the agent responsible for the secret choreography of its life could not be found—nowhere to be seen. This apple, as my Other, resists giving up its secrets. Its very essence eludes me. Even if I were to further probe into the depths of its seeds by any number of contemporary technologies to determine its genetic structure, the choreography that structures an apple's life would still escape me. A remainder remains. "Something" eludes the visibly apparent ontogenetic development from seed to tree to fruit. The impossibility of the apple's total self-objectification, of its complete transparency, is *precisely* what makes the apple "real" to me. Now to pun: It is real because it is Real. Its very resistance—the mark of its secrecy, of its non-transparency, enables my imagination to constitute it, to "make it up," to construct it. We could say that this very resistance is what gives it *life*, what makes it unique and sensual. It lures my eye and I "light" it up. And what is this "life," this "light," if not an organic energy, a vital force that in higher sentient beings takes the form of Freud's libidinal sexual energy, better known as Lacanian *jouissance*; or perhaps Walter Benjamin's idea of the aura of the optical unconscious?

This is the place of the Lacanian Real, and the imagination cannot exist without the place of its *impossibility*. The Real, therefore, can only *show* itself; that is, *present* itself alongside my picture as a *site* [sight/cite] of its existence, as a by-product, a prelinguisitc or extralinguisitic dimension as something that escapes me, a pure unknowable specter. This unknowability of things (Kant's *noumena*) which *coexists* with our apparent knowability (*phenomena*) of things can be illustrated simply but dramatically. As soon as a mark is made on a sheet of paper, dividing one side from another, a border—an impasse or abyss—is formed. We can illustrate this rather easily by drawing a line (Figure I.1) and magnifying it X times (Figure I.2).

Figure I.1

Figure I.2

Our perception of the line is at once modified by the second figure. We see a crevice, a chasm which looks remarkably like a "cut" made by the stylus (pen, pencil) itself due to the "touch" of my hand. The "line weight" asserts a particular pressure. It demonstrates that a line is incapable of causing a simple dualism; rather, it creates a third space. In a "good," vibrant drawing this line dances around the figure according to the undulations of its weight, introducing the fluctuations of time into that very space. In this way, the figure comes "alive" by virtue of having it "stand out," "show" itself lit up through the vibrancy of its interior/exterior relationship. These, then, are the effects of a "thing's" unknowability, its Real. Its sensuous Being shows itself by site [*sight*] cite. As Lacan (1992) remarks, there is a "mystery" in the way Cézanne painted his apples (*S VII* 114, 141). These apples as *die Sachen* (objects) can be raised to "the digity of *das Ding*"— to the level of the Real and become an impossible (non)object of desire. Ordinary apples take on a certain "dignity." They become special, lit up. We see and desire them in a new and different way.

OBJET A OF PEDAGOGY[1]

My first pedagogical thought bubbles up. As teachers we love and *hate* our students for precisely what "shows" itself, what "stands out," what "vibrates" in them. As Lacan (1979) famously said, "*I love you, but, because inexplicably I love in you something more than you—the objet petit a—I mutilate you* (*S XI* 263). Silverman (2000), dwelling only on beauty of such a relationship, writes: "We confer this gift of beauty when we allow other people and things to incarnate the impossible nonobject of desire—when we permit them to embody what is itself without body, to make visible what is itself invisible" (17). Isn't it strange the way our "good" student can become "bad," instantly it seems, and vice versa? Or, the way they can "turn around" as the teaching year progresses? But the teacher could also become a "transitional object" (Winnicott) to the student—affectionately cuddled, excitedly loved—but also mutilated and then eventually discarded! Wasn't this Lacan's idea of successful therapy?

The psychoanalyst is hugged, mutilated, and then finally dumped! The student, like the analysand, is able to produce his/her own master signifiers and confront the "truth" of his/her own questions; to move from *the* answer given by the Master teacher to *an* answer given to the self where there is no guaranteeing Other. A separation has been achieved and the choices the student makes can only be decided on ethical grounds. As a teacher one never knows when such a point is reached, when the production of signifiers has been sufficient enough to arrive at a moment where they are no longer satisfactory and in their failure produce a new birth.

The mark, cut, or line, as in the above illustration, is a delimitation—a frame of perception to distinguish the inside from the outside, one side from another. Often when we look, we dwell on the starkness of difference, the border or frame that has been created enabling a differentiation to maintain itself, rather than on the paradoxical nature of the Real chasm which is formed as a by-product of such action. This chasm presents us with the paradoxes of a tensional hybridity if we only look at it awry, as when, for instance, one juxtaposes complementary colors together. For example, a certain red and green combination achieves a *Schein* (a glare), a vibration of vitality that achieves the pulse light of *jouissance*. Or, perhaps another combination of colors brings with it an abhorrence and rejection as the chasm issues forth a death cry. There is no logic of taste. Like love and hate, beauty and abhorrence coexist. In both cases the effect emerges from the depths of the in-between—the elusive Real, registered by the perceptual signifier—our look—which *can* make the effects of the Real affectively present and bodily felt. Primal impressions issuing from the Real seem to defy the order of the signifier as privileged by Lacan, as site, sight [*cite*]. They appear nonmediated, direct, like the "grain" of the voice (Barthes), its timbre and rhythm only as pulsation, the intensity and shade of color, the smell and taste of the "thing," *avant la lettre* as "something" that can only be sensed. But this "sense" is non-sense, atemporal, like Levinas's "instant," Freud's *fort*, and Lacan's master signifier (S_1), empty of meaning, like the zero, for instance. As Kristeva (1980, 280–286) claims, music is prior to the syntax of language acquisition. The expelling of sounds of pleasure and pain by the infant are a direct release of the drives—a "protomusic." The Real emerges from the holes, pauses, and cavities while perception awaits the achievement of meaning.

PEDAGOGICAL VOICES

I immediately think of the voice of the teacher. What gives It Its authority? Why does It compel me to listen? Why am I drawn into Its orbit? Its spell? When It speaks and touches, It does so from the very depths of my teacher's Being and seems to penetrate deep inside me where I am moved. Its "touch" seems immediate. Is this love? It is not *only* the meanings of her words—there is something else that hovers in and around them governed by a sublime incomprehensibility—something *excessive*, outside of the transparency of the words that are issuing from my teacher's mouth. If It seduces me—I am stirred, moved. It is melodious and I am swept away into Its song. But if It frightens me, makes me cower and anxious, that same voice becomes a *remainder*, a noise, a buzz in my head, a source of horror and terror. I become haunted by It. It keeps repeating inside my head. In both cases, the voice as *excess* and *remainder*, meaning has been eclipsed (see Žižek 1996b, 147–155). The voice is therefore both fascinating and deadly at once.

How this excess and remainder of the Real in the voice circulates as drive (*Trieb*) and/or desire has fundamental pedagogical consequences, for It establishes discipline, Logos or Law, as well as transgression, *which is the fundamental antagonism in education as exemplified by the many competing curricular ideologies*. As the *excesses* of the drive (i.e., Kristeva's "semiotic") when the subject (S) is no longer barred ($), It can be a transgressive hysterical voice of feminist pedagogies in Its insistence against the Symbolic Order. As an outLaw voice It refuses to accept the master signifiers (S_1) that are offered to It to complete Its identity formation, a refusal to identify fully with the object as to who she "is." It is a disruptive, dangerous, and shrill voice in the way It sounds to the established patriarchal institutions (Church, State, Medicine, Education, etc.), recalling the singing of the Sirens (Salecl 1998). However, this is a voice that enjoys Its own meaning as unsatisfied desire—It doesn't need the Other as such. It enjoys Its disruption as a self-consuming enjoyment which Lacan coined *jouis-sense* (enjoyment-in-meaning). But this is only half the story. It is a voice that tries to seduce the Other as well, to provoke the Other's desire for her, which will never be satisfied. "Am I a man or a woman?" plagues the hysteric so as not to buy into the system's signifiers. This *excessive* feminine pedagogical voice of the drive in regard to patriarchal Law presents a never-ending *insistence* regarding the foreclosure of feminine *jouissance* as being *outside* the Symbolic Order, like the complaint of Lilith, who was locked outside the Garden of Eden; that is to say, an access to a maternal genealogy of woman rather than the "murder" of the Mother in our current Symbolic Order (as developed by the writings of Luce Irigaray). These are Daughters answering their Fathers, insisting that a new symbolic relationship be formed with Mothers. Against the "supplementary" feminine *jouissance* Lacan theorizes, in *Seminar XX, Encore*, "complementarity" in all of its complexity that such a relationship could bring is searched for.

The *remainder* (and reminder, cf. Žižek) outLaw voice of the drive is exemplified by obsessive pedagogies like critical emancipatory education, often referred to as social constructivism (e.g., Trifonas 2000). Such a voice often appears heroic, noble, challenging, and revolutionary. It is troubled by the danger It sees of being seduced by the desire of the Other (i.e., global capitalism and the hegemony of instrumental reason). It rejects the seduction of such a sell. The strategy is to become the master of one's own desire, to set up an alternative desire (i.e., socialism, Green politics, etc.) to fill the lack which is never quite reached but which one is always on the road toward. The obsessive pedagogue is the hysterical necessary Other who represses hysteria in himself. Being an impossible desire this is a strategy to negate the Other's desire, and a way to become preoccupied with ways to complete himself, to fill the lack through his own self-sufficient *jouis-sense*; hence to challenge the Law from the fringe, as non-mainstream and on the edge. Faced with the death drive, "Am I dead or alive," the obsessional pedagogical voice strives to be in charge of the situation. The rigor of his preparation is never underestimated. Obsessionals make good academics and excellent scholars, since constant production is required to keep the desire of the Other at bay. This requires constantly mastering the desire of the Other and generating his own voice. Constant critique with rhetorical assimilation is one such strategy; the Other is recognized only as a thing that is useful to him so that his unity and wholeness is continually restored. The Other's *jouissance* (i.e., the way the Other enjoys) is continually being "stolen," appropriated, assimilated as a strategy of differentiation. In this way such a voice doesn't "fade," vanish, or become annihilated as a subject, which would happen if he "bought" into the Big Other's desire.

How is this driven voice a *remainder* (and a reminder) of the Real as related to the Law? The voice of the obsessional pedagogue is compelled to address the desire of the Other as Authority, as Law, as Logos which would otherwise overwhelm him, for he has rejected the desire It offers. This Authority of the Other (Lacan spoke of the Discourses of the Master and the University which are discussed in a number of the the chapters in this volume) *must* be recognized, otherwise the foreclosure of the Law would result in psychosis. He would become an outLaw in the most radical sense of the term—criminal, outside participation in the given order. His transgression remains tied to the Law. However, this relation to Authority is split, for this voice hears the Big Other "laughing," mocking, enjoying at the expense of others. It is greedy and gluttonous, wanting it All—an omnipotent Law, corrupt, evil, and totalitarian. This is the psychic "remainder" of being totally dominated by the Other as developed by Freud's myth of the patricide of the "anal father," and as experienced by the boy as Freud had shown through his analysis of the "beating fantasy." Such a critical pedagogical voice is that of a son addressing the "shadow side" of his Father (and of himself)—the Father of unbridled *jouissance*—raising the paradox of the superego itself, split as it is between a demonic agency which thirsts for domination, omnipotence, mastery, and control and the good, loving Father of social justice and equality.

Is this not, then, the structure of the Hegelian master–slave relationship governed by the phallic signifier (ø) of the Name-of-the-Father? (see esp. Benjamin 1988). It may be read that way; however, the death drive as played out in the struggle between justice and domination leads to criminal transgression only when the aggression (hate) has not been sublimated, turned into "democratic" rather than demonic forms which would channel *jouissance* in a creative (aesthetic) and ethical way; where what may result is an agonistic compromise—beautiful and elegant in its resolution rather than a continued antagonism. It becomes "ugly" and pathological when this doesn't happen.

In the tonality of the voice the student encounters the teacher's *jouissance*. Its grain is sex/gendered in the very complex tensionality that this dualistic word suggests: the Real of sex and the symbolic signifiers of culture as mediated by an Imaginary fantasy played out through the performativity of the body. Most hysterics are women while most obsessionals are men. They complement one another. The student, therefore, encounters the abyss of the teacher's desire. S/he finds a place within it, transfers love and/or resistance, by being silent for instance. What does my teacher want from me, anyway? Why is she making me do this? Why is he saying this to me? Why do I hate this teacher? His hygiene is so bad! The voices (and bodily smells) are grained by *jouissance* that unconsciously speak the student's desire, as s/he searches for completeness, love, and confirmation.

We should be reminded that schooling, be it public or private, is done by teachers *in loco parentis*. As such the sex/gender of a teacher is significant to the way pedagogical drive and desire circulate in and through the curriculum discourses that, to use Pierre Bourdieu's (1990) term, shape the *habitas* of education. If we characterize the dominant curriculum of schooling as being predominantly logocentric, heterosexist, and nationalistic, then its hegemony is maintained by the teacher as a structural placeholder within the accepted kinship structures which, economically speaking, reproduce and maintain, more or less, its stability through the countless ways any curriculum is reproduced. In this sense the two insistent drive positions described above meet up against two positions where the drives have already been sublimated under the Law of acceptable desire. The grain of the voice has already taken on symbolic meaning, screening the effects of the "semiotic drives" into self-assured, completed speech. Here, of course, I am referring to the Law of the Father that is already installed as curricular Authority mandated by the "will" of society (Big Other) which requires the vigilance of an oppositional pedagogy, as well as the position of the Phallic Mother which then erases sexual/gender difference (hence the vigilance of the nurturing Mother of the maternal breast), a position which predominates among feminist pedagogies.

There are then "two" Fathers and "two" Mothers—minimally four positions which could be fruitfully explored through a Gremasian "semiotic square" producing various logistic fantasies of pedagogic "holdings and handlings," to use Winnicottian (1982, 131, 153) terms, so as to generate a number of scenarios of possible transferences and counter-transferences in the pedagogical relationship read as the "family romance" of parenting (jagodzinski, 1996b). One can, for instance, imagine the phallic push of the finger behind a student's neck as s/he attempts something new and falls into the loving safety net of the Mother's arms should something go wrong; one can point to instances where kindergarten boys are able to bad-mouth a woman teacher as bitch and "dragon lady" to put her in her "place," predicated on the masculine fear of the all-powerful mother (Walkerdine 1986, 4); one can point to instances where sport is no longer a sublimated game to channel aggression but a coach's own sadistic desire to win at all costs caught up in the throes of his own deadly *jouissance*—the superego's devilish whisper of "Go ahead, do all that it takes to win, use all the dirty tricks that you know"; and one can also see the *collapse* of the "right" pedagogical distance into the space of a sensuous erotic relationship as teacher and student become lovers (see Campbell, Chapter 6 in this volume).

The matrix of possibilities, each defined by its own pedagogical distance, while not endless, would serve to map out instances from which we educators can learn the way our drive/desire circulates in relation to our *jouissance* (painful pleasure), to our sufferings and joys when teaching. *Our symptoms uniquely define each of us as teachers.* Some of us stay after class too long talking with our students, seemingly never coming home; others leave as quickly as they can, never paying attention to the voices they hear. Some of us continually worry that we are not "reaching" all our students, not meeting their needs and igniting their desires. We blame ourselves and suffer burnout. Our ego ideals are in conflict with what we thought the Other wants of us. We never seem to reach our wished for self-image. Idealization rather than sublimation defines our work, and we suffer terribly when we get the feeling that our principal, teacher's union, or school board has let us down (Vanheule, 2001). Yet, others seem oblivious to classroom dynamics, disavowing their responsibility to their students by hiding behind the "objectivity" of knowledge (see Bracher, Chapter 7 in this volume).

What is missing from the above discussion is the grain of the voice that is not allowed to be heard, a voice undetected, repressed, not given much of an ear in public schooling: the queer voice. This voice, from the position of the heterosexual Big Other, is misplaced—not in the proper body, discordant, threatening, and intolerable. Its gay feminine *excesses* and lesbian masculine *remainders* appear especially dangerous and unnerving since they throw the structural logistics of the pedagogical family romance into disarray. It exposes the suppressed eroticism that already circulates within those boundaries, for surely the fantasy is that gay and lesbian teachers are wildly promiscuous and will "infect" students with their erotic lifestyle. Raising children in a same-sex marriage undermines and stains the preserve of marriage as a site/sight/cite of procreation which, especially for the Moral Majority, now takes on the fantasies of perverse debauchery, the same moral corruption that would be carried into the classroom. Schooling *in loco parentis* as it is currently defined is exposed for what it fears most—namely, after Freud, the so-called "negative Oedipalization."

What, then, should be the voice of the teacher's call? Can the teacher escape these antagonisms that abound in education? The answer is "no," but there is a place from where the teacher should position him or herself in relation to these complex of transferences and counter-transferences that take place. In the Lacanian psychoanalytic transference the student's love for the teacher is initiated when s/he perceives in the teacher something that s/he doesn't have: namely, the *objet a*, the inexplicable "something" in the Real. The teacher is an Authority figure who is "supposed-to-know." The loving student presupposes that this object is in the teacher "more than in him/herself," creating the fantasy—the spell of transference. The proper response of the teacher under Lacanian suppositions is to insist there is *nothing* in him or herself that is worthy of love. *What the student falls in love with is the way that the teacher enjoys*—the way the teacher "gets off," her/his *jouissance*, which comes through the teacher's bodily comportment, voice, and gaze. *It is this eroticism which must be displaced elsewhere*, namely, to the "love" of the subject (the discipline), to literature, to art, or to the love of teaching itself (see MacCannell 1991, 76; McWilliam 1996, 134–135) but *never* to the bedroom (see Campbell, Chapter 6 in this volume). In brief, the eroticism must be channeled toward the student's own desire: *the objet a*. The teacher must *refuse* love since the object that is perceived in him/herself is a pure nothing, an emptiness. It is to be found elsewhere. The student misperceives where his/her desire lies. Hence the teacher must try to retain this emptiness since the student's transference usually emerges *only when s/he does not want to encounter his or her own desire*. Instead, s/he offers him/herself as the object of love to the teacher— as in "teach me," "fill me up with knowledge." By refusing this demand for love the teacher has to maintain the presentment of emptiness so that rather than returning love, the teacher might be able to return the student's desire in the form of the enigmatic *objet a* s/he seeks—in the subject matter, in the question, or in the search. This does not mean acting as some sort of inhuman sounding board. Rather, pedagogically this means knowing "not how not to transmit but how to *suspend* knowledge" (Johnson 1987, 85) and *displace eros*. This requires performing a speech act which Lacan (1998) coined "le mi-dire de la vérité," (*S XX*, 193), the truth can only be "half said." Such a suspension and displacement of knowledge allows for the analytic exploration of the *objet a* of fantasy, the cause of the passion, the question, the inquisition, the search, the fascination with the teacher in the first place. It enables the student to continue to deal further with his/ her own desires. Such a "not knowing" on the student's part (misperception of his/her love object) can be understood as a *negative* sense of ignorance (i.e., as result of unconscious repression). But ignorance can also be understood *positively* as well, as "the pursuit of what is forever in the act of escaping, the inhabiting of that space where knowledge becomes the obstacle to knowing" (Ellsworth 1997, 85), a coming to terms with one's own drives and the fantasy objects of desire. That is, to take *ownership* of them, for they define the Real of your identity (Bracher 1999c).

The impossibility of delimiting the apple as an object also means the impossibility for theory itself to control the object, of knowing it completely. All perception in this Lacanian sense is a *méconnaisance* (misrecognition), which itself retains a paradoxical stance. On the one hand, mis(recognition) enables multiple possibilities to happen, like the sensuous representations of Cézanne's apples, for instance, and other potential "misrecognitions" which decenter an apple's accepted associations and common meanings. This is the Imaginary's great strength, for there are multiple, perhaps endless possibilities for its representation, none of which would definitively give us the Real apple. Rather, each representation is a mask, a screen, a site/*sight*/cite that enables the apple to exist as an object of desire. Each representation captures "something" that escapes the object, something of its Real which it "screens." (I have an artist friend, Harold Pearse, who painted his dog every day for a year. The exhibition, "My Year as a Dog," showed 12 months—365 paintings of living with his dog, even, of course, when he was traveling and his dog wasn't with him.) On the other hand, mis(recognition) can also be interpreted as a necessary need to anchor down a signifier's meaning. This is its great weakness, for theory as a frame of containment stubbornly enables us to stereotypically and categorically perceive and name reality through master signifiers (S_1 in Lacan's lexicon), the *point de capiton*—/apple/. We see and act toward the object in particular, predetermined, set ways, thus "framing" our perception and limiting possibility. However, in the Hegelian sense, just as there is a "murder" of the thing through the *captionnage* of the signifier, there can also be a new creative birth of the thing, a *creatio ex nihilo* through a deliberate unhinging of its meaning (signification), to look at it anew, "to create from zero, a will to begin again" (Lacan *S VII*, 212). *Méconnaisance* is a door that can open both ways: it is janus-faced, looking one way toward desire and the other way toward the drives.

It is here that Lacan's distinction between the "look" and the "gaze" as developed in *S XI* (sessions 6–9) becomes particularly interesting, for it suggests that even the experience of a common apple can become a "strange encounter," as it was for me when I first cut into it. Lacan attributed the look to "natural" perception. That is, to the initiative and power of the subject as *moi*. This meant the ability to place people and things at a proper distance from the self, constitute them as objects at the ego's disposal. As such, the ego (as *moi*) has the capacity to continually misrecognize itself. The look more properly belongs to the working of the spectacular *imagination*. For Lacan the psychic register of the Imaginary also implies a framing by the limits of perception itself—by that which threatens the very stability of the ego. We can never occupy this zone outside framed perception, or "true infinity" in Hegelian terms; we can only perceive the illusionary false infinity of geometrical space. In other words, the Imaginary presupposes the inclusion of a *screened*, non-spectatory dimension which Lacan attributes to the unconscious Real, specifically naming it *object a*, a skewing of geometrical space into non-Euclidean possibilities of ex-timate space/time. The *imagination* remains confined to the preconscious *cognito* (I think), whereas Descartes' *cogito* (I am) is rendered as the subject of the unconscious. The *Je* becomes the "true" subject of the symptom.

When we come to the gaze our mastery over perception fails. Proper distance collapses as "something" is found not to be in its proper "normative" place. An ordinary apple can now become extraordinary. It stands out as *object a*, metaphorically speaking, as a bit of the Real. It has become either "too close" or unthinkably distant, "too far" away since the ego cannot grasp or contain it. It enters into the twilight zone of extimate space, a place of "impossibility." The experience is described as shattering of the ego's coordinates. Strangeness, uncanniness, and shock mark its effects. The *Je*, as the core of one's being, is directly affected by a psychotic moment where the object gazes or stares back. Lacan's memory of the sunlight beaming off the sardine can in the water during his summer vacation excursion with poor fishermen (as described in session 8) is presented as the paradigmatic example. Here Lacan's bourgeois sensibilities are dislocated. He does not fit in the tableau of the fisherman's lifestyle. He remains an imposter who does not belong on the boat with Petit Jean and the rest of the crew. It remained a "recollected" memory that only he, some 20 years later, was able to confront again in what can be identified as a classic example of Freudian *Nachträglichkeit* (deferred action).

René Magritte, as is well known, was one such artist who attempted to question and unhinge the capture of the signified by the signifier so as to place the viewer in an "extimate" position where the door is always quivering at the site/sight/cite of Lacan's three psychic registers, Real/Imaginary/Symbolic, respectively. The picture below, *Le Faux Savoir*, quotes Magritte on this possibility. The apple floats in a perfect Magritte-like blue sky that suggests the imaginary illusion of reality. The apple appears in an impossible space. It should not belong there, but somehow it does because of its "realistic" representation. At the place where the sun glistens on its surface appears the dark stain of the Real where no light penetrates—as represented by the figure of *Savoir*.

Le Faux Savoir

Such is what constitutes Lacan's notion of the Imaginary: imagination where "something" (*objet a*) has been excluded from perception which, nevertheless, (non)exists in a "warped" or "enfolded" space-time dimension where the inside/outside duality collapses into ambiguity and paradox. It is the (non)place of the unconscious structured by a both/and, neither/nor logic; an excluded middle where a part can seemingly be greater than the whole; where condensation and displacement are at work in nonlineal ways. The logic of this enfolded space/time is not well understood. It exists on the "other side" (*jenseits*) of both letter and number where, for instance, the mysterious and wondrous calculations and artistic achievements of savants defy any explanation. Its paradoxical, irresolvable dualisms, which define its non(territory)—masculine/feminine; beauty/ugliness; outside/inside; love/hate; sex/gender; nature/culture; absence/presence; death drive/life drive—butt up against deconstruction's very claim of endless semiosis—of Derridean *différance*; of the signifier's difference (spatial) and deferment (temporal)—defying any emerging *indécidables*; that is to say, terms that cannot be said to be one or the other because they either refer to the conditions under which such dualisms are possible at all, or because it is not possible to say that they are (or are not) one or the other of the two terms. Instead, Lacan presents us with another anti-dualism: the maddening deconstructive logic of the impossible gap between them as represented by the lozenge form (<>) of his mathemes; the "k(not)" of their coexistence and complementarity, subtly demonstrated through the rhetorical play of his performative and stylistic teachings where, when any one assertion is posited, ambiguity, indeterminacy, and evasion are immediately introduced into the signifier so as to defy its certainty. Certainly, no term more so than the phallus (ø) has received such endless debate as to its transcendental status in his system, yet its very status was continually "unhinged" from its mooring throughout Lacan's career, both veiling and unveiling itself, at once agentic, authoritative, and fraudulent—just like its locutor. Its descriptive/prescriptive status was always left wanting, in flux, blinking in and out of existence, neither here nor there.

Yet, the distance between both Lacan and Derrida's deconstructive strategies is itself an impossible gap. Each theorizes interiority/exteriority—fundamental presence/absence in a complementary fashion. And if *différance* and its synonyms (invagination, arche-writing, dissemination, hymen, iterability, supplement, parergon, and trace) are not concepts in the traditional sense, neither are Lacan's mathemes of Other, screen, *objet a*, A, phallus (ø), and so on, which present and hide at the same time, and cannot be grasped once and for all. They are like the "black holes" of his thought out of which their definitions disappear and reappear in new guises, doing and undoing new theoretical work.

For Derrida of *The Post Card* (1987, 123–124) the letter (signifier) may never arrive to complete its message (signified) but may be lost in the limitless folds of *différance* or laid waste in the *poste restante* (dead letter office). Whereas for Lacan the letter will always eventually arrive to deliver its message, to complete its signification—as the haunt of death until a "proper" burial is given to its unanswered insistence.[2] If Derrida's deconstruction can be said to be a son addressing the void of his Mother, as Spivak (1983) suggests, then Lacan is a son addressing the "cut" of the Name-of-the-Father. One might risk the claim that Derridean deconstruction is life-enhancing in this respect, prolonging possibilities and opening up new ones, while Lacanian "passion" for the signifier is tragic and death inducing. But both have to be taken into account, for one doesn't exist without the other.

THE APORIAS OF PEDAGOGICAL CROSS-DRESSING AND CROSS-SEXING

The practice of pedagogy is also a question as to how much "cross-dressing" and "cross-sexing" is allowed when the fundamental antagonism between masculine and feminine is taken into account (jagodzinski 1996a; see also Aoki, Chapter 3 in this volume). The question of identity politics, which surrounds sexual difference in educational discourses, is of utmost importance. This can be both frustrating and challenging since, for Lacan, sexual difference has nothing to do with anatomy per se. Man/Woman as desiring subjects are not equivalent to Male/Female in any straight and forward way. Embodiment becomes a question of the way unconscious desire is set in motion, which can be and often is in contradiction to the subject positions assigned by the Symbolic Order. Desire and identity are never completely settled and collapsed into one another.

For Lacan, sexual difference is the Real of a fundamental antagonism. Masculine and feminine—*as logical positions*—are irretrievably separated and deadlocked, defined as different kinds of relations to the Symbolic Order. Sexual difference treated as binaries (active/passive, rational/irrational, reason/emotion) always *fails* for there is no signifier for sex in the unconscious. *Every* culture structures a myth to explain the incomprehensible gap which exists between sex/gender (Moore 1997). The Oedipus complex happens to be the West's variant, while the yin/yang of Tao is the East's. Both of these unconscious psychic structures emerged as patriarchal genealogies supplanted matrilineal (perhaps matriarchal) ones, and have consequently subordinated women's relationships to men's and are subject to change (Goux 1992; Laqueur 1990).

Lacan's "formulae of sexuation" (*S XX*) address the riddle of sex (Fink 1995, 98–125). Masculine and feminine positions are theorized as "closed" and "open" contradictory systems respectively, governed by asymmetical logics.[3] They articulate two separate responses in the way language "fails" to signify sex, posing questions that are forever unsettled and unsettling. The impossible chasm between them is breached only at the level of fantasy—in the Imaginary, through love.

In a nutshell, masculine logic as a closed system of order addresses how a certain Particular is able to claim to be a/the Universal by being extracted from the system (as -1), yet seemingly remaining in it. This element has a paradoxical existence of being both in and outside the system at once, in the Real. An erasure of this constituting master signifier (S_1) takes place to enable the system to enclose itself. Its apparent "openness" is a *conditional* one, based on what Hegel identified as a "false" infinity rather than a "true" one. This means the All as the Symbolic Order (or Big Other) refers to symbolic norms *as well as their transgressions*. Masculine logic is caught by the transcendental phallic signifier (Φ) and defined by a *phallic or symbolic jouissance* associated with the play of the *signifier*. It is entirely caught by the symbolic, locating its desired *objet a* on the side of the feminine Real—in the non-All. The dominant reading of this position is to claim that in Western discourse the allegory of "truth" for Man is Woman, and its correlate stated negatively: Woman is the absence of truth, which is the truth of castration.

Feminine logic is structured by an asymmetry. Feminine logic addresses the particularity of the phenomenal world, the heterogeneity of phenomena (Particulars) that are accessible to sensible intuition. In the attempt to grasp the real existence of objects as a whole from *within* the system, the antinomy of "non-All" of the phenomenal field emerges. Despite there being no object (Particular) given in intuition which does not belong to the phenomenal field of particularities, there are no assurances to say that there isn't one. The "All" is never complete, hence the system remains open. It is "non-All." Feminine logic always requires the addition of yet another element (+1, some Particular) to the seemingly closed field. As an additive operation (as against the masculine logic's subtractive one), it is the inherent *inconsistent* character of the phenomenal field—as opposed to masculine logic of *incompleteness* of the noumenal one—which is at issue.

Both logics are governed by Lacan's notorious notion of the symbolic phallus (Φ) differently and asymmetrically, which has caused so much controversy (see Campbell 2000 for a review). Each side is subject to castration, which in the broadest sense means giving up the narcissist claim to the complete fullness of Being. Some *jouissance* must be given up to enter the Symbolic Order. The most important aspect of Lacan's explication of feminine logic is its asymmetry with the masculine one. Woman has a *dual relation* both to the phallus (Φ) and to the signifier of the lack/and or desire that exists in the Law, (written as S (Ø), meaning lack/desire in the Other) which is said to be "beyond" the phallus—non-phallic *jouissance* is possible. If she so chooses to subject herself to the phallic signifier, and define herself in relation to a man through a *masquerade*, she remains, according to Lacan, an *hommosexuelle*,[4] subject to masculine desire. This is where feminists of all persuasions have objected to such a characterization as being precisely where women is said to "lack." By "being" the phallus her subjectivity comes only in the form of seductive performativity (i.e., a protective masquerade of appearances).[5] The *femme fatale*, especially, becomes the dangerous creature who, by dropping her masquerade, is able to derail masculine desire, but at the expense of being punished by the Law. Surprisingly, it is at this "limit" position of Woman where a theorist like Žižek (1991) identifies as to exactly where a supplementary non-phallic *jouissance* "beyond" the Law emerges. Such a surplus *jouissance* pertains to the drive (*Trieb*), a satisfaction *not* concerned with or disregarding the phallic order. This is the point reached where the masquerade seems to "turn in on itself," for the *femme fatale* "presents a 'pure' nonpathological subject fully assuming *her own* fate" (p. 66). Becoming a subject means risking "symbolic death" (being placed outside the Symbolic Order). In unmasking herself, the *femme fatale*, demands the recognition of her subjectivity. The man has but two attitudes when facing such a woman. He can either reject her or identify with her "symptom" as her ethical complaint against the Symbolic Order, exposing its lack. This later decision seals his own fate.[6]

If Irigaray's (1993) project is to escape the phallic transcendental signifier by developing a contradictory *female* syntax, Lacan's asymmetry of feminine logic attempts to preserve nonidentity and the possibilities of cross-dressing and cross-sexing. Feminine logic escapes the phallic function just as long as it remains an open infinite set. The paradox here being that the phallic castrating function (Φx) must remain operative "in the last instance" otherwise the subject would become psychotic, locked out from the Symbolic Order. Woman is capable of such a supplementary *jouissance* "*without losing its reference to castration*" (Zupančič 2000a, 295). However, should some Particular singular (+1) become a Universal, it seems to me the phallic function comes into play in this "last instance," for feminine logic has inversely mirrored a masculine one (e.g., the historical moment when feminism spoke for *all* women). A new "regime of truth" in Foucault's sense is established. But in this scenario, the "beyond" of the phallus suggests that it is *only* "in the last instance" where the phallic Law is *truly* challenged. She remains self-sufficient, not needing the Other only to a point. The creation of a new master signifier (S_1) in a "true" and not spurious sense is when the addition of another element (the +1 *as* S_1) restructures the entire system to become a "universal singularity" (ibid., 287–290). *An evagination or implosion takes place.* It is no longer *some* Particular but a Singularity (*Einzelheit*) that is the cause. This is an ethical *act* proper for Lacan; the singularity (*Einzelheit*) of Antignone's act (S VII) is taken as a paradigm case, whose *até* (madness or drive) places her in between "two deaths," a place that, in effect, questions the entire symbolic system. Antigone, in this sense is already "dead," in all the nuances of meaning that this brings. The feminine *jouissance* of such a singular Universal is sublimely beautiful—both horrific and blissful at the same time, as well as traumatic. This is why Žižek (1999, 247–312) can accuse Butler of not recognizing an ethical *act* proper that escapes the limits of the Symbolic Order. But at what price?[7]

Non-phallic feminine *jouissance* points to Hegel's "true" infinite as opposed to his "false" or "spurious" (masculine) infinite, or to what Žižek (1996b, 91), following Lacan, identifies as Cantor's "transinfinite" object. We enter a realm where the satisfactions of the drive (as "pure desire")— outside the Law as opposed to desire (and its transgressions) still caught within the Law—are operative. We also enter perhaps the most difficult and dangerous of territories when it comes to sociopolitical and ethical change that could be considered for education since such challenges to the Law are stalked by the "death drive." Each "singular" incident of transgression of an ethical act *proper* in the realm of freedom brings with it an unexplainable event that changes the course of history, or the "singularity" of one's existence, a transformative experience in the proper sense when one's or a society's fundamental fantasy that holds its Being is traversed.

Such a radical act also raises the question of "radical evil" (Copjec

1996; Žižek 1993, 83–124), for at the heart of an act of free will lies the contradiction that Kant at first identified and then avoided in the superego itself. Non-phallic *jouissance* is subject to the very ethical conflict that lies at the heart of being a "split subject" (*$*). For Kant, *Wille* referred to our moral conscience which was still under the Law. Guilt here appears as a reminder that there *is* a Law, that is the only way we know of its existence. In contrast *Willkür* is the very limit of *Wille*, the place where we are never sure if we want to obey our inner conscience or not. This is when the superego tells us simply to "enjoy" the fullness of our *jouissance*. It puts us on the edge of freedom (free will proper), for it confronts our choice of "no choice" under the Law. The "choice of the Worst changes the very standards of what is good and bad" (Žižek 1999, 307 n.25).[8]

Closely entwined with the "subjective destitution" of the act described above is the supplementary feminine *jouissance*, which comes through the sublimation of the drives as "pure desire" through artistic means where full satisfaction is achieved (Dean 2000, 275–278; Fink 1995, 115). The "genius" artist in this sense is "driven" to create a new master signifier (S_1), either as its own embodiment or as the output of the work itself. Through this work of love the artist discovers the relationship to "*das Ding* somewhere beyond the Law" (Lacan *S VII*, 84), through a striving which can equally be placed "between two deaths."[9] Lacan's purposeful neutral naming of *das Ding* (the Thing), taken from Freud, refers to *Life* itself (and not just to the Mother as is often interpreted), as the nonsublimated life-substance of the drives, pure libido which he called *lamella*. The ordinary object is raised to "the dignity of the Thing" but at a cost. The attempt is to reach an impossible mythical first satisfaction of an undivided subject (S) of the primary fantasy. Artistic sublimation which is so "driven" reaches a point where it can turn into its obverse: a desublimation experienced as a desexualized zone, subject to mysticism and ecstatic states of bliss and horror. There is a certain hysteria attached to this feminine *jouissance* in its striving to become a full subject; for it promotes the idea that subjects are all alike and equal beyond the Law. *It cancels out sexual difference.* The *lamella* as an "organ-without-body" is beyond sexual difference, a necessary myth to keep the fundamental notion of justice open.[10]

Butler's position of mimetic performativity of identity as developed through her numerous writings (1990, 1993, 1997, 2000) is where the Lacanian Real is most emphatically challenged and dismissed. Butler does away with the Real, collapsing the sex/gender distinction into Imaginary (performativity) and the Symbolic Order (performance) only. Heteronormativity polices desire and identification (i.e., wanting the other and wanting to be the other) along strict dualistic lines. Same-sex desire and identification become the abjected and excluded other. Butler's ruse has the advantage of "short-circuiting" previous discourses of essentialism and social constructivism (where the subject was theorized merely an effect of social conditions) by introducing the possibility of not reiterating the norm or code that both constitutes the subject and reproduces the symbolic law.

Butler's theory of performative mimesis both opposes and challenges the Lacanian split-subject and supports Foucault's poststructuralist subject of discourse as the practice of a "technology of the self." The question of a psychoanalytic ethics (*S VII*), where the subject assumes a position as a cause of his or her desire so as to be able to deal with one's symptomatic *jouissance*, is replaced by an identity politics informed by Foucault's power/resistance couplet. The formation of subjectivity (ego) is understood along *early* Derridean lines of Austin's performative speech act where the value of force supercedes the authority of truth, while the "constitutive outside" refers to exclusionary positions formed in difference as a way of negotiating the dialectics of inside/outside as to what does and does not belong to the self, and what is and is not abjected from it. Her theory of melancholia (1990) of same-sex loss is a ruse to show that heterosexuality is an established norm *before* the incest taboo; while her notion of the lesbian *imaginary* phallus as fetish (1993, 57–92), largely indebted to De Lauretis's (1994) own theoretical formulations, serves to displace and de-center Lacan's *early* formulation of privileging the imaginary phallus (ø) in the 1950s with the possibility of having *any* body part (breast, clitoris, hips, and so on) become the phallic fetish. This is a formidable and powerful position.

Both Dean (2000, 174–214) and Žižek (1999, 247–312) have criticized Butler's misunderstanding of the Lacanian Real and her misconceptions of the "constitutive outside" in an attempt to defend Lacan and rescue the importance of the Real of sexual difference. Dean (192) points out that the "constitutive outside" as theorized by Butler (and by implication *early* Derrida) is not consonant with Lacan's own position: "The non-ego is not to be confused with what surrounds it, the vastness of the [R]eal" (*S XI*, 245). By eliminating the unconscious Real in *Gender Trouble* and *Bodies that Matter*, subjectivity becomes reduced to the imaginary and symbolic level. In *The Psychic Life of Power* (1997, 86–87) Butler attempts to rescue this elision of the unconscious by rethinking Foucault's notion of the "soul" as the psyche which includes the unconscious *as well as the ideal ego*. It is the unconscious in the psyche which resists normalizing discourses. But, as Žižek (1999, 265–269) points out, this ruse fails to account for the *jouissance* associated with resistance itself. The painful pleasure of transgression requires a different understanding of the superego than the one Butler offers, where it is defined as a mediating agency between the imaginary ideal ego and symbolic ego ideal. The Lacanian superego is attached to the choices that trouble *jouissance*. The burden is placed on *an act of freedom*. The subject is caught between acting on one's own fundamental fantasy—in this case the *jouissance* of masochistic resistance that defines the Real of desire which sustains being as long as it remains foreclosed and repressed—or accepting the subjectivization (symbolic identification) that is offered by the Big Other. Conscience is always plagued by indecision and undecidability because of this uncompromising position. Should I? Shouldn't I? In the final analysis, there is no knowledge to rely on to make a sure decision. To traverse this fundamental fantasy is to undergo a "subjective destitution." In contrast, performativity does not get at the *jouissance* of unconscious desire that sustains being. Rather, by consciously identifying the contradictions between ideal ego and ego ideal (as mediated by Butler's definition of the superego) through different performative iterations, it simply recycles and reconfirms the *jouissance* that supports the being of transgressivity in the first place. From this Žižek can claim that performativity is not an authentic *act* in the Lacanian sense. It is not a true *act of freedom* which more properly belongs to the Real and "beyond" the Law, but inadvertently as an identity politics in opposition to dominant heterosexuality simply reconfirms the binary that is already in place. Rather than metaphorically displacing the symbolic Law, it is only reconfigured and not radically changed. Performativity fails to engage the *objet a* of unconscious desire by remaining as a contradictory dialectic between the ego (Imaginary) and the superego (formulated as the Symbolic Order).

To unhinge Butler's claim that the primordial foreclosure to homosexuality leads to the constitution of the melancholy heterosexual subject as opposed to the homosexual subject who is able to mourn the same subject loss by finding substitutes for it in the external world, Žižek (1999, 269–273) questions the logic which emerges when the claim that the heterosexual subject overcomes same-sex loss through an identification and incorporation of the lost sex—man for the boy, woman for the girl—is taken seriously. Does the masculine melancholy heterosexual identification, Žižek queries, result because of desiring another man as a man? (the homosexual resolution), or does it take place because of the desire to be a woman who is then desired by a man (the transsexual resolution), or yet a defense against the fear of becoming a woman (the heterosexual resolution)? It seems the possibilities are ambiguous and undecidable. Sex, when left to the Imaginary and Symbolic levels where it becomes a "positive" identity defined in opposition to the other sex in various ways as homosexual or heterosexual, leads to a claim saturated with ambiguity. Lacan reads "loss" not in terms of the differentiated sexual difference of identity politics, but as the "loss" of possibility of ever closing masculinity and femininity once and for all. By interpreting sexual difference in terms of identity politics, Butler, like her counterparts Dollimore (1991) and Edelman (1994), once again inadvertently equates (and thereby affirms) sexual difference with the heterosexual norm they are trying to topple.

For theorists like Dean (2000) and Champagne (1998), Lacan is already a queer theorist through his radicalization of *objet a*, which leaves identity an open issue. Freud as well can be radicalized by taking his claim concerning "perverse polymorphous sexuality" seriously (SE 7, 145, 220; see also Shepherdson 1994). As soon as a "body" is attached to perversion in terms of a queer identity, *it loses its subversive effects*. "The pervert does not exist except as an ideological construction, an imaginary misrecognition" (Dean 2000, 246). By aligning sex with the unconscious it always remains "refractive, maladpative and always, to some extent perverse" (245).

Lacan and Butler present contrasting positions on the question of sex/gender: radical non-identity against radical identity of mimed performativity, with contrasting politics and ethics. These intricacies surrounding sex/gender lie at the very heart of schooling which is shaped by heteronormativity, where sex/gender along dualist lines of male/female remains in place and where cross-dressing/cross-sexuality is not tolerated and often policed. Despite the complexities that I have briefly outlined, Copjec (1994b) must still rely on the tendencies of the two sex/genders to fall one way or the other in relation to desire and identity.

[T]he male subject is more apt to seek a resolution [to his desire] in the impostures of masculinity—that is, in the deluded belief that there might be a universal without exception—while the female subject is more likely to look for a solution [to her desire] in the masquerade of femininity—that is, in the misguided belief that the particular can forever evade inclusion in the universal, in public space. (p. 5)

In terms of teaching authority, this suggests that the masculine position is most often *heroic* (which incorporates the factors of race and ethnicity) as typified by any number of Hollywood narratives (*To Sir with Love, Teachers, Stand and Deliver, Stand by Me, Dead Poets Society*, and so forth). But it is one where phallic power is typically *fraudulent* (most often dressed in a suit) and needs to be continually recuperated because of its failure to sustain any claims to omnipotence, commensurability and universality. The heroic teacher (-1) who stands outside the system cannot sustain his assumed authorial status indefinitely. An impasse is always reached. The teacher is not a Master. Yet, he must ethically attempt to act as though he has the "last word" in the belief that he is being as comprehensive as possible. Should something escape him, he tries to account for its exceptionality, to bring it in to a universal space of comprehension. The Discourse of the University, one of the four discourses Lacan discusses in *S XVII*, places the teacher as someone who is always involved in "second-hand" knowledge (S_2)—knowledge whose initial production (as S_1) must be disavowed (Salecl 1994; see also Samuels, Chapter 4 in this volume).

A masculine ethic would continually perform an ideology critique, attempting to displace master signifiers for more just ends. However, there are moments of sheer heroism when the masculine sublime seems to achieve a subjective capacity to outstrip nature itself, where the drive (as "pure desire") is to establish a master signifier *ex nihilo* to ground a new school. The teacher as a rebel or an artist speaks to a Universal singularity of such an ethical act. How else are we to understand a figure like A. S. Neil (1969) and his radical philosophy of raising adolescents in *Summerhill*? Or someone like Jaime Escalante (jagodzinski 2001), or Lacan's grounding the *École freudienne de Paris* (Freudian School of Paris) by resorting to a simple tick? (Roudinesco 1997, 309–310). Can these be read as ethical acts proper "beyond" the Law in their singularity?

The counterpart to the heroic masculine teaching position of heteronormativity are the conflicting subjective positions between the performative masquerade of feminine pedagogy and the nurturing mother. The "phallic mother" or "bearded lady" makes her appearance in the primary and elementary classrooms as the conflict between nurture and discipline emerges when the boys attempt to put the woman teacher in her "place" (Walkerdine 1986). The "truth" of this stereotype was represented in the comic strip *Calvin and Hobbes*, where the phallic teacher regularly appeared as an elderly lady holding the phallic pointer. (Miss Grundy from *Archie* comics is yet another exemplar.) Although the nurture/discipline conflict—the smile and the frown—is never fully resolved, the feminine masquerade becomes more predominant in the upper grades.

To achieve the "right" distance with her students, the female teacher is not to be seen as a sexually desirable object; hence a certain asexuality and professionalism in dress and style mark the signifiers of authority along masculine lines. Respect, order, superior knowledge, and status come with these signifiers of performativity of a "man" in drag. At its extreme, some all-girl schools go as far as miming boys' school uniforms, where plain skirts replace pants. The all-female staff is required to wear white shirts and a tie. Feigning the phallus can also take the form of displaying complete confidence and control of knowledge, always being well organized, well prepared, and competent. Scholarship supercedes popularity.

In contrast to the nurturing mother, the masquerade of sexuality—playing with the phallus—presents its own dangers. Even the Barbie doll as student teacher (Weber and Mitchell 1995, 110–114; see also Couture, Chapter 9 in this volume) is presented as a dutiful teacher, a "saviour" who helps girls overcome their problems of belonging and eating disorders. Here it is feminine seduction as opposed to masculine power that collapses the "right" pedagogical distance, and the teacher tips easily onto the side of the bitch and *femme fatale* to be punished. The "good" breast of nurturance becomes the "exposed" breasts of the "bad" teacher (Gallop 1995). A film like *Dangerous Minds* (John N. Smith, 1995) presents Mich-

elle Pfeiffer's character, LouAnne Johnson, as the woman whose authoritative control of male students comes through seduction. Both "being"
and "having" the phallus come together in the fantasy of her being an ex-
marine capable of taking care of herself physically, as well as wearing
sexy sartorial attire accompanied with the right flirtatious body comportment.

Feminists of all persuasions have tried to present a hysterical discourse
that struggles to formulate new master signifiers consonant with a
woman's teaching culture that opposes the feminized masculine one. Can
those feminist pedagogical discourses based on caring and nurturing (e.g.,
Noddings 1981) that form a new ethics overcome the "feminized" classroom that is already in place? Irigaray's own problematic would support
such an attempt. In this regard it is rare to see a film like *Music of the
Heart* (Wes Craven, 1999) which demonstrates a supplementary feminine
jouissance. Roberta Guaspari (Meryl Streep) is "driven" to establish a
violin school in New York where each and every child is given the chance
to play in the orchestra. There are moments when the school's funding
would fail and Guaspari suffers her own "subjective destitution" in the
attempt, for she is given no support by those administrators in charge. Yet,
with the help of a network of community support, the school's music
program eventually becomes a reality.

The duality of sex/gender that hegemonically circulates in schools—
between masculine "hard" subjects like the sciences and feminine "soft"
subjects like the arts; between abstract, neutrally delivered knowledge of
technology and experiential relational bodily knowledge; between mind
and body—are certainly under constant challenge by educators. The broad
issue of questioning the "labeling" that goes on in schools (Hudak and
Kihn 2001) is part of the attempt to continually unhinge the categorical
signifiers which deny children from becoming full ontological subjects. A
psychoanalytically informed queer pedagogy in its most disruptive sense
is an ethics and politics of the struggles against normative notions of
identity and desire. Sex as a "calling" (Taubman 2001) needs to be made
more inclusive our schools. The logical paradoxes between masculinity
and femininity as the Real of sexual difference need to retain their antagonism in order to change the deep psychic structure of phallogocentrism
in the future anterior.

Lacan's neologism for the unthinkable territory of radical anti-dualism
was *extimité* (extimacy) (Evans 1996, 58; Miller 1994), a non-Euclidean
topology which presents a paradoxical, intersubjective structure where the
inside and outside turn on each other to create a confusion of opposites.
This was illustrated dramatically by Lacan's teaching through such figures
as the möbius strip, the torus, the inverted figure eight, the famous Bor-
romean knot, and his "mathematical" excursions into set theory and Fre-

gean numeration to grasp the elusive "language" of the unconscious (Fink 1995, appendixes 1 and 2; Miller 1977–1978). Lacan's similarities and precursory affinities with the topology of quantum theory, fractal spaces, and the "strange attractors" of chaos theory have been duly noted, explored, and applied, for example, to law and criminality (Milovanovic 1992, 1997). This structure of extimacy presents an approach to the paradox of "something"—of Being rather than Nothing—at the very "center" of our subjective world as a result of its very *exclusion* from both our imagination and signification. "[P]osited as exterior . . . something strange to me, although it is at the heart of me, something that on the level of the unconscious only a representation can represent" (Lacan 1992, 71). "That" which is most intimate inside us is, at the very same time, the most secretive; "that" which is most hidden is also "that" which is most strange, exemplifying, once again, the paradoxical logic of the Freudian unconscious characterized as being both at once *heimlich und unheimlich*. It is this alterity which is Other, but not only in myself, in the object as well. Lacan is attempting to theorize something outside ordinary discursive existence. Something ex-ists because it lies at a discursive limit, yet we can only get at it from within the very intimacy of discourse itself. The apple becomes the very structure of representation in my failure for it to be thought, which is the failure, impossibility, or impasse of cognition itself. In Lacan's lexicon this unconscious, nonspecular alterity is the psychic register of the Real, of the unconscious, and goes by the name of *das Ding*, and its antinomous forms as *objet a*.

FETISHISTIC SPLIT

So, what use is such theorizing to education? Derridean deconstruction, of course, has been fruitful in dismantling master signifiers (S_1) and unraveling the secondary significations they support (S_2 in Lacan's lexicon) by attending to the "constitutive outside" of what has been excluded. Pedagogically, however, there is left a perplexing question which psychoanalysis attempts to address. Why is it, for instance, that despite the exposure of a category's discursive overdetermination, the tendency to hold onto a myriad of "irrational" essentialisms is not diffused? For instance, the treatment of students simply as "empty vessels," as objects, or as just "statistics" as a longstanding educational practice refuses to go away, despite the multiple critiques of the damage that this causes. Why this compulsion to repeat? Or, why perpetuate the notion that the most valuable knowledge is what is practical and testable? Again, why hold onto such a value, given that it has been exposed for its narrowness? Is there something about power and control which, despite deconstructive critique, still holds reign over our behavior? The belief in "woman" as man's Other, in the worst-case scenario, has her deemed as male property, which justifies physical and mental abuse. Despite the Law, the abuse of women persists.

All such irrationalities have been deconstructed. But why do we continually repeat and update curriculum theory that reproduces subject positions that objectify students through evaluative standards of control? Or, recycle curriculae that are insensitive to ecological issues? One should think that, by now, with the continued emphasis by educators on Foucaultian discursive analysis, Derridean deconstruction, feminist pedagogies, and critical social theory, such educational practices and policies have been sufficiently exposed for their ideological racist, class based, sexist, patriarchal shortcomings. However, pointing out inconsistent and irrational behavior does not automatically lead to change. Mere knowledge at the level of the meaning of inconsistent behavior seems to do little to disrupt established patterns of behavior. As behaviors these are social symptoms which are manifested through the unique character (symbolic universe) of each individual teacher, for a subject is socialized as an individual through the process of imaginary and symbolic identification; (i.e., through the introjection of common social signifiers). An engagement with Lacanian psychoanalysis points to the Real of our subjecthood, *our internal antagonism* which is subject to our own extimate blockage, our own *jouissance*. Not only is there an impossible gap between the curriculum as planned and the curriculum as lived; there is a further impossible split within the curriculum as lived itself. The teacher may well *know* that s/he lives in a patriarchal, discriminatory society where boys in the classroom are more privileged than girls; where African-American students and First Nations students are less privileged than their "white" counterparts; where homosexual and lesbian students are really OK and just like any other student; and where much of what s/he does on a daily basis contributes to an impending ecological disaster. Nevertheless, s/he *believes* that in *this* class boys and girls are all equally treated; that in *this* class there is no discrimination; that the gay/or lesbian student is "different" but that's tolerable just as long as they keep it to themselves; and that the Earth will take care of itself because, after all, Nature is infinitely flexible. In other words, *the fetishistic split as conditioned by our disavowal shapes our human existence.* The recognition of the *irreducibility of antagonism and conflict* helps us to understand why we continually repeat our educational symptoms despite the powerful critique of deconstruction.

The first step toward pedagogy informed by Lacanian psychoanalysis would be to recognize the fetishistic split that constitutes our very human condition; and that we must first undertake to assume it rather than ignore or repress it. A psychoanalytic pedagogy for transformative change has to expose that which escapes the signification process: *jouissance* (enjoyment) and our relation to it. How can we locate this "surplus" enjoyment when examining its traces in the discursive medium through repetitions, inconsistencies, paradoxes, and circularity?

The Real, as "the grimace of reality," is the unconscious. Its distinction from our perceived "reality" defines the psychoanalytic endeavor and distinguishes it from psychology, relocating and splitting the Imaginary *moi* (ego) into the acephalic *Je* of the unconscious Real on the one hand, and thus raising the alienating question: "What am I?"; then further decentering the ego into the Symbolic Order of language on the other hand, where "Who am I?" is now supplanted by "Whose am I?" If language "speaks us" more than we speak it, where is agency to be found? If our seemingly unknowable *Je* is the seat of our symptoms, drives, and the "cause" of our desires, to what extent can one trust the egoic consciousness? One of the criticisms of Lacan is that subjectivity seems always overdetermined by a symbolic network, or always contained by Imaginary fantasy and caught up in the symptomatic Real. But Lacan's reply was that although the subject was continually caught by the defiles of the signifier, sublimation always allowed for both a creative and idiosyncratic response to desire.

Lacan's tripartite articulation of the "subject" and of identity formation complicates human existence and transformation by positing a *manque* (loss and lack)—a fundamental unknowability—at the center of our existence which speaks directly to our finitude and the paedamorphic nature of our species being. An infant's biological needs and demands for support, satisfaction, and nurture, or "cherishment" (Young-Bruehl and Bethelard 2000), have to be met in order for it to survive and enter the social order. Articulated most forcefully in Seminar VII, *The Ethics of Psychoanalysis* (1992), Lacan's Heideggarian-influenced articulation of *Dasein* is recast in terms of an encounter with the Freudian *das Ding*. The infant's interuterinal experience of wholeness, of ~~Being~~, of complete auto-eroticism, of presence, of a choral symbiosis within the mother's womb, bathed in the experience of the here and now, must eventually be experienced *retrospectively* as a loss, and therefore as a *manque-á-être* (loss/lack of being); that is to say, an "extraction" or a "giving up" of libidinal energy—the "psychic energy" of *jouissance* has to occur, when the umbilical cord is "cut." The Mother, although *not* immediately, eventually becomes a barrier for the full and total source of the infant's satisfaction which she once was. At the onset of the infant's first cry, the infant, in the Heideggarian sense, is "thrown" into the world, a process which starts the process of what Lacan called *alienation*, which then leads to *separation*. *Das Ding* for Freud presents itself as a scream—which, depending how it is read, is the trauma of birth and the sheer "silence" that follows. It is a scream from the Real. And isn't that the paradox of a silent scream—the notion that you are screaming but do not know why?

KRISTEVA'S PEDAGOGY

It is especially important to call on Kristeva here for the implications of a transformative, politically informed pedagogy grounded in psychoanalysis. Kristeva's ethics of identity difference is especially developed in *Strangers to Ourselves* (1991), where she argues that we must address difference within personal identity itself; to acknowledge the death drive by analyzing our aggression, frustration, and hate, as well as love. Her claim is "that" which is excluded from a society or nation so that the boundaries of identity may be preserved is, in actuality, interior to our very identity. It lies in our unconscious Real and hence, as abject, it is projected onto those whom we exclude from our society/nation so that a stable identity of our individual self and society and nation is preserved (see also Žižek 1993, 200–238). The stranger or foreigner is within us.

Kristeva is following the footsteps of Freud's reading of the *Nebenmensch* (neighbor) as "the absolute Other of the subject" that is simultaneously at the heart of the subject, the Other within the self that defines what is most central to the subject. What is most central is bound up with the world of desires. Just as an individual must deal with the return of the repressed—the excluded Other—so too must a nation. How then does one confront alterity pedagogically? In order to understand our social relations with others, we must understand our relation to the Other—the "stranger" within ourselves. How do we grapple with what we abject so that cohabitation is possible? How might a psychoanalytic understanding of difference enable teachers to help children live with their difference? (Richardson 2002). Being able to live with difference within ourselves, claims Kristeva, enables us to live with the difference around us. Her deconstructive strategy is to make the identity of the stranger "strange" so that transference can take place to the place of the stranger. We can then empathize with the Other. By doing so, the concept of the stranger makes it "strange" to ourselves—enabling a confrontation with our Real.

It seems that Kristeva has clearly been influenced by the philosophical writings of Emmanuel Levinas, the philosopher of alterity, although she does not seem to acknowledge it. "The Other in the same" is a Levinasian borrowing. Kristeva links ethics with "negativity," her complex term for the oscillations that can take place between Law and transgression; between the semiotic and the symbolic; between the drives and desires; between the Real and Imaginary-Symbolic. Her particular form of deconstruction for such an ethical disruptive praxis enables the "subject-in-process and on trial" to destabilize its narcissistic identity by harnessing the heterogeneity that exists in language, namely, the semiotic drives. Her "poetic language" points to the "heart" of the Real as an aesthetic envelope of music, tone, rhythm, and the mother's voice. For Kristeva, Lacan reduces the primary affect of *das Ding* to language, reducing semiotic to the symbolic—the preverbal affective energy of the drives to linguistic categories. The relation to *das Ding* is not the word but subjective affect of trauma. Yet, non-phallic, supplementary feminine *jouissance* as developed in Lacan's formulae of sexuation would point in the same direction.

Is such pedagogy of making the unconscious conscious possible so that we might confront the "horror" within ourselves? Should this be the way we interpret Freud's enigmatic saying: *Wo Es war soll Ich werden*? (Where the Id was the Ego should be) (see Schlender, Chapter 8 in this volume). Lacan would say that we can only know "half-truths" about ourselves. What remains especially difficult to grasp is the circulation of abject in Kristeva's system of thought, which may be somewhat misleading if to form one's identity is founded on the process of abjection. This means that the abject "object" of primal repression is the Mother. It is she who we both love and hate, abhor, and repel from as the undesirable Other in our effort to separate from her. There is an internal violence, a death wish in wanting to do so. Kristeva, like Klein, claims that the mother's own violence should not go underestimated. Yet, it is the love for the Mother as the *semiotic imaginary* available to both sexes, repressed in Lacan, which can disrupt the Symbolic Order.[11]

There is another sense of the abject, of course, which is to have our subjecthood placed at risk—to be shunned, ostracized, criminal, and locked outside the Symbolic Order. This paradoxical understanding of abject could be read as an ecological ethic—namely, that we are responsible for our excrement, both psychical and physical. We are responsible for the way we define ourselves in difference; always living with the possibility that we may mistakenly wrong the Other. It raises, as Kristeva points out, the hypocrisy that the abject brings to light in the way the Law can hide the terror it wreaks in the name of "the people"; that is to say, the way the Symbolic Order expels its abject to keep its "pure" identity (Nazi Germany, for example).

If the subject is defined in unity, it is the ambiguous abject which disturbs that unity dwelling in extimate space—neither one nor the other. I am reminded here again of Winnicott's transitional space and the objects that dwell in it—the common examples of the "blankie," teddy bear, huggable pillow, doll, and so on which are loved and mutilated at the same time, eventually abandoned and thrown away. Aren't they abject objects as well? They occupy the space of the "screen-image" Lacan theorized in *Seminar XI*. Isn't the transitional object—an object which is and is not the mother, and paradoxically is and is not the child—the kind of object that oscillates between abhorrence and bliss in terms of abjection and unity—another name for *objet petit a*? Finally, isn't the screen-image the limit, the enfolded space/time of the Real and the Imaginary, which ushers in and supports the Symbolic Order of language? So, wouldn't a pedagogy that takes seriously the *objet a* of desire and of the drive focus on this

Imaginary screen space of transition which either "lights up" or becomes "dark" and painful as one encounters the Real? It seems to me that this points to the tensions between the Real and the Imaginary—the "tain of the mirror," to use Gasché's (1986) term—where creative sublimation might take place. Kristeva's semiotic, associated with creativity, identifies a feminine *plus de jouir* that belongs to the maternal body.

There is a difference between mutilation and loving something until it has a "patina," a history. The ethics involves knowing just when to stop before it gets worn out, or when it needs to be refurbished, patched up. Eventually it may be discarded, but the parting would be friendly and perhaps melancholic and mournful. Could that be the space of living with difference, abject, and alterity? For the acquisition of knowledge and letting it go require similar questions (see Alcorn 2001 and Chapter 5 in this volume). Knowledge, like identity, has to be connected to desire. A pedagogy of abject as *objet a* would be vigilant to the ethical and political ramifications that follow, for anxiety is sure to bound as the Real self is approached. Only if the student confronts his/her *objet a* enacting an ethical *act* of freedom can one say that a "truly" transformative pedagogy is possible. Psychoanalytically speaking, only then does change take place. For Kristeva, psychoanalytic ethics is directed to a space where the analysand can brace the Other in her/himself in order to live out the crisis of values. The ethical dimension is commensurate with love. Maternity as the very embodiment of alterity within provides Kristeva with an explicatory "herethics" where the obligation of the self to the Other is based on the mother's love for her child.

The apple's seeds hold the kernel of the Real in its infinite depth, in its infinite vastness, or "true infinity" in Hegelian terms. They contain both "at once" the apple's life and its death. But just where is such information stored, if it is "information" as we know it at all? Deep ecology speculates the interconnectedness of all living and nonliving things, in symbiosis *as well as in conflict*. The Real may well be the impossible place where the historical memory inherent in nature dwells, as in the speculative theorizations of "morphic resonance" by Rupert Sheldrake (1988), for instance, who argues that there is a collective memory, much like Jung's collective unconscious, from all previous things of their kind. "The world is merely the fantasy through which thought sustains itself—'reality' no doubt, but to be understood as a grimace of the [R]eal," crypts Lacan (1990, 10). Obviously, humans cannot be compared to apples; however, the Real kernel of our being also subjects us to knowledge we cannot read nor foresee but which we nevertheless carry within us, for it spells our death. Freud names this the "death drive" in *Beyond the Pleasure Principle* (1920, SE 18). The death drive is a *savoir* (knowledge) within us of our own path to death, but it is a knowledge we are not cognizant of, and which we do not recognize, yet this *savoir* condemns us to death. We shall have occasion to return to the death drive and its importance for pedagogy. For now one can see how the neologism "w(hole)" captures this paradox of the Real, the both/and logic of something seemingly complete and yet with something missing that *co*-exists in an extimate site: again in the Lacanian lexicon *das Ding* and *objet a*, respectively.

PEDAGOGY WITH THE DEATH DRIVE

The death drive is perhaps one of the most important concepts when considering the importance of psychoanalysis for a pedagogy that would be informed by it. To undergo a transformative change (to traverse one's fundamental fantasy) is always to face one's "death," for it inevitably means a changed relationship to the Symbolic Order. One never quite "enjoys" (*jouissance*) in the same way again. Lacan's rereading of Freud's death drive is perhaps almost an antithetical reading of Heidegger's well-known notion of Being-towards-death in *Being and Time* (1962). In moments of "towards-death," when we "face" ourselves, claims Heidegger, we "hear" within ourselves a "guilty conscience" for we become acutely aware of how much we are indebted to persons and things around us, and therefore it is a call to care (*Sorge*). From this, phenomenologically and hermeneutically informed pedagogies have developed an ethics of moral intuitiveness and thoughtfulness (Huebner 1999; van Manen 1991). The pedagogue attempts to do "good" for the child/student through the practice of "tact." "Pedagogcial authority is really a designation of moral service" (van Manen 1991, 69). Lacan, however, has something more disturbing in mind in his call for an ethics of the Real (*S VII*; Zupančič 2000b). He begins from a different starting point by extrapolating the "good" which is lost to the subject and positing the paradox of the superego split by drive and desire. Is there any reconciliation to be found between these two very different positions, between phenomenology and psychoanalysis? Perhaps.

For psychoanalysis, the split subject is "subject" to a principle *beyond* the pleasure principle, to the pathologies of the drives. In this view we are not driven to seek our own good; rather, what is required is a reformulation of ethics on the principle of the death drive. How can we explain self-destructive conduct—the myriad of ways we self-deconstruct despite seemingly having it all (i.e., the good life as it is sold to us)? At the void of the Real is posited a fetishistic split; the warring eros and thanatos; life drive (love) and death drive (aggression, hate), a non-deconstructive (in the Derridean sense) binary.

Moral order is established, according to psychoanalysis, not in obedience to some reasonableness or compassionate command to sacrifice our pleasure to the state but because we recoil before the violence and obscenity of the superego's incitement to *jouissance*, to a boundless and aggressive enjoyment. The recoil before the commandment to love thy superego as thyself does not open up the floodgates of our aggression or our enjoyment; on the contrary, it erects a barrier against them, and places out of reach our object of desire. In resisting the superego, then, we insist on separating ourselves from, rather than surrendering to, this incomprehensible part of our being; we insist, in other words, on prolonging the conflict with ourselves. *The sole moral maxim of psychoanalysis is this: do not surrender your internal conflict, your division.* (Copjec 1994a, 92; emphasis added)

ETHICS/PEDAGOGY

This is a perpetual struggle with radical evil—*until death*, which is why Lacan in *Seminar VII* claims that the figure of Antigone is "beautiful," for she embodies such a struggle. Her action bathes her in "splendour," in an excessive *Schein* (glow) because of her ethical insistence and transgression against Creon's Laws. As an "aesthetic object" her sublimity "shows" the "shadow" of *das Ding*. She is "lit up" with excessive *jouissance* of the drive—"pure" desire. One could say she is "holy" (w(holy)) in this sense. We seem to be back to an extimate space of being brought to a limit where form dissolves into an "emptiness"; the mysticism Lacan spoke about concerning non-phallic *jouissance*. We could say it brings us to the "tain of the mirror" and the dissolution of the screen-image, for our "natural" everyday perception is on the verge of collapsing. Death knocks on life's door. It is only then, one could say, that the fantasy of the Imaginary mirror has been shattered—and the fantasy traversed, for isn't it only then that the "support" or "veil" that covers over *objet a* becomes lifted and the "truth" (*savoir*) exposed, the Real encountered? A pedagogy based on such an extreme position seems unlikely, for we are in the realm of religious ecstasy. However, each and every time we confront our own *objet a* in an ethical way we risk facing "death." It is a "spiritual" act. The paradox here is that "death" turns into the possibility of a new "life," and "life" for Lacan was the *lamella* of pure libido.

Ethics, in this reading, is the unconscious struggle itself! Antigone is placed in what Lacan called a "second death." Her action is an "event" which derails the established Symbolic Order. Like the crucifixion of Christ, the event "haunts" the established Law, insisting that the injustice caused be righted. Such a reading has a certain appeal and explanatory power in terms of chaos theory (i.e., some global "events" like the dropping of the atom bomb on Nagasaki and Hiroshima unquestionably charge world leaders with unprecedented responsibilities). (As mentioned earlier, who ultimately decides whether such an act was evil?) Small and seemingly insignificant "events" can also traumatize and (retroactively) lead to similar insistent haunts that are personal, but may become global as the acted out symptoms of world leaders. (Here one can think of the radical evil of a Hitler.) This was Freud's point concerning *Nachträglichkeit* (deferred action). The ethical surround of the "event" itself, however, is not free of the fundamental antagonism concerning sex/gender, nor free from continuous historical re-evaluation. While Lacan reinterprets Hegel's reading of Antigone, so do both Irigaray (1985a, 117–118, 214–226) and Butler (2000). Both, from different perspectives, have identified the kinship structures and the ramifications of Antigone's action in relation to the hegemony of patriarchal Law.

Like Cézanne's apples, rather than maintaining the illusion of them being "just" another signifier, they point to something else—a relationship to *das Ding*. Art doesn't teach us what we must do, moralizing as to what the good life is. It can only point us in relation to *das Ding*, thereby raising the object to the "dignity" of *das Ding*. It then becomes a *bien dire* (well saying) for Lacan (1990, 22). Pedagogy as *bien dire*. The possibility of pedagogical dialogue where new knowledge about the subject is produced that is life transforming. Now there's a thought (see Guerra, Chapter 1 in this volume).

The pathology of the drives grounds the "Good," making moral law possible (Žižek 1993, 95–101). The psychoanalytic view of freedom, then, is "oddly" defined as not to be motivated by one's self-interest in choosing Good! Lacan doesn't trust "nature" in defining the Good. Defined negatively, on the one hand freedom is a resistance to the pleasure principle and not submitting to the law of the death drive, the sadistic superego: the Kantian *Wille*. The argument is that the inaccessibility to the sublime *Ding* is *both* the founding *and* the repression of desire. As a primal repression (*Urverdrägung*) of desire it makes *das Ding* an impossible object. This, then, enables desire to be maintained through fantasy formations so that one doesn't fall into the pathology of self-completion—omniscience, a fall into a superegoistic ego. On the other hand there is the ethics of the drives which challenge the fundamental fantasies at the very core of our "being" in the Symbolic Order so that the Law can be changed. But the price is always high.

This maxim concerning *jouissance* surrounding desire and the drives is a rather sobering thought, for it is a tragic view of life. As Lacan says, we have a "passion" for the signifier; that is to say, human suffering, since there is no let-up. An encounter with the Real can derail our seemingly tranquil lives, engulfed and addicted by a newly found *jouissance* from which we cannot free ourselves. We have to live with our addictions, our pathologies, our symptoms. We are, in this sense, our own worst enemies, at war with ourselves. This moral interdiction is directly related to the prohibition of incest. The Good object that is lost is the Mother, who is split by the child as being both phallic and Good. The maternal breast is not always given. The child cries from want. And, although the interdiction appears to address both sexes, feminists and queer theorists alike have been quick to point out the differences of relationships to their primary caregivers and to the Symbolic Order which continually troubles Lacanian orthodoxy. So, for instance, Žižek (1993) can say (following Lacan's analysis of Freud's grandson's fort/da *Spiel* exemplifying entry into the symbolic) that "[t]he entry into the universe of symbols is therefore paid for by the loss of the incestuous object, of mother qua Thing" (91); Irigaray (1989, 135–136) goes to great lengths to reread this game and argue that this can only be a gesture of a boy, a girl's gesture is entirely different toward her mother. Worst perhaps is Irigaray's indictment on the death drive itself. "Woman *represents* death or the unthinkable for/by men" (in Whitford 1991, 115). For men, the aggression associated with the death drive is turned outward on objects—toward women. Women, on the other hand, turn their aggression inward, on themselves. They are masochists unable to sublimate their aggression and are typically self-sacrificing. It depends, therefore, how *das Ding*, as an empty signifier, the void itself, is being theorized—as the originary Mother's body (e.g., Cornell 1997, 1998; Irigaray 1985b) or the *lamella* of Life itself.

THE PEDAGOGY OF ALIENATION

One possible way out of this dilemma, and this is the position I will take here, is to suggest that *das Ding*, as the Real—as alterity as such—should be identified with the process of what Lacan called *alienation* and not *separation*. That is to say, to the moment *before* the figure of the Mother and the signifier of language emerges in full force (as S_2). Against Lacan, but certainly consonant with Kristeva's "semiotic" position, the time before the subject's identification with the signifier (\$), the "child of the drives," so to speak, of Being (S), experiences the Real as an aesthetic experience. As argued above, the Real as *das Ding* is experienced at the bodily sensate level as an impossible dualism of beauty–ugliness, hate–love, and so on. There is no sexual differentiation as yet, although as Stern (1985) points out, "selective attunements" by the parents are already at work.

Alterity has two sides—either as blissful terror or terrible bliss. I am referring to the span of time before the "drop" of the signifier, *avant la lettre*, when in Freud's terms, the pre-conscious and conscious receive the exterior visual and oral signifiers as "thing-presentations," as sensuous materiality; what Freud (1915) called (in his "Instincts and Their Vicissitudes," SE 14, 109–140) "ideational [imaginary] representatives." These can be viewed as the *psychical interior* processes homologous to the body's interior physical processes of acceptance and expulsion of abject material (feces, urine, wax). Strictly speaking, the resultant satisfaction/ dissatisfaction of *jouissance* (both bodily and psychically) is had at the body's orifices, the rim-like structure of the erotogenic zones where the drive aims at an object of desire to "fill" its cavity. In the phase of *alienation* the oral, anal, and scopic as *prephallic* drives take over and mark the first irresolvable dualism of nature/culture on the infant's body. This body of *demand* presents itself as an overlay between the physical (biological) body of need and the body as "civilized" by the signifier. The body's cavities (or holes) repetitively open and close to process and expel the material and cultural symbolic world alike (taken together, "reality" as such).

The loss and lack of what Freud called an "oceanic feeling"—as the infant's Being begins to "fade" as it "wakes up" to the world—is a process which becomes "installed" in the psyche retroactively as a deferred memory. The first attempt of the infant to come to terms with "what" it is— its "being there"—by way of an originary processed "ideational representative" is *necessarily* a repressed and *traumatic* event, for the infant confronts the void of non-meaning and non-sense. As such, this "ideational [imaginary] representative" is non-representable, which at first appears to be a contradiction in terms. We could call it a "pure" empty signifier, a phonetic letter, since it has no signified meaning as yet. But it is "full" of activity as it strives to be completed—both full and empty at once. Perhaps best to call it a neuronal trace. The infant first cries and whimpers before it smiles, for it confronts an unknowable and impossible outside (Other), an impossible non-object of desire, hence the term *das Ding*. Unable to make sense of "it," as an unconscious memory trace without any previous traces to refer to, its psyche is traumatized at once by difference (intruding is the "blissful" light of the here and now) and deferment of its meaning (a belatedness). This traumatic moment, which is generally defined by Freud as a response to an unexpected or overwhelming "violent" event or events that are not fully grasped as they occur, but return later as repetitive phenomena (flashbacks and nightmares), is already at the onset characterized by Derridean *différance*. It is an "empty," non-sensical trace of the event, the "non-representable representation" as the *Urverdrägung* which, paradoxically, acts as a "stand-in" for the initial loss of Being, and thus the primal ground of the unconscious and the subsequent secondary repressions as "meaning" comes to fore.

We can describe this space of subjective *alienation* in yet another way. From birth to eight weeks, the approximate time *before* the infant can begin to make direct eye contact with the Mother (Stern 1985), its perceptual world—the world of symbiosis with its mother—is characterized by an amodal, or cross-modal perception which enables it to transfer perceptual experience from one modality to another. For instance, time duration in relation to the intensity of both light and sound, audiovisual cross-modality for another, and the transference of touch to vision are ways in which the infant is trying to consolidate its "body ego" as these haptic-visual transfers become stronger as associative links are formed. At the earliest weeks, therefore, the experience of the Real as the pre-symbolic and pre-linguistic realm is characterized by synesthetic experience and the experience of the "surface" of things; their shapes, intensities, patterns, smells, tastes, temporal patterns, rhythms—in brief, "feeling perceptions," or affective "thing-perceptions" (see also Silverman 2000), where the timbre of the Mother's voice is heard simply as a musical surround. There appears to be no "loss" and "lack" here as yet, but the trauma of birth has already taken place and the primal repression of a "bit" of *jouissance* has already begun. A part of the need cannot be articulated by the infant's demand, and its caregiver is unable to totally meet its demand. Not all the infant's needs can be 100 percent assured and gratified, but the Mother *is* "good-enough," to use Winnicott here, in attending to her infant.[12]

Isn't this world of the infant, then, somewhat "magical" in feeling and appearance? Affective states of joy, distress, disgust, surprise, interspersed by cries for help and moments of terror—heaven and hell at once? The Real here is not a static or inert *site* [sight] [cite] but constantly "bubbling" up with *vitality affects* that the infant experiences as "explodings," "fadings," surgings, and rushes (Stern 1985). It is presided over by anal, oral, and scopic drives—and the touch of the skin. Frustration and accomplishment, need and demand structure its space and time. The Real is, therefore, characterized by bodily affects—what is smellable, touchable, tasteable, and poetically by the timbre of Lacan's *lalangue*, the "voiced breath" that fastens the child to an undifferentiated maternal body through its rhythms, intonations, and echolalias (Kristeva 1980, 173–180). In this characterization, the unconscious Real is most "open" to the world, registering various bodily sensorimotor physiognomic sensations through drive mechanisms as visual perceptual schemas or as "activation contours" (Stern 1985). These are clusters of trace memories which have the potential to be activated as "thing representations" by pre-conscious and conscious processes. A child feels and sees before it "knows." The breast, to follow Kristeva (1987), is not an object but an incorporated "model," a "pattern," in Stern's (1985, 97) terms a Representation of Interactions that have been Generalized (RIG) which constitutes a basic unit of representation of the infant's core self. The Real as *das Ding* in this regard is the place of human *sentience* and the realm of affect and the sensuous aesthetic. I am in full agreement with the importance of Kristeva's recognition of the auto-erotic pre-Oedipal body and "semiotic chora" as the repressed maternal body that is associated with the child's relation to its mother's breast.

Such an imaginary space that is being described here is more auratic and loving, provided that the caregivers attend to the child. At a moment before the full development of the scopic drive that establishes Lacan's mirror phase, it seems to me what Kristeva does, in *Tales of Love* (1987), is to theorize the very lining of that mirror—again, the mirror's tain. Within the two- to six-month structure it is possible to see the significance of Kristeva's narcissistic transference between mother and infant prior to the spectacularization of the mirror stage (Lacan 1977, 1–8)—a moment of "pre-separation"—a transition from the Real of the unconscious being-in-itself to a full accounting of the specular Imaginary development of the ego as a being-for-itself in *separation*. This space/time is characterized by the infant's imaginary (in the sense of it being semiotic) identification with the mother. It is within that space/time that the infant is identifying with the pattern of the Other (mother's pattern of language) through forms of imitation. Kristeva calls this a "narcissistic reduplification," which creates a space between the infant as not-yet-subject but not-yet-object. Such an imaginary structure of narcissistic love fills the space between the mirror and the infant. It is a place of metaphoric transference prior to Lacan's claim that desire is characterized by endless metonymic displacements. But why metaphor before metonymy? As a figure of displacement (sub-stitution of one object for another) metaphor establishes the pattern of displacement in language, and thereby characterizes the transference of language that takes place between mother and infant through the structure of primary narcissism. Moreover, it is the infant's affective bodily states— Stern's "vitality affects," Kristeva's semiotic—its drives that are put into the place of language. Kristeva is pointing to the grasping of the image by the child as being already embodied, the synesthetic affects of the touch of the skin, the timbre of her voice, the taste and smell of her milk, and so on. In brief, the Real of the drives and the *affect* they embody give greater importance to the movement toward the Other and to mutual at-traction than the Lacanian desire as lack and the identification of the ideal ego in the mirror. For Kristeva, love rather than lack is what is required.

At two months old and onward—when mutual "gaze behavior" between mother and child becomes fully established at about three to five months— only then can the full implications of desire emerge and *separation* begin as the infant takes control over the initiations and terminations of direct visual engagement. The more orthodox understanding of *das Ding* emerges as fully realized alterity of the primal caregiver (most often the Mother). Fear, for example, is not experienced until about six months of age (Stern), and between the seventh and ninth month infants share sub-jective experience or intersubjectivity. The signifier has not as yet fallen since this is a time of holophrastic speech acts where communication be-tween the infant and caregivers is being established.

To make the transition of the child into the Symbolic Order of language and the Law of the Father, Kristeva posits the passage by way of a meta-

phorical "imaginary father"—the fantasy structure of father who loves like
a mother. Opposed to the stern Lacanian father (superego or God) is this
archaic, pre-symbolic imaginary father who gives support to the mother's
desire which is ultimately for the phallus. (This is where objectives to her
position by feminists begin to incur.) The imaginary father is a fantasy of
wholeness—a mother-father conglomerate, so that the transference is an
identification that is whole and complete since it combines both maternal
gratifications and paternal prohibitions against a mother who would covet
her child. If this weren't the case, passage into the symbolic would not
be playful and sublimational but characterized by mourning and melancholia for the loss of the maternal body. The imaginary father—as an
Imaginary Third who is neither mother nor father and yet both father and
mother—is the mother's love in disguise, a "metaphor for love" as she
"gives up" her own narcissism to shift the child to the Other, from the
demand on the mother's body to desire in language.

The emergence of Self and Other in *separation* introduces all the nuances that desire as related to the Other suggests in Lacan: as desire of
the Other; that is to say, desire originating in the symbolic Big Other, or
inhabiting the unconscious as Other, or in the Other as a subject "who-is-
supposed-to-know" (*sujet supposé savoir*) as the one who provides the
illusion for the guaranteed meaning and truth. Regardless, satisfaction is
always impossible because it lays in the field of the Other, and it is from
this Other that psychoanalysis teaches us whom each of us might be said
to "be." What is at issue for feminists concerning Kristeva's position, of
course, is whether that *screen* or support that she establishes as a mother
simply enables the dominance of male fantasies to proceed where women,
as mothers, fall back into a subservient role. But this place of *alienation*
is also the place of creativity and the aesthetic itself. It brings us closest
to the Real when changing who we are by sublimating our experiences
through artistic means (e.g., Press 2001).

With this reading of *das Ding*, the ethical moment Lacan stages is related
to the encounter with the Real, which is always *traumatic* and repetitive.
It is important that trauma here be understood not only in its most dramatic and tragic forms (i.e., the loss of a loved one, the horror of war
neurosis, a disabling accident, etc.), but also as a pedestrian experience
where an unexpected, unanticipated, and seemingly unexplainable event
occurs; something very simple as when, pedagogically speaking, a student
reacts strongly to a story you have introduced in your English class. S/he
refuses to read it (Berman 1999); parents complain to you, the teacher,
about the treatment of their child, and you are accused of being prejudiced. An art student refuses to work with clay, another hates the charcoal
as a drawing medium. Such incidents are not usually seen as "traumatic
events" but they are all encounters with the Real. This is simply another

way of reminding us that the Real is not some suprasensible realm existing in some unfathomable place. Rather, its presence infiltrates both the Imaginary and Symbolic psychic registers that form our "normative" perception.

This traumatic moment, as Lacan (1979) develops it in "The Unconscious and Repetition" (S XI), must be understood in relation to the two senses of its future repetitions: as a *Wiederholen* and as a *Wiederkehr* (48–50). As *Wiederholen* (repeating) the traumatic experience is a missed encounter with the Real. This repetition is necessary, for the traumatic event in some significant sense has not been grasped. And one wonders here whether all learning is based on such a necessary but "ignorant" repetition; whether we keep on repeating something, again, and again, rehearsing it by the drive process—"aiming," as it were—until we sublimate and achieve our goal. Drive/desire; process/goal; *jouissance*/ satisfaction—are these tensions not fundamental to learning that informs the struggle between process and product, struggle and achievement? The small release of felt satisfaction after so much work of painful *jouissance* is the sublimated product. The *Wiederholung* of the event serves to "screen" the Real. We might call it a perceptual gloss, for in the repetition there is some loss of affect. We say to ourselves, "that isn't it." There is something missed, not remembered, a(voided) in the recalling. For example, the art student stubbornly refuses to engage with clay no matter what you as a teacher might try. It is the student's repetition of the repressed as symptom or signifier. S/he does this automatically—as an automaton. What has "caused" this aversion to this material? Repetition as refusal here serves to "screen" the *objet a* that has been abhorrently projected into the clay. Unlike my apple, the clay "looks back" here as an abjected, horrible substance whose form cannot be contained. It is almost a paranoid extimate moment when inside/outside collapse. Mundanely, the teacher might offer the student a pair of surgical gloves—another form of "screen"—which would enable the distance, the proximity to the abjected Thing to be somewhat breached. An acquaintance with the clay as "material" might begin, a dialogue started, a touch made. Eventually a beautiful object may emerge as the student comes to terms with the "ugliness" at first encountered. In a sense, this would constitute an ethical act, and a *Weiderkehr*, or encounter with student's anxiety, would take place.

In contrast, then, a *Wiederkehr* is a repetition with a difference (*kehr* in the German meaning a turning around, a coming back). It is beyond the *automaton* or a *Doppelgänger*-effect where "a repetition that succeeds perfectly may be fatal because the space difference between model and copy has been eliminated, collapsing both terms into one entity and abolishing the singularity of each separate term" (Bronfen 1993, 104). Rather, following Aristotle, it is a *tuché* (S XI, 55)—a chance encounter, a touching. Between perception and consciousness the subject is "touched" by the Real as the "object," metaphorically speaking, "looks back" now in an entirely different way. This is a *constructive* repetition that emphasizes difference, rather than a *destructive* one that emphasizes sameness (*Wiederholen*). Like the movie *Groundhog Day*, the day's events keep repeating themselves because an encounter with the Real has been missed. No Real learning has taken place, no *objet a* confronted. I interpret such learning as an aesthetic experience, one which itself is governed by the dualistic and paradoxical tensions of beauty/ugliness, of bliss/horror, of pulse light/death ray.

When I first cut into the apple I was immediately *struck* by the vulva-like cavity holding the apple seeds and the delicacy of its form. At the same time, an exposure, a vulnerability of the apple itself emerged. Upon reflection, I realized that this encounter with the Real raised the question of sexual difference. *Where was the so-called masculine presence of the apple in all of this?* I ended up deliberately drawing the stem as if it were an intrusive phallic symbol (see the opening figure). My relationship to/with the apple seemed to be split into the irreconcilable gap between a masculine and feminine approach to the sublime Real. On the one hand the very sensuousness of the apple had touched me. Its sentience is what I felt—the aesthetic surfaces of its features drew my eye, but it was the masculine cut, the trauma of opening it up which shocked me. It is this double-bind of identity which is always and already at issue; the drive of *jouissance* and the screening of desire.

A rapprochement between phenomenology and psychoanalysis might be made as pedagogically dealing with the two moments of *alienation* and *separation*, one based on maternal Law of the "support" of the mirror, the other on the paternal Law, the prohibition against *jouissance*: care and love tempered with the firm voice of the Law. This sounds very traditional, but it need not be so if the conflicts of *jouissance* are kept in mind in the way our student's pain might be caught up in the repetition of the drive rather than being sublimated. Or transgressions understood as a call for justice, a demand that is not realized in the Symbolic Order as yet. To undo such repetition, the drama educator and social activist Augusto Boal (1995) introduced the figure of the "Joker" into his plays. The Joker, a character who plays in the extimate space of being both in and outside the play at once, disturbs the play's characters by making them rethink their actions through evoking memories, stopping and rearranging the action, playing devil's advocate, and so on, so as to provoke an encounter with the Real as a *Wiederkehr* experience. There are never any assurances. Is the Joker sex/gendered? I would say yes. As a literalized superegoistic voice, its playfulness would need to be identified and evaluated in the ethics of the Joker's intervention. "Passion branding" is another attempt at sublimating the drives through drama. In front of witnesses (the Big Other), students (and adults alike) enact a narrative in the way they have overcome some trauma in their lives—be it sexual abuse, addiction, a disability—thereby facing their own pain and turning it into a creative performance which is then shared with the audience.

The trauma of *alienation* and *separation* to which the ethical relationship must answer requires the repair of the "narcissistic wound," the repair of the cut, so to speak. Such trauma is continually experienced on many minute levels that call on the teacher to act. We revisit here again the *paradoxes* of the two ethics that are at work both grounded on the fundamental split within ourselves. On the side of the Law of the Mother—because the subject is alienated from itself—is the loss of the wholeness of Being that one can speak of a "beyond." The goodness, transcendence, and compassion of a non-phallic *jouissance* can recapture the originary loss through aesthetic means. This requires an ethics of love which phenomenologically sensitive pedagogies respond to. On the side of the Name-of-the-Father we see that the "devilish" superego calls us to transgress, not foreclosing *jouissance* via our desired fantasies. Yet, this same transgression can become an ethical act, a way to challenge the Symbolic Order itself. The first grounds ethics in uncompromising love, the second in abhorrence; the same conflictual oscillation Freud had struggled with in the figure of the *Nebenmensch* (neighbor). It is a fundamental antagonism within us. Either way the split subject—because it *is* split—is always already being challenged, called upon, summoned, troubled, commanded, and interrupted for an ethical response to oneself via the Other as a relation that exceeds simple satiation, the pleasure principle. But with this conclusion it seems we are back to the idea of the "two mothers" and "two fathers," the deadlock, or double-bind of the fundamental antagonism in pedagogy that continually must be reconciled as we teach.

This conflict, of course, *defines a pedagogy that is informed by a psychoanalytic understanding.* It is unresolvable once and for all, like the mystery of Being and its Beyond. We have already discussed some of the differences and sameness between Lacan and Derrida, and one wonders whether Lacanian psychoanalysis doesn't present the complementary face to the "maternal" phenomenology of Levinas, the philosopher of an uncompromising alterity whose face-to-face relationship forms the cornerstone of his ethics. His warnings against "the other in the same" and "the inside of the inside that is outside" certainly sound like explications of an extimate space. Levinas's position of ultimately being responsible to God, however, is not shared by Lacan.

The touchstones that exist between Levinas and Lacan have been usefully explored in *Levinas and Lacan: The Missed Encounter* (Harasym 1998), where various philosophers work out both the sameness and the differences in their respective approaches to ethics. Some critics, like Drucilla Cornell, reject outright Lacan's position,[13] claiming that Derrida's deconstructive approach to the Real does it better, a position I have already argued against. Donna Brody develops the similarity between Levinas's *il y a* (there is) and Lacan's Real.[14] Levinas's the Saying and the Said is explored by Paul-Laurent Assoun. The Saying cannot exist without the Said, yet the Said always undermines the Saying, always betrays its intention, renders it Other which is close to Lacan's notion of the subject as always "fading" under the signifier. The subject is always searching to signify his or her intentionality but remains caught up in the throes of signifiers which always withdraw from what was "truly" meant to be said. However, in another context Critchley (1999) aptly demonstrates that Levinas's seemingly overt rejection of psychoanalysis can be deconstructed to show that there is an extraordinary agreement in their view that an initial trauma constitutes the subject. Further, Levinas developed a concept of the unconscious in his *Otherwise than Being* (1981, 99–130) if his chapter on "substitution" is read against the grain. The infant is "passive" toward the "non-intentional affectivity" of the Other (constitutional outside) which then "tears" into its subjectivity. Such a transference experience of an "original trauma" of the outside world is experienced pre-ontologically. The Other exceeds all representation, intentionality, equality, and reciprocity. For Levinas the ethical relationship is an attempt to imagine a non-dialectical concept of such a transference (Critchley 1999, 190), rather than the Hegelian master–slave relationship which Lacan is often accused of adopting. Ethics as the disposition toward alterity does not take place on a conscious level of reflection; rather, it takes place at the level of sensibility, at the pre-conscious level of sentience. The bond with the Other is affective. Despite Levinas's more "maternal" ethic, he does not escape the question of sexual difference, leaving the question as to its resolution in doubt, even for Irigaray, who was highly influenced by his thought (see Chanter 1995).

Significantly, Critchley works out another response to the Real of the death drive rather than the tragic one Lacan offers, and that, not surprisingly, is humor, the other side of the drama masks. Humor as a pedagogical tool is indispensable for reversing the effects of the superego. Critchley reminds us: "It recalls us to the modesty and limitedness of the human condition, a limitedness that calls not for tragic affirmation but comic acknowledgement, not heroic authenticity but laughable inauthenticity" (224). As Critchley goes on to explain, from the Lacanian perspective the only possible happiness that can be offered is through sublimation, a satisfaction without repression (Freud). Sublimation is creative, a realization of one's desire, yet paradoxically, knowing that one's desire will never be fully realized. One faces the lack of being that one is. Shouldn't that be the moral goal of education informed by psychoanalysis? To put the student in relation to his/her desire, of confronting the lack of being—the split within ourselves which is always bound up with a relation to death as human finitude—a pedagogy, as it were, between laughing and crying?

The reader will certainly take due note that I have not presented the customary introduction where the gist of an author's argument in the book is summed up. Each contributor has his own take as to what is a fruitful encounter of psychoanalysis and education. However, a word must be said regarding the last chapter of this collection. The reader will be challenged by an essay as enigmatic as any to be found in the Lacanian archives. The use of neologisms push and stretch the signifier to its limit so as to capture the horizon of new possibilities. It is a reminder, for me at least, the interminable task of an educator dedicated to the "practice of freedom," the question of ethics in its most profound sense.

A praxis of education informed by psychoanalysis has only just begun (e.g., Ragland, 1994; Berman, 1994, 1999; Bracher, 1999a, 1999b, 1999c). Others, like Appel (1999), Britzman (1998), Todd (1997), and Taubman (1990, 2000, 2001), to name a select few, have made contributions to its philosophical possibilities. To take psychoanalysis seriously would be to turn pedagogy "on its head" in the way we now practice it in North American schools, with our *emphasis* on cognitive knowing. It would require shifting the emphasis onto bodily affect and imaginary desire—onto the registers of the Real and the Imaginary—so that a politics of the symbolic might be renewed. As Butler (1993) has argued, this would require taking imaginary positions that have been abjected by the dominant Symbolic Order. This would mean recognizing that this process is always already troubled by a fundamental antagonism, the fetishistic split within us, and the sexual difference that informs it. We can close this somewhat, at times, arduous introduction with a remaining figure of an apple, *Connaisance*, wondering whether pedagogy will abandon the body, its sensuousness and the ethics that exceed it in favor of a digitalized constructed world of information. It is through "art" that we have access to the Real, and teaching is an art.

Connaissance

NOTES

1. I have indented and introduced a different font here to present an inquiring pedagogical voice against the academic voice which attempts to articulate the Lacanian Real utilizing the trope of the apple.

2. The polemic between Lacan's and Derrida's discourses remains a complex

and unresolved issue. Do we pit Lacan's transcendental signifier against Derrida's transcendental signified? Are their positions much closer than we think? See Nobus (2001) for a thoughtful re-evaluation of the debate, and Derrida (1998, 57–59) for his eight criticisms of Lacan's theoretical edifice.

3. Both Žižek (1991, 42–46; 1993, ch. 2) and Copjec (1994c) have identified the Kantian-Hegelian influences on Lacan's "formulae of sexuation." Kant's paradoxes of the universality of "pure" reason which end in the limits of mathematical and dynamic sublime turn out to be precisely the expression of Lacan's development of feminine and masculine logic, respectively. Hegelian antilogies between some Particular (*das Besondere*), the/a Universal (*das/ein Allgemeine/s*) and Individual (*das Einzelne*) inform masculine and feminine position in more specific ways.

4. *Hommosexuelle* conflates man (*homme*) and homosexuality. Irigaray (1985a, 1985b) in particular has taken exception to this characterization.

5. Irigaray has tried to develop a specifically female imagery of the "two lips" in order to provide a transcendental signifier for a renewed relationship of mother–daughter genealogies. In this regard she reaches back to the time prior to the Chalcolithic age, during the time of goddess worship. By doing so she skirts a biological essentialism.

6. It is here where the biological body and body of desire can easily slip into normative identities, for we immediately think of heteronormativity in such a scenario. However, cannot the figure of Dil, the black fe.maler in the film *The Crying Game* (Neil Jordan, 1992), be read as a *femme fatale*? Did s.he not risk "exposure" (h.er unmasking) to be a subject by continuing and pursuing the relationship after Ferguson's initial shock? And did not Ferguson, by eventually returning h.er love and identifying with Dil's symptom as an abjected object of the Symbolic Order, end up in jail, thereby enacting his own symbolic death? It is such a gesture of "limitless love" which ends Lacan's *Seminar XI* as existing "outside the limits of the law" in the Real "where alone it may live" (276). Here it is a transsexual and her heterosexual lover who enact an ethical act that is "beyond" the phallic Law, and not a performative dissimulation that is within it. But at what price? You pay with your life.

7. It seems that Žižek most often casts this event as the "subjective destitution" of Woman. The only subjectivity she has is either suicidal or pathological when she commits such acts of "pure desire" (drive) (Chisholm 2001, 246). "Truth" of man once again appears as Woman, but it need not be if we keep biological identity at bay, as the example of Dil in note 6 above suggests.

8. How does one judge the dropping of the atom bomb on Nagasaki and Hiroshima? As an act it certainly was a sublimely beautiful event that changed the geopolitical world forever. Was it an act of radical evil? In contrast, the "axial age" which produced the figures of the current world religions (Confucius, Buddha, Christ, Mohammed) certainly qualify as events of non-phallic *jouissance* where political structures gave way through a singular Universal. Their ethical actions qualify as the very "mysticism" Lacan refers to as a response "beyond" the phallus. In these cases the paradox of terror and fascination comes together as the body comes under a "death drive" as the Law is being challenged.

9. Salecl (1998, 63–64) offers the example of the diva, where the voice can achieve "the status of the object detached from the body. The singer has to approach 'self-annihilation' as a subject in order to offer himself or herself as pure voice."

10. This is where Lacan's position, once more, is a precursor to Derrida's own writings on justice and sexual difference. The myth of the *lamella* is the question of the metaphysical kernel of *life* itself. It points to an unrepresentable *alterity* as being beyond the transcendental signifier of the phallus as Being. Such a position is consonant with Derrida's *latter* Levinasian-informed interpretation of sexual difference as the ethical encounter with the Other as always "otherwise than being." In *Spurs* (1979) sexual difference is theorized along two mutually exclusive performative forces. The logic that Lacan identified as masculine is related to Derrida's own discussion of generality of the Law, or norm, while the logic of non-phallic feminine *jouissance* is related to Derrida's concern for the fundamental alterity of the Other (i.e., to singularity). In "Choreographies" (1985) he presents sexual difference based on non-identity. Derrida, like Lacan, has been accused by feminists for cross-sexing, of appropriating Woman for masculine gains (e.g., Feder and Zakin 1997; Whitford 1991, 126–135).

11. Kristeva has been criticized for her conservative position on motherhood, essentially supporting a "soft" imaginary loving father as against Lacan's "hard" paternal father. Feminists have rebuked her for valorizing male avante-garde writers as exemplars of semiotic disruption. Kristeva's stance on lesbianism has also been controversial, claiming it to be violent and psychotic.

12. The Mother's breast, gaze, and voice become the most immediate lost objects of *jouissance* when it comes to the pre-conscious perceptual Imaginary. What is primarily repressed becomes desire—a longing for what cannot be articulated, Lacan's infamous *objet a*. Who one "is" in terms of desiring the loss of missing *jouissance*, therefore, depends on what and how one desires. And what and how one desires is to be found both "outside" as well as "inside" oneself—in the Other (unconscious and Symbolic Order). Later images and language will "stand for" (fill in) this Real of desire. But we are now talking of the processes of *separation*.

13. It seems that the +1 as S_1 of feminine logic is the response of Lacan's most persistent critic, Drucilla Cornell (1992, 110), who reads "Woman" as "more" (*mère/mehr*), as already always "more" than any categorization of gender identity that can be assigned to her. In "Where Love Begins" (1997) Cornell confines her critique of Lacan to his *S VII* (*Ethics*), where she selectively reads the moral Law as being grounded on the foreclosure of Woman. Lacan's *das Ding* is interpreted as the body of the Mother. She seems to pay no attention to the other side of the sexuation formulae, where it is clear that a different ethics of the Real has been worked out. There is no discussion of Antigone, for instance. She misreads the paradox of S (Ø) as only lack and not of desire as well, and theorizes the imaginary phallus (ø) as the opposed symbolic notion of castration (Φ).

14. I follow Critchley's (1999) argumentation that the Levinasian notion of alterity is akin to Lacan's Real, rather than Ziarek (1997, 134–135), who argues to the contrary but fails to read the full implications of the sexuation formulas; rather, she remains within the Kantian antinomies as developed by Copjec (1994c).

REFERENCES

Alcorn, Marshall. 2001. Ideological Death and Grief in the Classroom: Mourning as a Prerequisite to Learning. *Journal for the Psychoanalysis of Culture & Society* 6(2): 172–180.

Appel, Stephen, ed. 1999. *Psychoanalysis and Pedagogy.* Westport, Conn.: Bergin & Garvey.

Benjamin, Jessica. 1988. *The Bonds of Love: Psychoanalysis, Feminism, and the Problem of Domination.* New York: Pantheon Books.

Berman, Jeffrey. 1994. *Diaries to an English Professor: Pain and Growth in the Classroom.* Amherst: University of Massachusetts Press.

———. 1999. *Surviving Literary Suicide.* Amherst: University of Massachusetts Press.

Boal, Augusto. 1995. *The Rainbow of Desire: The Boal Method of Theatre and Therapy,* trans. Adrian Jackson. New York: Routledge.

Bourdieu, Pierre. 1990. *The Logic of Practice.* Cambridge: Polity Press.

Bracher, Mark. 1999a. Adolescent Violence and Identity Vulnerability. *Journal for the Psychoanalysis of Culture & Society* 5(2): 189–211.

———. 1999b. Psychoanalysis and Education. *Journal for the Psychoanalysis of Culture & Society* 4(2): 175–192.

———. 1999c. *The Writing Cure: Psychoanalysis, Composition, and the Aims of Education.* Carbondale: Southern Illinois University Press.

Britzman, Deborah P. 1998. *Lost Subjects, Contested Objects: Toward a Psychoanalytic Inquiry of Learning.* Albany, N.Y.: SUNY Press.

Bronfen, Elizabeth. 1993. Risky Resemblances: On Repetition, Mourning, and Representation. In *Death and Representation,* ed. Sarhah Webster Goodwin and Elizabeth Bronfen (pp. 103–129). Baltimore: Johns Hopkins University Press.

Butler, Judith. 1990. *Gender Trouble: Feminism and the Subversion of Identity.* New York: Routledge.

———. 1993. Arguing with the Real. In Judith Butler, *Bodies That Matter: On the Discursive Limits of "Sex."* New York: Routledge.

———. 1997. *Psychic Life of Power: Theories in Subjection.* Stanford, Calif.: Stanford University Press.

———. 2000. *Antigone's Claim: Kinship Between Life and Death.* New York: Columbia University Press.

Campbell, Jan. 2000. *Arguing with the Phallus: Feminist, Queer and Postcolonial Theory.* New York: Zed Books.

Champagne, Rosaria. 1998. Queering the Unconscious. *The South Atlantic Quarterly* 97(2): 281–296.

Chanter, Tina. 1995. *Ethics of Eros: Irigaray's Rewriting of the Philosophers.* New York: Routledge.

Chisholm, Dianne. 2001. Žižek's Exemplary Culture. *Journal for Psychoanalysis of Culture & Society* 6(2): 242–252.

Copjec, Joan. 1994a. *Read My Desire: Lacan Against the Historicists.* Cambridge, Mass.: MIT Press.

———. 1994b. The Cogito, the Unconscious, and the Invention of Crying. *New Formations* 23 (Summer): 1–12.

———. 1994c. Sex and the Euthanasia of Reason. In *Supposing the Subject,* ed. Joan Copjec (pp. 16–44). London: Verso.

———. 1996. Introduction: Evil in the Time of the Finite World. In *Radical Evil,* ed. Joan Copjec (pp. 1–29). London: Verso.

Cornell, Drucilla. 1997. Where Love Begins: Sexual Difference and the Limit of the

Masculine Symbolic. In *Derrida and Feminism: Recasting the Question of Woman*, ed. Ellen K. Feder, Mary C. Rawlinson, and Emily Zakin (pp. 161–206). New York: Routledge.

———. 1998. Rethinking the Beyond of the Real. In *Levinas and Lacan: The Missed Encounter*, ed. Susan Harasym (pp. 139–172). Albany, N.Y.: SUNY Press.

Critchley, Simon. 1999. *Ethics-Politics—Subjectivity: Essays on Derrida, Levinas and Contemporary French Thought*. London: Verso.

De Lauretis, Teresa. 1994. *The Practice of Love: Lesbian Sexuality and Perverse Desire*. Bloomington: Indiana University Press.

Dean, Tim. 2000. *Beyond Sexuality*. Chicago: University of Chicago Press.

Derrida, Jacques. 1979. *Spurs: Nietzsche's Styles/Eperons*. Barbara Harlow, ed. Chicago: University of Chicago Press.

———. 1985. Choreographies. In *The Ear of the Other*, ed. Christie McDonald (pp. 163–185). Lincoln: University of Nebraska Press.

———. 1987. *The Post Card: From Socrates to Freud and Beyond*. Alan Bass, trans. Chicago: University of Chicago Press.

———. 1998. *Resistances of Psychoanalysis*. Peggy Kamuf, Pascale-Anne Brault, and Michael Naas, trans. Stanford, Calif.: Stanford California Press.

Dollimore, Jonathan. 1991. *Sexual Dissidence: Augustine to Wilde, Freud to Foucault*. Oxford: Clarenden Press.

Edelman, Lee. 1994. *Homographesis: Essays in Gay Literary and Cultural Theory*. New York: Routledge.

Ellsworth, Elizabeth. 1997. *Teaching Positions*. New York: Teachers College Press.

Evans, Dylan. 1996. *An Introductory Dictionary of Lacanian Psychoanalysis*. New York: Routledge.

Feder, Ellen K., and Zakin, Emily. 1997. Flirting with the Truth. In *Derrida and Feminism: Recasting the Question of Woman*, ed. Ellen K. Feder, Mary C. Rawlinson, and Emily Zakin (pp. 21–52). New York: Routledge.

Fink, Bruce. 1995. *The Lacanian Subject: Between Language and Jouissance*. Princeton, N.J.: Princeton University Press.

Freud, Sigmund. 1905. Three Essays on the Theory of Sexuality. In *The Standard Edition of the Complete Psychological Works of Sigmund Freud*, ed. and trans. James Strachey (vol. 7, pp. 123–243). London: Hogarth, 1953–1974. (Cited as SE 7.)

———. 1915. Instinct and its Vicissitudes. In *The Standard Edition of the Complete Psychological Works of Sigmund Freud*, ed. and trans. James Strachey (vol. 14, pp. 109–140). London: Hogarth, 1953–1974. (Cited as SE 14.)

———. 1920. Beyond the Pleasure Principle. In *The Standard Edition of the Complete Psychological Works of Sigmund Freud*, ed. and trans. James Strachey (vol. 18, pp. 7–64). London: Hogarth, 1953–1974. (Cited as SE 18.)

Gallop, Jane. 1995. The Teacher's Breasts. In *Pedagogy: The Question of Impersonation*, ed. Jane Gallop (pp. 79–89). Bloomington: Indiana University Press.

Gasché, Rudolphe. 1986. *The Tain of the Mirror: Derrida and the Philosophy of Reflection*. Cambridge, Mass.: Harvard University Press.

Goux, Jean-Joseph. 1992. The Phallus: Masculine Identity and the "Exchange of Women." *Difference: A Journal of Feminist Cultural Studies* 4(1): 40–75.

Harasym, Sarah, ed. 1998. *The Missed Encounter: Levinas and Lacan.* Albany, N.Y.: SUNY Press.

Heidegger, Martin. 1962. *Being and Time,* trans. John Macquarrie and Edward Robinson. New York: Harper & Row.

Hudak, Glenn, and Kihn, Paul, eds. 2001. *Labeling: Pedagogy and Politics.* New York: RoutledgeFalmer.

Huebner, Dwayne. 1999. *The Lure of the Transcendent: Collected Essays by Dwayne E. Huebner,* ed. Vikki Hills, intro. by William F. Pinar. Mahwah, N.J.: Lawrence Erlbaum Associates.

Irigaray, Luce. 1985a. *Speculum of the Other Woman,* trans. Gillian C. Gill. Ithaca, N.Y.: Cornell University Press.

———. 1985b. *This Sex Which Is Not One,* trans. Catherine Porter with Carolyn Burke. Ithaca, N.Y.: Cornell University Press.

———. 1989. The Gesture in Psychoanalysis. In *Between Feminism and Psychoanalysis,* ed. Teresa Brennan (pp. 127–138). New York: Routledge.

———. 1993. *An Ethics of Sexual Difference,* trans. Carolyn Burke and Gillian C. Gill. Ithaca, N.Y.: Cornell University Press.

jagodzinski, jan. 1996a. *The Anamorphic I/i.* Edmonton, Alberta: Duval Publishing.

———. 1996b. The Unsaid in Educational Narratology: Power and Seduction of Pedagogical Authority. *Journal of Curriculum Theorizing* 12(3): 26–35.

———. 2001. The Best Teacher Stands and Delivers: The Case of Jaime Escalante. *Journal for the Psychoanalysis of Culture & Society* 6(2): 232–241.

Johnson, Barbara. 1987. Teaching Ignorance: L'ecole des Femmes. In Barbara Johnson, *A World of Difference.* Baltimore: Johns Hopkins University Press.

Kristeva, Julia. 1980. *Desire in Language: A Semiotic Approach to Literature and Art,* ed. Leon S. Roudiez, trans. Thomas Gora, Alice Jardine, and Leone S. Roudiez. New York: Columbia University Press.

———. 1987. *Tales of Love,* trans. Leon Roudiez. New York: Columbia University Press.

———. 1991. *Strangers to Ourselves,* trans. Leon Roudiez. New York: Columbia University Press.

Lacan, Jacques. 1977. *Écrits: A Selection,* trans. Alan Sheridan. New York: W.W. Norton.

———. 1979. *Seminar XI, The Four Fundamental Concepts of Psycho-Analysis,* ed. Jacques-Alain Miller, trans. Alan Sheridan. Harmondsworth: Penguin Books. (Cited as *S XI.*)

———. 1990. *Television: A Challenge to the Psychoanalytic Establishment,* ed. Joan Copjec, trans. Denis Hollier, Rosiland Krauss, Annette Michelson, and Jeffrey Mehlman. New York: W.W. Norton.

———. 1992. *The Ethics of Psychoanalysis. Seminar VII,* ed. Jacques-Alain Miller, trans. Dennis Porter. New York: W.W. Norton. (Cited as *S VII.*)

———. 1998. *On Feminine Sexuality, the Limits of Love and Knowledge, 1972–1973. The Seminar of Jacques Lacan XX, Encore,* trans. with notes Bruce Fink, ed. Jacques-Alain Miller. New York: W.W. Norton. (Cited as *S XX.*)

Laqueur, Thomas. 1990. *Making Sex: Body and Gender from the Greeks to Freud.* Cambridge, Mass.: Harvard University Press.

Levinas, Emmanuel. 1981. *Otherwise than Being: Or, Beyond Essence,* trans. Alphonso Lingis. The Hague: M. Nijhoff.

MacCannell, Juliet Flower. 1991. Resistance to Sexual Theory. In *Texts for Change: Theory/ Pedagogy/ Politics*, ed. Donald Morton and Mas'ud Zavarzadeh (pp. 64–89). Urbana: University of Illinois Press.

McWilliam, Erica. 1996. Eros and Pedagogical Bodies: The State of (Non) Affairs. In *Pedagogy, Technology and the Body*, ed. E. McWilliam and P. G. Taylor (pp. 123–132). New York: Peter Lang.

Miller, Jacques-Alain. 1977–1978. Suture (elements of the logic of the signifier). *Screen* 18(4): 24–34.

———. 1994. *Extimité*. In *Lacanian Theory of Discourse: Subject, Structure, and Society*, ed. Mark Bracher, Marshall W. Alcorn, Jr., Ronald J. Corthell, and François Massardier-Kenney (pp. 74–86). New York: New York University Press.

Milovanovic, Dragan, ed. 1992. *Postmodern Law and Disorder: Psychoanalytic Semiotics, Chaos and Juridic Exegeses*. Liverpool: Deborah Charles Publications.

———. 1997. *Chaos, Criminology, and Social Justice: The New Orderly (Dis)order*. Westport, Conn.: Praeger.

Moore, Henrietta L. 1997. Sex, Symbolism and Psychoanalysis. *Difference: A Journal of Feminist Cultural Studies* 9(1): 68–94.

Neil, Alexander Sutherland. 1969. *Summerhill: A Radical Approach to Education*. London: V. Gollancz.

Nobus, Danny. 2001. Littorical Reading: Lacan, Derrida, and the Analytic Production of Chaff. *Journal for the Psychoanalysis of Culture & Society* 6(2): 279–288.

Noddings, Nel. 1981. *Caring*. Berkeley: University of California Press.

Press, Carol. 2001. Creativity, Self Psychology, the Modern Dance Choreographer, and Transformative Education. *Journal for the Psychoanalysis of Culture & Society* 6(2): 223–231.

Ragland, Ellie. 1994. Psychoanalysis and Pedagogy: What Are Mastery and Love Doing in the Classroom? *Pre/Text* 15(1–2): 47–78.

Richardson, George. 2002. *The Death of the Good Canadian: Teachers, National Identities and the Social Studies Curriculum*. New York: Peter Lang.

Roudinesco, Elizabeth. 1997. *Jacques Lacan*, trans. Barbara Bay. New York: Columbia University Press.

Salecl, Renata. 1994. Deference to the Great Other: The Discourse of Education. In *Lacanian Theory of Discourse: Subject, Structure and Society*, ed. M. Bracher, M. W. Alcorn, Jr., R. J. Corthell, and F. Massardier-Kenney (pp. 163–175). New York: New York University Press.

———. 1998. *(Per)versions of Love and Hate*. London: Verso.

Sheldrake, Rupert. 1988. *The Presence of the Past: Morphic Resonance and the Habits of Nature*. London: Collins.

Shepherdson, Charles. 1994. The *Role* of Gender and the *Imperative* of Sex. In *Supposing the Subject*, ed. Joan Copjec (pp. 158–184). London: Verso.

Silverman, Kaja. 2000. *World Spectators*. Stanford, Calif.: Stanford University Press.

Spivak, Gayatri Chakravorty. 1983. Displacement and the Discourse of Woman. In *Displacement: Derrida and After*, ed. Mark Krupnick (pp. 169–195). Bloomington: Indiana University Press.

Stern, Daniel. 1985. *The Interpersonal World of the Infant: A View from Psychoanalysis and Developing Psychology*. New York: Basic Books.

Taubman, Peter. 1990. Achieving the Right Distance. *Educational Theory* 40(1): 121–133.

———. 2000. Teaching Without Hope: What Is Really at Stake in the Standards Movement, High Stakes Testing, and the Drive for "Practical Reforms." *Journal of Curriculum Theorizing* 16(3): 19–33.

———. 2001. The Calling of Sexual Identities. In *Labeling: Pedagogy and Politics*, ed. Glenn Hudak and Paul Kihn (pp. 179–202). New York: Routledge-Falmer.

Todd, Sharon, ed. 1997. *Learning Desire: Perspectives on Pedagogy, Culture, and the Unsaid*. New York: Routledge.

Trifonas, Peter Pericles, ed. 2000. *Revolutionary Pedagogies: Cultural Politics, Instituting Education, and the Discourse of Theory*. New York: Routledge-Falmer.

Van Manen, Max. 1991. *The Tact of Teaching: The Meaning of Pedagogical Thoughtfulness*. Faculty of Education. University of Western Ontario: The Althouse Press.

Vanheule, Stijn. 2001. Burnout and Psychoanalysis: A Freudo-Lacanian Point of View. *Journal for the Psychoanalysis of Culture & Society* 6(2): 265–270.

Walkerdine, Valerie. 1986. *Schooling Girl Fictions*. London: Verso.

Weber, Sandra, and Mitchell, Claudia. 1995. *That's Funny, You Don't Look Like a Teacher: Interrogating Images and Identity in Popular Culture*. London: The Falmer Press.

Whitford, Margaret. 1991. *Luce Irigaray: Philosophy in the Feminine*. New York: Routledge.

Winnicott, D. W. 1982. *Playing and Reality*. Harmondsworth: Penguin Books.

Young-Bruehl, Elizabeth, and Bethelard, Faith. 2000. *Cherishment: A Psychology of the Heart*. New York: The Free Press.

Ziarek, Ewa Plonowska. 1997. From Euthanasia to the Other of Reason. In *Derrida and Feminism: Recasting the Question of Woman*, ed. Ellen K. Feder, Mary C. Rawlinson, and Emily Zakin (pp. 115–140). New York: Routledge.

Žižek Slavoj. 1989. *The Sublime Object of Ideology*. London: Verso.

———. 1991. *Looking Awry: An Introduction to Jacques Lacan Through Popular Culture*. Cambridge, Mass.: MIT Press.

———. 1993. *Tarrying with the Negative: Kant, Hegel, and the Critique of Ideology*. Durham, N.C.: Duke University Press.

———. 1996a. "I Hear You with My Eyes": or, The Invisible Master. In *Gaze and Voice as Love Objects*, ed. Renata Salecl and Slavoj Žižek (pp. 90–126). Durham, N.C.: Duke University Press.

———. 1996b. *The Indivisible Remainder: An Essay on Schelling and Related Matters*. London: Verso.

———. 1999. *The Ticklish Subject: The Absent Centre of Political Ontology*. London: Verso.

Zupančič, Alenka. 2000a. The Case of the Perforated Sheet. In *Sexuation, SIC 3*, ed. Renata Salecl (pp. 282–296). Durham, N.C.: Duke University Press.

———. 2000b. *The Ethics of the Real*. London: Verso.

Part I

Psychoanalysis with Pedagogy

Chapter 1

Psychoanalysis and Education?

Gustavo Guerra

At the end of *The Lacanian Subject: Between Language and Jouissance*, Bruce Fink (1995) provocatively summarizes a line of thinking that he has somewhat hinted at throughout his text. "In the United States," writes Fink, "Lacanian psychoanalysis is little more than a set of texts, a dead discourse unearthed like ancient texts in archeological finds, the context of which has been washed or eroded away. No quantity of publications can change that. For Lacan's discourse to come alive, his clinical approach will have to be introduced alongside his texts, through analysis, supervision, and clinical work, that is, through subjective experience" (p. 152). Fink's obvious point here is that any attempt to understand Lacanian thought without the clinical context that should accompany it is doomed to fail. Without this clinical context Lacan is, for Fink, a "set of dead texts," and those texts will remain dead as long as Lacanian thinkers keep forgetting the clinical aspect of Lacan's work: the aspect where, Fink continues, "clinicians can observe Lacanian practitioners at work," or see "the immediate benefits at the clinical level of Lacan's distinctions and formulations" (p. 151). And "no quantity of publications can change that" because without the clinical context such publications will be simply more "dead text." Although Fink's words make sense, not many have heeded his warning, since it is almost expected to see much "dead text" these days where Lacanian psychoanalysis is used primarily as an epistemological tool, as a method of reading that yields interesting results. Thus there are "readings" of, for example, *Moby Dick*, or any other work, from the perspective of, say, *Seminar VII*, or *XI*, or *XX*, or whatever seminar or Lacanian article happens to sound "cool" and appealing. From the looks of it, it seems that psychoanalysis is only just one more of the latest fashions in literary criticism these days; and any mere resemblance between psychoanalysis and a clinical method used to cure what Colette Soler (1991) has called "the subject of suffering," is perceived as uninteresting and illusory. One of the immediate dangers of the unexamined application of a particular set of axioms from one discipline to another is an unfortunate reduction of the complexity of either discipline. And although I do feel that there is something to say about the value of reductionism on occasion, I am not convinced such is the case in the areas of psychoanalysis and education, specifically for reasons I hope will become clearer as my argument develops.

I felt, therefore, at first slightly curious as I started thinking of the relationship between psychoanalysis and education, and later on skeptical when I began to read some of the claims made in the name of psychoanalysis, particularly in the field of composition theory nowadays. Pedagogical theory seems to have fallen in love with the idea that psychoanalysis is the antifoundational discipline per se; with the idea, that is, that all that psychoanalysis teaches is that there are no absolutes, that there are only perspectives, individual histories, and no transcendental center that one occupies. Any psychoanalytically oriented pedagogy, in this version of psychoanalysis, serves to advance the claim that there is no foundation to knowledge, that teachers occupy no privileged position, and that whatever students say is correct as long as it derives from some strange place within themselves, frequently called "the students' inner experience." This line of thinking often argues that teachers cannot, or at least should not, teach students directly; rather that they should allow students to create the circumstances in which learning can occur; that professors should encourage students to come to their own conclusions about, for instance, what constitutes good or bad writing, and why this is so and, in the most extreme cases, that the best thing teachers can do for students is to get out of their way. Recently, however, and because of the perceived failure of this pedagogical strategy, the opposite stance has been adopted. A number of institutions of higher education have designed composition programs where the teacher's role is more like that of a dictator telling students exactly how and what they should be thinking and writing. In some extreme cases the teacher's position is almost elevated to that of "the subject who really knows," to use a well-known Lacanian maxim. This is, for example, the position of writing theorist George Trail (2000), who writes that we should go back to those times when teachers were considered "masters." Even though Trail concedes that he does not expect those of us who teach to call ourselves "masters," he thinks our students should. "The master, or sensei," Trail writes in what we might call a Zen moment in his argument, "herself would not consider an area mastered, but would expect that that title be employed by those seeking to study under an individual whom they recognize as particularly distinguished in a given area of endeavor" (p. 1). Although Trail does not invoke psychoanalysis directly, he often talks about writing in relation to what he calls "psychological complex processes," which he clearly believes are related to a version of psychoanalysis where the analyst's job is simply to tell the analysand what to do or how to behave in a given situation or context. In case we run into the temptation of dismissing his thoughts as too simplistic, Trail makes sure to remind us that such is not the case, finishing his argument with the supposedly powerful sentence: "nothing about the process is simple" (p. 6), although it seems as if the process will indeed be simplified as long as we adopt the attitude of all-knowing scholars objectively imparting our hard-earned knowledge to whoever students fall into our hands. Those who think Trail is an isolated case would do well to read Alan Frances's (2000) recent "Dialectics of Self: Structure and Agency as the Subject of English." Drawing on Newman's ideal of liberal education "for the cultivation of the intellect for its own sake" (p. 146), Frances asserts that "composition specialists tacitly assume that rhetoric and writing instruction performs disciplinary work essential to the study of language and literature" (p. 146). Besides revealing a deep anxiety that composition not be viewed as a sub-discipline within English departments—something that concerns Frances throughout his essay—the assertion makes clear that such disciplinary attitude is essential for the construction of a pedagogy whose aim is "the student who must learn to assemble and assimilate the fragments of post-modern experience into a coherent, self-conscious identity in order to communicate, or to join discourse communities" (p. 149). The question is, what exactly *is* the student going to communicate after she has miraculously "assembled and assimilated the fragments of postmodern experience?" Frances, of course, avoids this question because answering it would place his argument in a fragile position. After such "defragmentation" process occurs nothing would have changed because such learning cannot have any bearing on the way the students write. Or, to put it in philosophical terms, finding some transcendental horizon from where to make sense of yourself does not avail one of any practical knowledge about how to run your life, and least of all about how to write. Or, to put the matter slightly differently, Frances's basic problem seems to lie in that he thinks that you need to become something other than what you are in order to become productively involved in a certain discursive community. But doing so will simply allow you access in a different community and nothing else. Once no longer fragmented, Frances's students, although they may gain access to the community of unified selves, will lose entrance to the community of "fragmented" selves. Or, perhaps more accurately, they will have recourse to two discourses instead of one. They will, in sum, be able to be both fragmented and defragmented as the need arises. They will honor the title of Frances's essay in that they will be able to engage in a "Dialectics of Self," a dialectics which, by the way, does not seem to appeal much to Frances himself, since he is so concerned to restate the centrality of the self through the activity of teaching. This is why at the end of the essay Frances tells the hypothetical reader outside an English department that the central role of composition studies is to "teach students how they can decide for themselves what is true" (p. 163). The central words here are "teach" and "outside." Despite all the echoes of Foucault in words like "disciplinary," "discourse," and so on, what Frances calls for is an old-fashioned, teacher-centered pedagogy. What is true for Frances's students is what he tells them it is. In placing the teacher in that center role, he can justify the teaching of composition to those "outside" English departments.

Now these two antithetical positions in writing theory are often largely dependent on what task we believe pedagogy should perform. The first line of thinking assumes that the aim of education is to unsettle and disturb the students' complacency and sense of self so that they can become, *à la* Nietzsche, something other than what they are. The second line assumes that the students are already unsettled and disturbed enough when they begin higher education, and that the aim of education is to actually help students find their "center" so that they can also change and become different from what they were before. What is interesting about these two positions— which we might call the "decentering" and the "centering" positions—is that, although they apparently present opposing ways of thinking about education, they are in fact alike. Both of them, for instance, rely on various principles of communication that underlie their central pedagogical claims. For the both of them, however, the communicative function is quite alien to any psychoanalytic process. Insofar as both positions start from the premise that the teacher will be able to change students in some fundamental ways, it is fair to claim that they attempt to determine the conditions of reception of a particular kind of discourse. In this particular model, the listener or student is, more specifically, simply an empty head—or *tabula rasa*, in philosophical terms—receiving information from a sender. This particular view of pedagogy would have the classroom as the location where messages get sent to a group of receivers. And, if there is any dialogue whatsoever, it usually takes only the form of an exchange of the same role between two persons so that the sender and the empty receiver take turns at performing either one role or the other.

Readers conversant with basic psychoanalytic theory will be quick to recognize this particular scenario as radically alien to anything psychoanalytic. This is alien to the psychoanalytic process as defined by Lacan because the fundamental aim of psychoanalysis is *to help the subject acknowledge and take responsibility over her unconscious desire*. In so doing, psychoanalysis places subjectivity within an ethical framework of responsibility and caring alien to the mechanical and univocally oriented educational process I described above. But, if this is unjust in its representation of the nature of psychoanalysis, it is as disturbing, I propose, to the nature of any committed educational process. For in creating such a rigid communicative hierarchy, both the decentering and centering positions make the professor an absolute authority—indeed, a master, in Trail's words—and the students simple receptacles for the transmission of a pre-constituted, unexamined, and unquestionable knowledge. Education is perceived as the development and training of blank minds who never analyze or question the purposes and function of their particular educational process. So, instead of either centering or decentering, ostensibly the original goal of this line of thinking, we end up with the achievement of a mimetic identity where the student is either a replication of the professor or of his place in the communicative chain.

One reason for the appeal of psychoanalysis for teachers is that it is the only model that I can think of where the teacher–student relationship can be said to parallel the analyst–patient relationship. Because the psychoanalytic process does produce a different kind of subjectivity, it seems natural to claim the same of the educational process. This parallel becomes even more obvious when one points out the shared interest between psychoanalysis and education in the workings of language. Even though it is hard to disagree with the fact that psychoanalysis presents us with what Bruce Fink calls a "radically new theory of subjectivity," it is hard to reconcile that subject with that one imagined to come out of composition classes. This radical new theory is based on a linguistic model which, for lack of a better term, I will call dialogic. By dialogic I mean simply that the addressee's (or student's or analysand's) head is already full of language so that the Saussurean (Saussure 1966) model of communicative transmission cannot describe effectively what happens in either a classroom or a psychoanalytic setting. Communication, in other words, cannot be the transfer of a prefabricated meaning. What someone says or writes takes place among a crowd of ideas, thoughts, linguistic expression. That explains why in Lacan's writing, the word "subject" appears often in between double quotes. The quotes are meant to represent the fact that the subject is always something already rhetorically marked insofar as we understand rhetoric as a dialogical exchange. This is even clearer in the clinical setting itself where, in the words of Fink:

If the analyst offers up something along the lines of meaning to the analysand, he or she nevertheless aims at something capable of exploding the "analyst-provides-the-meaning-of-the-analysand's discourse" matrix by speaking equivocally, at several levels at once, using terms which lead in a number of different directions. By intimating several, if not a never-ending panorama of, successive meanings, the register of meanings is itself problematized. (p. 67)

Therefore, conversation or writing takes shape in a discursive sense in which neither participant is a master. The "new" subject that comes—or should come—out of this process is not the poststructuralist, decentered or deconstructed subject posited in the "decentered" mode, but instead one in which the notion of meaning or understanding has undergone a fundamental revision; one arrived at not through a process of indoctrination or decentralization, but of a dialogue that produces what Lacan has called "*bien dire*," which is often translated as "well saying," and which Soler (1991) clearly explains thus:

Well-saying [*bien dire*] concerns the relation between words and being, between words and who you are. Well-saying [*bien dire*] produces something new which was not present before, a new knowledge about the subject. The new subject produced by psychoanalysis is one who has changed his mind. About what? About what matters in life. It is a subject whose values have changed, a subject who has decided it is worth knowing who he is. (pp. 30–31)

In the educational scenario this new subject should also change her mind. And, even though I would not want to make the ambitious claim Soler makes, it is fair to say that the aim of education is to produce students who can make their own meaning. The key word here is "own." For in this particular scenario it is the students who bring their truths, choose their topics, or, in the words of Jeffrey Berman (1994), "the students control how much of the genie they want to release at a time" (p. 32). Marshall Alcorn (1994) puts it beautifully when he writes that "as a result of textual identifications," which are, of course, the result of an educational process, "people come to fantasize about themselves differently, to define themselves differently, to act differently, and to have ideas about an ideal community. They adjust their self-image and form bonds with like-minded people and begin to argue with others. They engage in politics. They formulate new definitions of authority and morality to justify the new visions of self and society that they have come to embrace" (p. 21). They accept, in psychoanalytic terms, something alien as their own. *In making and accepting something alien as your own lies one of the most fundamental principles of both psychoanalysis and education.*

One of the many objections that I can anticipate to some of my observations here is that neither of the positions I described earlier represents a truly psychoanalytic theoretical or practical account. Neither do they represent accurately what a committed educational process entails. But if this is true, it is hard to understand why statements like that of Gregory Jay, in a 1987 essay of *College English*, is still considered relevant today. Jay affirms that the teacher's role is to "undo certainty":

A pedagogy of the unconscious must dislocate fixed desires rather than feed us what we think we want to know. . . . [T]his means that the teacher's task is to make the student ill (which we often do unknowingly anyway). Where the psychoanalyst seeks to stabilize a shattered self, the pedagogue hopes to unsettle the complacency and conceptual identities of the student. Education becomes subjective in the sense that the student experiences his or her existence as being subjected to various discourses, including that of the teacher. The disturbance that ensues includes the split between the self-as-subject and the subject-of-knowledge, since the latter comes into being in skeptical reflections on the former—even to the point of finally doubting the value of such reflection. Like psychoanalysis, education can only begin with self-doubt, and its disciplinary self-analyses should be interminable. (p. 790)

When Jay drops the idea that teachers often make students ill with a casualness that is frightening, it really does make one wonder to what kind of psychoanalysis or education he refers. This is precisely why Mark Bracher (1999), in *The Writing Cure*, together with Jeff Berman's (1994) *Diaries to an English Professor: Pain and Growth in the Classroom*, are perhaps the most sophisticated, if not the only, explorations of the complexity of the relationship between psychoanalysis and education. Bracher cautions several times throughout the book that much which passes for psychoanalysis these days is simply a misrepresentation. The book is full of statements like "so and so misrepresents psychoanalysis in crucial ways," or "in a truly psychoanalytic pedagogy, this and that would happen," or "a truly Lacanian pedagogy offers this and that." Even though Bracher's well-intentioned anxiety to clarify the difference between true and false or misguided pedagogical strategies goes a long way toward clarifying what is at stake in a thorough understanding of both psychoanalysis and education, it still does not erase the fact that when both psychoanalysis and education are so poorly understood and made to interact with each other, the question of why this should be the case becomes even more urgent. So my point is made precisely to raise the question of why it is that a misrepresented psychoanalytic pedagogy is so often invoked as a basis for educational practice. As Berman points out, "since the 1960s, the writing classroom has become socially and politically charged, with teachers advancing their own ideological agendas. Students sometimes find themselves caught in the middle, not knowing which ideology to espouse or resist" (p. 28). It is only natural that the students themselves should be confused when, as Bracher points out, the teachers seem to be as, sometimes even more, confused than the students. It is somewhat embarrassing to confess that I do not have the answer to that question. But as long as we use psychoanalytically informed pedagogies that, whether we like or acknowledge it, produce replicas of ourselves, we are going down the wrong path. Students will not be able to benefit from what can be considered, broadly speaking, an underlying premise of both education and psychoanalysis: the ability to be able to engage others in such a way that, as a result of productive encounters, they become different from what they were before. Without that capacity, students will never be able to engage in arguments and think of themselves any differently from the way they did before participating in their own educational process; they will never, rephrasing some of the statements from Alcorn cited above, be able to create imagined communities. I worry—should I encounter students of Berman or Bracher who I know have been able to make their own meaning, who think for themselves, who have been able to engage argumentatively with others, and who have created such communities—in case they ask me that question I have posed here, but with a rather different intention than mine, one reflecting not intellectual inquiry or curiosity, but boredom and indifference.

REFERENCES

Alcorn, Marshall. 1994. *Narcissism and the Literary Libido: Rhetoric, Text, and Subjectivity*. New York: New York University Press.

Berman, Jeffrey. 1994. *Diaries to an English Professor: Pain and Growth in the Classroom*. Amherst: University of Massachusetts Press.

———. Forthcoming. *Risky Writing: Self-Disclosure and Self-Transformation in the Classroom*. Amherst: University of Massachusetts Press.

Bracher, Mark. 1999. *The Writing Cure: Psychoanalysis, Composition, and the Aims of Education*. Carbondale: Southern Illinois University Press.

Fink, Bruce. 1995. *The Lacanian Subject: Between Language and Jouissance*. Princeton, N.J.: Princeton University Press.

Frances, Alan. 2000. Dialectics of Self: Structure and Agency as the Subject of English. *College English* 63(2): 145–165.

Jay, Gregory. 1987. The Subject of Psychoanalysis: Lessons in Psychoanalysis and Politics. *College English* 49: 785–800.

Saussure, Ferdinand de. 1966. *Course in General Linguistics*, trans. Wade Baskin. New York: McGraw-Hill.

Soler, Colette. 1991. Ethics in the Cure. *Lacanian Ink* 2: 29–36.

Trail, George. 2000. *Rhetorical Terms and Concepts: A Contemporary Glossary*. Orlando, Fla.: Harcourt Brace.

Chapter 2

The Teaching Imaginary: Collective Identity in a Post-Prefixed Age

Derek Briton

Every society up to now has attempted to give an answer to a few fundamental questions: Who are we as a collectivity? What are we for one another? Where and in what are we? What do we want; what do we desire; what are we lacking? Society must define its "identity," its articulation, the world, its relations to the world and to the objects it contains, its needs and its desires. Without the "answer" to these "questions," without these "definitions," there can be no human world, no society, no culture—for everything would be an undifferentiated chaos. The role of imaginary significations is to provide an answer to these questions, an answer that, obviously, neither "reality," nor "rationality" can provide. (Castoriadis 1987, 146–147)

THE CURRENT IMPASSE

Of late, questions such as "Who are we as a collectivity?" "What are we for one another?" "Where and in what are we?" "What do we want?" "What do we desire?" "What are we lacking?" have become acutely pertinent to North American teacher educators. No longer is it taken for granted that teaching is a field of endeavor worthy of study in the university. It seems as if the very notion of teaching as a profession, as a research-based discipline that proceeds from "a specialized, authoritative, and counterintuitive professional knowledge base" (Labaree 1992, 135) is slipping from popular consciousness. The very *idea* of teacher preparation in North America seems in danger of reverting to one that flourished prior to the institution of Teacher Education[1] at the turn of the twentieth century. Until teacher educators better understand the reasons for this inversion, the question of how best to respond to populist, reactionary attacks on the field will remain a point of contention and will inevitably promote in-fighting and further fragmentation of the field. This chapter looks to events leading up to and proceeding from the institution of teaching as an area of specialization in North American universities and colleges, and draws on central concepts from the psychoanalytic tradition, and the work of several theorists working in that tradition—Castoriadis, Copjec, Lacan, La-clau and Mouffe, Lefort, and Žižek—to explore this perplexing problem and outline a potential course of action that will allow teacher educators to move beyond the impasse currently immobilizing the field.

IN THE BEGINNING

Early in the nineteenth century, well before Teacher Education as a dis-tinctive area of study was even imagined, a craft-based mode of teacher preparation flourished in normal schools across the North American con-tinent.[2] An offshoot of mass public schooling in the Unites States, the first normal schools appeared in the 1820s, opened by proponents of public schooling who believed existing secondary schools and liberal arts colleges were incapable of supplying the number, and perhaps more importantly, the *kind* of teacher public education demanded—the more affluent second-ary school and college graduates tended to be unsuited and ill-prepared for the less cerebral demands of public schooling, and those who did take teaching positions usually abandoned them forthwith for more lucrative professions.

Normal schools, "on the other hand, recruited a class of students who had limited opportunities for advanced education elsewhere or for achieve-ment in other professions than teaching," and made no pretense to prepare their graduates for "educational leadership, which was still a function of talented amateurs like [Horace] Mann"; their goal was to produce teachers who "would remain in the classroom, teaching a curriculum prescribed by the board of education, through texts selected by that board or provided on a chance basis by parents, and according to methods suggested by mas-ter teachers or educational theorists, most of whom had been educated in the colleges" (Borrowman 1965, 19–23).

Unlike the liberal arts colleges and universities, which sought to instill in their graduates the ideals of the Good or Contemplative life, "the American normal school glorified and supported the ideal of superb craftsmanship in classroom management" (Borrowman 1965, 23).[3] Academic limitations notwithstanding, normal schools offered the only course of study devised specifically for teachers, and the only alternative to the traditional "teach-ers' degree"—the Bachelor of Arts (B.A.) degree offered by liberal arts col-leges and universities. It was the establishment of normal schools, then, that brought the preparation of teachers to public consciousness, and made it possible, for the first time, to *imagine* Teacher Education as a distinctive area of study.

INSTITUTIONAL REFORM

The idea of Teacher Education as a distinctive area of study did not coalesce, however, until late in the nineteenth century, when America's institutions of higher learning succumbed to reform—initially, to the mounting pressure to broaden the traditional liberal arts curriculum to include such new fields of endeavor as modern languages, English grammar and literature, history, political economy, the natural sciences, and education; and later, to the swelling demand for "useful knowledge," as the nation expanded westward and "those destined for leadership in any occupation—including manufacturing, commerce, and teaching—required higher education tailored to their vocational needs" (Borrowman 1965, 17). Initially, it was advocates of agricultural and engineering education who imagined introducing "practical" fields of study into the new Midwestern state universities.[4] To such people, it made perfect sense to use the new universities "to augment the supply of teachers for a rapidly expanding common-school system. It is not surprising, therefore, that the new universities moved quickly into the field of teacher education" (p. 18).

Not all, however, supported this course of action. W. C. Poland, of Brown University, for example, maintained that "the traditional BA degree, which required study of the 'laws of the mind,' was in fact a teachers' degree," and that any "specialized technical skills that the professional teacher had to learn . . . should be taught in a separate graduate school" (Borrowman 1965, 18). But reform was in the air, and previous ideas of teacher preparation were soon sublated by that of Teacher Education—an area of specialization worthy of study in the academy: "by 1900, the normal-school and liberal arts college traditions of teacher education were coming together," and "in the half-century that followed . . . , the normal school moved from the position of a secondary school to that of a collegiate institution, and the study of education found a place in virtually every American university and in most of the liberal arts colleges" (p. 27).

THE IMPACT OF PRACTICAL EDUCATION

The impact of practical knowledge on universities proved so great that by the turn of the century, empiricism had eclipsed reason as the touchstone of truth, and the "scientific method" had established itself as the only assured path to truth's door.[5] This prompted a number of teacher educators to imagine Teacher Education anew—as neither a liberal art, a profession, nor some amalgam of the two—but as a science. Educational psychologist Edward Thorndike, who published his *Principles of Teaching, Based on*

Psychology in 1906, typified the new scientific teacher educator. Thorndike (1965, 175) was convinced that "just as the science and art of agriculture depend upon chemistry and botany, so the art of education depends upon physiology and psychology. A complete science of psychology would tell every fact about every one's intellect and character and behavior." Some three years later, Franklin Bobbit, an advocate of "scientific training," imagined Teacher Education based on the principles of scientific management popularized by efficiency engineer, Frederick Winslow Taylor. Bobbit was "an extraordinarily prolific writer and influential reformer" who insisted that "education would be governed by SCIENCE—scientific management in the administration of schools, scientific curriculum-making, and the scientific discovery of the qualities of a good teacher" (Kliebard 1973, 11).

A SCIENCE OF EDUCATION

Many teacher educators readily identified with this new idea of Teacher Education,[6] and convinced that "a 'science of education' was waiting to be discovered, . . . set about, with a rather unscientific show of faith, trying to quantify the field, searching for the 'laws' and irrefragable principles they supposed governed the ways in which learning took place"; consequently, when the noted psychometrician, Charles H. Judd, declared in 1918 that "all that was necessary for solving educational problems . . . was the systematic application of the scientific method," few voices were raised in opposition (Koerner 1965, 28–29). Thus, as the 1920s roared into vogue, and science-based curricula rose to prominence in American colleges and universities, the idea of Teacher Education became an almost exclusively "scientific" one. Now, as never before, the field looked to *reality* and the *rational* for answers to such fundamental questions as "Who are we as a collectivity? What are we for one another? Where and in what are we? What do we want; what do we desire; what are we lacking?" to "define its 'identity,' its articulation, the world, its relations to the world and to the objects it contains, its needs and its desires" (Castoriadis 1987, 147–148).

According to Koerner (1965, 29–30): "the efforts of educationists to develop a bona fide discipline lured them for many years into the trap of scientism." In the beginning, few even attempted to hold their ground against scientism's blitzkrieg of "reason" and "reality,"[7] and even though opposition grew steadily throughout the 1930s, 1940s and 1950s, Teacher Education was construed in scientific terms well into the 1960s.[8] But the 1960s proved also to be a time of change for Teacher Education. It was during the 1960s, according to Wilfrid Carr (1995, 30), that the "orthodox view of educational theory was subjected to a barrage of heavy-handed attacks by an army of philosophers and denounced as 'confused', 'vague', 'pseudo-theory'," resulting in the field "being purged of its unacceptable features, and replaced by a somewhat arbitrary collection of academic disciplines . . . the philosophy, psychology and sociology 'of education'." As a result, Teacher Education was re-imagined as "education departments were reorganized; courses were restructured; professional identities were changed; new journals and academic societies were established, all displaying total allegiance to the view that educational theory was nothing other than the application to education of these 'foundation' disciplines." But as early as the mid-1970s, "the puritanical zeal with which the disciplines approach had originally been pursued began to be tempered by a growing realization that many educational problems were not accessible from the narrow confines of any single theoretical discipline" (Carr 1995).

IN SEARCH OF NEW ANSWERS

A number of teacher educators, it seems, had come to share Castoriadis's (1987, 147–148) conclusion that when it comes to such definitional questions as "Who are we as a collectivity? What are we for one another? Where and in what are we? What do we want; what do we desire; what are we lacking?"—that is, for the field to "define its 'identity,' its articulation, the world, its relations to the world and to the objects it contains, its needs and its desires"—these are answers "that, obviously, neither 'reality,' nor 'rationality' can provide." Consequently, in spheres once the exclusive domain of the orthodoxy—teacher education publications, journals, and conferences—the institution's modernist "answers" were subjected to ever greater scrutiny by an increasingly vocal lobby of educators committed to alternative forms of knowledge and pedagogy.[9]

Inspired by the successes of feminist and civil rights initiatives in other arenas, this alternative lobby struggled unremittingly to strip the establishment's answers of their essentialist guise; to unveil the exclusionary interests at play behind their universalist gloss; and to expose their insensitivity to specific differences, whether of time, place, gender, race, class, ability, sexual preference, or age. But, to coin one of Marx's favorite Hegelian turns of phrase, their victory proved, at once, to be loss. Once the modernist answers that had long served to unify the field were discredited, the power of the orthodoxy began to wane—but so, too, did that of the alternative lobby. Having lost its *raison d'être*, the alternative lobby began to dissipate into a plethora of special interest groups engaged in various forms of identity politics. Thus, stripped of its oppressive, but also defining, characteristics, Teacher Education is suffering an identity crisis, a crisis that some teacher educators fear threatens the very being of the field.[10]

THE PROBLEM OF LEGITIMACY

The problem confronting teacher educators, as researchers such as La-baree (1992) note, is one of legitimacy: If the very *idea* of Teacher Education has no legitimacy, can never be grounded in the modernist ideals of reason or reality, it would seem that all *post*modernist modes of teacher preparation are equally valid:

The context-bound and particularistic accounts of instruction that emerge from postmodern research simply do not provide an authoritative, foundational, and technical justification for policy interventions in the same way as those scientistic accounts that philosophers love to deconstruct. This conflict poses an intellectual and professional dilemma for teacher educators. While empirically and theoretically the science of teaching is increasingly difficult to defend, to abandon it in favor of the postmodern approach is to give up the very thing that gives their works a privileged status within educational discourse. If they are not speaking authoritatively from the platform of positive science, then why should their ideas on education be accorded any greater weight that those of laypersons such as teachers, parents, and citizens? (Labaree 1992, 143–144)

But given that most teacher educators reject populist, reactionary calls for a return to a craft-based mode of teacher preparation, we need to investigate the nature of Teacher Education further if we are to discover how such rejections can be substantiated.

THE NATURE OF IDENTITY

What is it that makes a "Canadian" distinctly different from an "American"? While members of both collectivities will protest and defend their "differences," just *how* they are different is often a mystery to Canadians and Americans alike. The same is true of members of other nations. In fact, according to Benedict Anderson (1991, 3–6), the concepts "nation, nationality, nationalism—all have proved notoriously difficult to define, let alone to analyse." Such concepts, Anderson contends, are "cultural artifacts of a particular kind"; consequently, "to understand them properly we need to consider carefully how they have come into historical being," and "in what ways their meanings have changed over time." Descriptors—or, to use Castoriadis's (1987) term, imaginary signifiers—such as Nation and Teacher Education, then, refer not to a set of objective or *real* features but *imaginary* relations. Why? Because teacher educators, not unlike "the members of even the smallest nation will never know most of their fellow-members, meet them, or even hear of them, yet in the minds of each lives the image of their communion."

However, just as the members of most nations consider themselves part of *real* rather than *imaginary* communities, so too do teacher educators. But if the reality of imaginary signifiers such as Teacher Education is not quantifiable and objective, as Anderson (1991) suggests, how does one arrive at their "truth"? According to Howard (1977, 249), who draws extensively on the work of political theorist Claude Lefort, much of which remains unpublished, through a process of philosophical interrogation, because "it is the nature of the *reality* in question to only expose itself in this manner: it is an historical reality."[11] Lefort construes history in neither objective nor teleological terms, but rather as

the repetition of the project which constitutes society: the assembling of men who situate themselves as depending on the same public thing, acquire a collective identity, inscribe their respective positions in a common natural space, their institutions in a private community vis-à-vis foreign people, find a certain equilibrium in the relation of forces (even if they constantly put it into question), and are led by the will of the Master, that of the most powerful or that of the majority among them, to find the means for their security and their development. (Lefort, cited in Howard 1977, 249)

Although Lefort is concerned primarily with the coming-into-being, or institution, of societies, his analysis is equally applicable to the institution of Teacher Education, for the establishment of that community likewise involves

the assembling of men [educators] who situate themselves as depending on the same public thing [Teacher Education], acquire a collective identity [as teacher educators], inscribe their respective positions in a common natural space, their institutions in a private community [establish faculties of education within the university] vis-à-vis foreign people [in relation to "other" academics], find a certain equilibrium in the relation of forces (even if they constantly put it into question) [agree on the need for a curriculum but differ on its content], and are led by the will of the Master, that of the most powerful or that of the majority among them [advocates of scientism], to find the means for their security and their development [a science of education]. (ibid.)

THE INSTITUTION OF COMMUNITY

However, the institution of any community, according to Lefort, is co-terminous with a fundamental breech that bifurcates the community into two seemingly distinct, yet intimately related, components: the Social and Political. The institution of Teacher Education, for example, entails the establishment of a mode of collective being that must obfuscate its origins on the level of the Social in order to appear to its constituents as "a public thing"—an ideal image, an imaginary signifier—on the level of the Political. This somewhat puzzling relation between practitioners (the Social) and

Figure 2.1
Lacan's Schema L

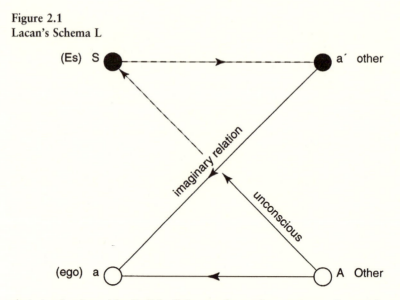

their institutions (the Political) is not the easiest to grasp. It may be useful, therefore, to look to a graphic representation of a similar relation between the ego and ego ideal that Lacan maps in his Schema L (see Figure 2.1).

If we look to Lacan's Schema L, it soon becomes apparent that the Social/Political axis Lefort posits at the core of collective being is homologous to the Imaginary/Symbolic axis Lacan identifies at the root of individual being. In Schema L, the Social corresponds to the Imaginary axis a—a': the realm of consciousness, of the signifier, of the ego or "me" and its specular correlative or "other," the ideal ego. The Political, on the other hand, corresponds to the Symbolic axis S—A: the realm of the unconscious, of the signified, of the thinking subject or "I," and the ego ideal.

We learn from Lacan (1977, 193–194) that individual being, the subject, "is stretched over the four corners of the schema: namely, S, his ineffable, stupid existence, a', his objects, and a, his ego, that is, that which is reflected of his form in his objects, and A, the locus from which the question of his existence may be presented to him."[12] If the collective being of Teacher Education is extended across Schema L in a similar fashion, we find: S represents the undifferentiated, pre-institutionalized community; a', the community's objects ("other" academic disciplines); and a, the community's image of itself in relation to those "other" fields of endeavor. These three elements are all located within the Imaginary or Social dimension. A, on the other hand, is located in the Symbolic or Political dimension and represents the imaginary signifier, "the public thing" members of a community must identify with to constitute its very being: the founding principle or Law of the community—the place from which the question of its existence can be presented to it.

A LACANIAN NOTION OF LAW

It is important to recognize, however, that the Lacanian notion of Law at play here is not merely prohibitory but also enabling, something "conceived as an agency of 'disalienation' and 'liberation': it opens up our access to desire by enabling us to disengage ourselves from the rule of the Other's whim" (Žižek 1991, 265). Under the Law, the emergence of Teacher Education as a Law-governed practice allows teacher educators to distinguish themselves from the Other, to identify with one another and see themselves as distinct from all other fields of academic endeavor.

However, before teacher educators can recognize themselves in an idealized representation of their collective desire on the level of the Political—in the re-presentation of that desire as a Law—the Political ideal of Teacher Education must appear greater than, and qualitatively different from, the various instances of teacher education that emerged from and compete on the level of the Social—liberal arts–based, craft-based, and professional-based modes of teacher education. The institution of Teacher Education entails, then, the coming into being of a concrete instance of teacher education that must repress all knowledge of its origins on the level of the Social in order to be able to re-present itself as an objective set of defining characteristics, the Law, on the level of the Political. In other words, a Particular instance of teacher education must begin to *function* as the Universal form of every instance of teacher education. In Platonic terms, then, an imaginary signifier is a Particular that *functions* as a Universal.

The inversion that elevates a Particular to the rank of Universal was of singular interest to Marx, who attributes the birth of German Idealism and the commodity form to just such an inversion. Writing of value, Marx notes:

This *inversion* through which what is sensible and concrete counts only as a phenomenal form of what is abstract and universal, contrary to the real state of things where the abstract and the universal count only as a property of the concrete—such an inversion is characteristic of the expression of value, and it is this inversion which, at the same time, makes the understanding of this expression so difficult. If I say: Roman law and German law are both laws, it is something which goes by itself. But if, on the contrary, I say: THE Law, this abstract thing, realizes itself in Roman law, i.e., in these concrete laws, the interconnection becomes mystical. (Marx, in Žižek 1989, 32)

If we modify Marx's example and substitute liberal arts–based teacher education for Roman law and craft-based teacher education for German law, it becomes only too clear how, through an act of inversion, an ideal can be abstracted from a number of concrete instances that emerge in the Social and function as an ideal or Master Signifier in the Political—Teacher Education. In retrospect, it is not difficult to see that the particular model of teacher education that began to function as the universal standard of teacher education is the pseudo-scientific model that emerged in the 1950s. This is the Master Signifier, the Law that the alternative lobby railed against.

THE QUILTING POINT

That this Master Signifier to which all other signifiers refer can somehow be cashed-out in terms of a set of objective features—the *true* definition— was long the unquestioned belief of the field. But the field, in fact, this "multitude of 'floating signifiers' . . . is structured into a unified field through the intervention of a certain 'nodal point' (the Lacanian *point de capiton*) which 'quilts' them, stops their sliding and fixes their meaning" (Žižek 1989, 87). It is the Political ideal image, the signifier Teacher Education, that serves as this "nodal point." It may be easier to grasp this process of "quilting" if we take the term "radical democracy" as a corollary of the term "teacher education" and observe how this signifier, this ideal image, serves to "quilt," to sustain the *identity* of diverse fields of political endeavor, in the work of Ernesto Laclau and Chantal Mouffe (1985). Slavoj Žižek (1989) offers the following account of this process at play:

Let us take the Laclau/Mouffe project of radical democracy: here, we have an articulation of particular struggles (for peace, ecology, feminism, human rights, and so on), none of which pretends to the "Truth," the last Signified, the "true Meaning" of all the others; but the title "radical democracy" itself indicates how the very possibility of their articulation implies the "nodal," determining role of a certain struggle which, precisely as a particular struggle, outlines the horizon of all the other struggles. This determining role belongs, of course, to democracy, to "democratic invention": according to Laclau and Mouffe, all other struggles (socialist, feminist . . .) could be conceived as the gradual radicalization, extension, application of the democratic project to new domains (of economic relations, of the relations between sexes . . .). *The dialectical paradox lies in the fact that the particular struggle playing a hegemonic role, far from enforcing a violent suppression of the differences, opens the very space for the relative autonomy of the particular struggles*: the feminist struggle, for example, is made possible only through reference to democratic-egalitarian political discourse. (88–89; emphasis added)

In the case of Teacher Education, "the dialectical paradox lies in the fact that the particular struggle playing a hegemonic role [that of the orthodoxy], far from enforcing a violent suppression of the differences, *opens the very space* for the relative autonomy of the particular [class, gender, race . . .] struggles" (p. 88; emphasis added). The irony in the current situation, then, is that the alternative lobby, in struggling to shatter the orthodoxy's image of Teacher Education, threatens to destroy that which "opens the very space for the particular struggles" that constitute the alternative lobby. This strange turn of events has arisen in Teacher Education, and arises in other institutions, when those in power, whether in a democratic or totalitarian manner, declare the Political ideal—as they are inevitably inclined to do—*actually* rather than *apparently* greater than, separate from, and independent of its origins in the Social.

THE PROBLEM OF THE POLITICAL

Of course, divorcing the Political from the Social generates legitimation problems. In the name of what, for instance, might the ideal, the Law, be imposed—individual freedom, the common Good, faith(s), pragmatism, Truth? If those in power simply impose the ideal, those in the Social will inevitably revolt; but if those in power admit the ideal to be no more than a competing instance from the Social, it can no longer serve as the Law. The bifurcation into Political and Social is a conundrum all institutions must contend with: Any institution, in the act of distinguishing itself from other fields of endeavor, comes into being through a Political representation that *appears* greater than, separate from, and independent of its concrete origins in the Social. But, as Howard (1977) notes:

Politics is not the sum and substance, the totality, of everyday life; it is and must remain different. At the same time, it cannot be isolated in its difference, either determining directly daily life from on high or being the simple addition or representation of the atoms which compose the social. It is the locus of Power, *the place where society represents itself to itself*: but at the same time that it is constitutive of the form of the society, it is constituted by and dependent on the society itself. Neither identical with, nor separate from the society, the political is not for that reason simply nothing: it is a *process* which is unending—and whose end could mark only the advent of a totalitarianism—in which the society and its members seek to define and structure their relations. In its concern with the good life of the citizens, it is universal; in its dependence on and relation to the individuals, it is particular and open to change. (p. 36)

CHOOSING A COURSE OF ACTION

The issue of concern to many teacher educators is one of Power: in the name of what is Power to be exercised, and on whom and by whom? Lefort maintains that while Power *must* be represented, it is neither something that one can, nor should try, to determine empirically: it is a derivative of *L'imaginaire*, the Imaginary, whose "function is to neutralize the conflictual origins of the social, to create the illusion of permanence and necessity" (Howard 1977, 256). The function of the imaginary, then, is to diffuse the divisive forces inherent to the institution, and it is in situations where Power is separated absolutely from the social, usually through an appeal to some form of transcendental legitimation, that institutions are most stable.

The price of such stability, however, is the blind imposition of Law on the Social. But Lefort contends that if *lived experience* is ever reduced to— that is, explained and determined solely in terms of either the Political or the Social—the institution is being governed *ideologically*. For Lefort, "ideology is articulated in the attempt to re-create the . . . [institution] without history. The neglect of origins, the denial of the division, and the pretence of rendering the social space self-transparent are its characteristics" (Howard 1977, 256). Any attempt to situate and occupy Power in either the Social or Political sphere is ideological: To attempt to do so in the Political is to identify oneself as an expert/leader; to attempt to do so in the Social is to identify oneself as an activist/militant. If we consider the course of action open to teacher educators in this light, it becomes possible to identify which of the competing Master signifiers are ideological attempts to situate and occupy Power in either the Political or the Social.

LEADER, MILLITANT, OR TEACHER EDUCATOR?

The first course of action open to teacher educators is to identify with the orthodoxy, to assume the mandate of expert/leader. This is to situate Power in the Political and divorce the Political from the Social by legitimating Power in terms of the "scientism" of the Western empirical-analytic tradition. While this will undoubtedly provide the institution with a greater measure of stability, it is an ideological course of action because, in attempting to bridge the gap between the Political and the Social, it subjugates lived experience to the Political and in so doing diffuses the creative potential between the two poles.

The second course of action open to teacher educators is to identify with the alternative lobby, to assume the mandate of the activist/militant. This is to situate Power in the Social and to reduce the Political to the Social, making it impossible to legitimate the Law in terms of something that appears greater than and different from the Social. This course of action too, then, is ideological because it tries to mask the difference between the Political and the Social and in so doing it, too, diffuses the creative tension generated between these twin poles.

According to Lefort, the only non-ideological course open to the teacher educator is to pursue a theory of the institution that s/he knows can only be philosophical. To think one can do more is self-deluding and *dangerous*. A theory that ignores its own limits inevitably falls prey to ideology of one variety or the other. The task, according to Lefort, is to participate from "one's own place: one analyses, writes, talks. No more can be done. . . . To want to be the leader, or to think of oneself as the militant, is to be open to contradiction in one's own attitudes and from the social reality itself" (Howard 1977, 260). The challenge lies in resisting the temptation to diffuse the creative tension between the poles of the Political and Social by attempting either to dispel or ignore the difference between the two poles: in pursuing a *philosophy*.[13] Does this mean, then, that progressive teacher educators must relinquish the idea of collectively pursuing non-exclusionary, mutually beneficial ends?

COUNTERACTING BUREAUCRACY

Unlike Lefort, Castoriadis (in Howard 1977, 265)[14] maintains that while bureaucratization is a constant threat to progressive organizations, it is something they must simply learn to counteract because social change requires collective action. For Castoriadis, "it is the stunting of the creative imagination of individuals, due to the existence of a socially legitimated collective representation—an *imaginaire social . . . —*which must be analysed." This is because everyday life is neither static nor predictable; it is "praxical:"

the educator, artist or even doctor does not know the final result he/she seeks; nor does he/she simply follow material lines of force as if they could be somehow read directly from the given, as if the given were immediately and univocally signifying, as in the dream world of the positivist. There is an indeterminateness in every praxis: the project is changed as it encounters the materiality of the works; and the visage of the world is altered once my project contacts it. (p. 287)

Castoriadis is singular in his insistence that the action of *individuals* does not constitute praxis. Individuals are *always-already* social beings, embodied agents plagued by the unconscious, the multivalency of representation, and desire. That humans must contend with such "impurities," that they can never have complete knowledge of themselves, is overlooked by those of a rationalist persuasion in their zeal to escape humanity's "tainted" state of embodiment. This leads them to ignore the more important question of what exactly our relation to the unconscious, the multivalency of representation, and desire really is. Castoriadis, however, insists that we "can relate to them, act on and through them, only because they *are* Other, always already present and continually changing. They are the horizon that gives sense to thought and action, *the condition of the possibility of creation*" (p. 287; emphasis added). It is through embodiment that humans partake in an intersubjective world of symbolically mediated discourse, since the body opens human beings to not only the discourse of the Other, but also the unconscious.

As Howard (1977) notes, for Castoriadis, Otherness is the condition of possibility of praxis, and alienation is not simply a result of the domination of the Other, but the fact that the Other to whom we relate "disappears, slides into an anonymous collectivity (the law, the market, the plan, etc.)" (p. 288). While some forms of alienation are unquestionably supported and fostered by those who benefit most from them, the fact remains that it "is concerned fundamentally with the relation of society to its own institutions," with "a struggle for the transformation of the *relation* of society to its institutions," with "the phantasm of the organization as a self-reforming and self-expanding machine" (p. 289). Castoriadis thus contends that

[T]he kinds of struggle which one finds occurring today, in all spheres of society, from the family to the military, from the ecological to the ethnic, including many of those at the workplace [not to mention the realm of teacher education], find their unification in a revolt against the manner in which bureaucratic society perpetuates itself through this phantasm.

Consequently, "they can be seen as attempts to reinstitute a praxical relation to the social institution" (ibid.) Castoriadis cautions, however, that

[I]t is doubtful that one can directly grasp this fundamental phantasm; at best it can be reconstructed from its manifestations because, in effect, it appears as the foundation of the possibility and unity of everything that makes up the singularity everything which, in the life of the subject, goes beyond its reality and its history. It is the ultimate condition permitting the *surging forth* [*survenir*] of a reality and a history for the subject. (p. 291)

Castoriadis's project is to reveal how the institution comes to ignore its own nature as instituting, and how alienation is the constitutive lack around which it is structured. For Castoriadis, the organization, once instituted, only *appears* to be an inert object, and the struggle is to help the organization

recognize itself as instituting, auto-institute itself explicitly, and surmount the self-perpetuation of the instituted by showing itself capable of taking it up and transforming it according to its own exigencies and not according to the inertia of the instituted, to recognize itself as the source of its own alterity . . . , [to] go beyond the frontier of the theorizable . . . [to] the terrain of the creativity of history. (p. 299)

THE CHALLENGE: MAINTAINING REFLECTION

What a collectivity of progressive teacher educators can do, then, is change the relation of Teacher Education to its institution by making apparent, and opening to debate, what has been theretofore mystified and repressed—to "reinstitute a praxical relation." The task of the organization is not so much to lead as to open and maintain reflection. If specific demands are advanced, they must be understood not as legislative imperatives but in terms of their interrogatory effect. What Castoriadis, in contradistinction to Lefort, offers progressive teacher educators is a new way of exploring collective forms of practice, forms wherein, however, the fundamental task remains, always, to rethink the theory on which the collectivity's political activity has been built. As Žižek (1993) notes:

the duty of the critical intellectual—if, in today's "postmodern" universe, this syntagm has any meaning left—is precisely *to occupy all the time*, even when the new [Political] order (the "new harmony") stabilizes itself and again renders invisible the hole as such, *the place of this hole*, [the void the Political masks], i.e., to maintain a distance toward every reigning Master-Signifier. (p. 2)

NOTES

1. I use the term "Teacher Education" to distinguish the field from its various instances of practice—"teacher education."

2. The emergence of normal schools is intimately related to the spread of mass public schooling in the United States. Often referred to as the common school movement, this initiative—dedicated to bringing moral and civic education to every American—was championed by Horace Mann (1796–1859). The movement's central purpose was to reduce group conflict arising out of interdenominational, religious, class, and ethnic factionalism; and to forge, on the principles of the Protestant Ethic, a national identity that would brace American society against the waves of immigration, urbanization, and industrialization that threatened to swamp the infant nation. Mann, a self-professed Whig, opposed the educational policies of the nation's first truly democratic president, Andrew Jackson. Jackson argued that all Americans should be prepared not only to vote in public elections but also to run for public office. This liberal vision of public education was rejected by the Whigs, who "feared that Jacksonian democracy could easily degenerate into 'mobocracy,' or rule by uneducated, unlettered, ignorant frontiersmen." Thus, the Whigs, who also feared that "the growing number of immigrants from Ireland and Germany would become pawns of political bosses or 'papist' priests," looked to common schools to "instill the 'right attitude and values' into the young and make them orderly, civil, and industrious citizens in a nation modeled on the mores of upper middle-class, English-speaking Protestants." In other words, "the dominant socioeconomic classes would use public schooling to mold the outlook and values of the lower classes and control the nation socially" (Gutek 1997, 201). Hence the preference for "normal" as opposed to liberal schools of teacher education. According to the *Oxford English Dictionary* (*OED*), the term "normal" came into English from Latin through French, and is derived from words that meant "rule," "model," or "pattern." Normal schools inculcated teachers with middle-class, Protestant norms, models of thinking and behavior that they, in turn, instilled in their students to promote a conflict-free society.

3. This, as Borrowman (1965) notes, was more perhaps through necessity than choice,

given students with limited knowledge, even of the elementary subject matter they would be required to teach, and a brief period of from six weeks to two years to train them. It was perhaps enough to hope that the student could be made a master of the elementary-school subjects, given a 'bag of tricks'—the more sophisticated title was 'the art of teaching'—by means of which [her/]his knowledge could be transmitted, and provided with an opportunity to practice [her/]his art under supervision. It should be noted that normal schools offered one of the few career alternatives available to women of the day. In fact, the inaugural class of the first normal school comprised of twenty-five female students. (p. 54)

4. Cornell's founder, "Ezra Cornell, a hard-working craftsman and part-time farmer who had fought his way to the top of the telegraph empire, nicely represented the attitudes of those who controlled the new universities," and who "believed that *immediate* utility was an appropriate educational goal" (Borrowman 1965, 17–18).

5. The *American Heritage Dictionary* defines the scientific method as: "the principles and empirical processes of discovery and demonstration considered characteristic of or necessary for scientific investigation, generally involving the observation of phenomena, the formulation of a hypothesis concerning the phenomena, experimentation to demonstrate the truth or falseness of the hypothesis, and a conclusion that validates or modifies the hypothesis."

6. Readily, because as Labaree (1992, 137) notes, teacher educators, being new to the academy, had to establish their professional status very quickly if they were to compete with other fields of endeavor and conform to the new academic norms that required them to conduct research and publish their findings:

Fortunately, a model of how to assert a claim to professional status successfully in an educational setting was close at hand. Since the turn of the century, educational psychology has been one area within education schools that has been able to establish itself as a credible producer of academic knowledge and, thus, its faculty as legitimate members of the university professoriate. Consequently, it is not surprising that the push for professionalization of teacher educators began with applying the methods of educational psychology to the problems of teaching. (Labaree 1992, 137)

7. Scientism did, however, spawn some apostates as early as the 1930s. In 1934, for instance, a teacher educator whom Koerner describes as "one of the most perceptive professors at Teachers College, who began his own career with faith in a science of Education," remarked rather pointedly that "the 'laws of learning' have an irritating habit of collapsing as evidence accumulates" (Bagley 1934, cited in Koerner 1965, 30). And, with the passing of time, the number of apostates grew, as did their suspicion of "scientific" curricula: "the search for incontrovertible laws on which education and instruction could be based has not been and probably will never be successful and the hope of developing a science of 'human engineering' is fortunately unrealizable" (Kandel 1957, cited in Koerner 1965, 30).

8. The impact of scientism on education was such that Koerner, writing as late as 1965, notes: "everywhere in the research and writing of the field, more so now than ever, is the drift toward quantification, toward classifying all things educational, measuring them, counting them, listing them, finding their modes, means, and medians, and coefficients of correlation" (p. 31).

9. See, for instance, Anyon (1980); Apple (1975, 1979); Aronowitz (1973); Bourdieu and Passeron (1977); Carr (1979); Elliot (1978); Hamilton et al. (1977); Huebner (1976); Pinar (1975); Schwab (1977); Warwick (1974); Wilson (1975). In that such critiques condemn "answers" based on the modernist, instrumental rationality of the Western empirical-analytic tradition, they are sometimes referred to

as *post*modernist. It should not be assumed, however, that such "postmodern" critiques have much else other than chronology in common.

10. In response to this crisis, the *Carnegie Task Force on Teaching as a Profession* and the *Holmes Group*, tabled in 1986, were reports that recommended teachers in the United States reassert their identity as professionals. But as Labaree (1992, 146) notes:

Even for teacher educators at research-oriented universities, the timing of the movement [professionalization] poses a problem. Teacher educators have come to the professionalization process rather late in the game, when the field is glutted and many predecessors have staked out the prime positions. Within the university, humanities has a strong hold on high culture, natural science has a claim to technology and the scientific method, and social science has a lead in the application of research to problems of social policy. Education is left to play catch-up, with borrowed equipment and a rookie's track record. In addition, teacher educators are coming late to the adoption of the scientific-rationalist model of research, *which is now under attack and in partial retreat in the waning years of the twentieth century*. (emphasis added)

11. Lefort's notion of philosophical interrogation has much in common with Foucault's (1980, 117) notion of genealogy, since it, too, posits a form of history which can account for the constitution of knowledges, discourses, and domains of objects, without having to make reference to a subject which is either transcendental in relation to the field of events or runs in its empty sameness throughout the course of history.

12. The terms "a" and "a' " have been reversed to correspond to the version of Schema L that appears above—taken from Lacan (1988, 243). In the extract from *Écrits* cited, Lacan (1977, 193) refers to an adumbrated version of Schema L, wherein the positions of ego and other are reversed—perhaps to stress the specular, interdependent, and interchangeable nature of the two. Another version of Schema L appears in Lacan (1993, 14).

13. As Howard (1977) notes: "philosophy is no longer the unveiling of a truth which was always there but somehow occulted; it is the continual process of interrogation, destined to ambiguity, prohibited from absolutising its results" (p. 241); consequently, "the task of philosophy (or theory) becomes an eminently moral one, social and engaged, which consists in uncovering the moments of praxis within a given social and historical structure" (p. 9). It is important, therefore, that this notion of philosophy be distinguished from that of the Western empirical-analytic tradition—from that of *theoria*: the pursuit of timeless, placeless, abiding Truths.

14. All page references in this section, unless indicated otherwise, are to Castoriadis in Howard (1977).

REFERENCES

Anderson, B. 1991. *Imagined Communities: Reflections on the Origins and Spread of Nationalism* (rev. ed.). London: Verso.

Anyon, J. 1980. Social Class and the Hidden Curriculum of Work. *Journal of Education* 162: 67–92.

Apple, M. W. 1975. Scientific Interests and the Nature of Educational Institutions. In *Curriculum Theorizing: The Reconceptualists*, ed. W. Pinar (pp. 120–130). Berkeley, Calif.: McCutchan.

———. 1979. *Ideology and Curriculum*. Boston: Routledge.

Aronowitz, S. 1973. *False Promises*. New York: McGraw-Hill.

Borrowman, M. S. 1965. Liberal Education and the Professional Preparation of Teachers. In *Teacher Education in America: A Documentary History*, ed. M. S. Borrowman (pp. 1–53). New York: Teachers College Press.

Bourdieu, P., and Passeron, J.-C. 1977. *Reproduction in Education, Society and Culture*. London: Sage.

Carr, W. 1979. Philosophical Styles and Educational Theory. *Educational Studies* 5(1): 23–33.

———. 1995. *For Education: Towards Critical Educational Inquiry*. Buckingham: Open University Press.

Castoriadis, C. 1987. *The Imaginary Institution of Society*, trans. Kathleen Blamey. Cambridge: Polity Press.

Elliot, J. 1978. What Is Action Research in Schools? *Journal of Curriculum Studies* 10(4): 355–357.

Foucault, M. 1980. *The Foucault Reader*, ed. P. Rabinow. New York: Pantheon.

Gutek, G. L. 1997. Horace Mann: Leader of the Common School Movement. In *Historical and Philosophical Foundations of Education: A Biographical Introduction* (2nd ed.), ed. G. L. Gutek (pp. 196–216). Upper Saddle River, N.J.: Merrill.

Hamilton, D., Jenkins, D., King, C., MacDonald, B., and Parlett, M. 1977. *Beyond the Numbers Game: A Reader in Educational Evaluation*. London: Macmillan.

Howard, D. 1977. *The Marxian Legacy*. New York: Urizen.

Huebner, D. 1976. The Moribund Curriculum Field: Its Wake and Our Work. *Curriculum Inquiry* 6(2): 228–234.

Kliebard, H. M. 1973. The Question in Teacher Education. In D. J. McCarty and Associates, *New Perspectives on Teacher Education* (pp. 8–24). San Francisco: Jossey-Bass.

Koerner, J. D. 1965. *The Miseducation of American Teachers*. Baltimore, Md.: Penguin.

Labaree, D. F. 1992. Power, Knowledge, and the Science of Teaching: A Genealogy of Teacher Professionalization. *Harvard Educational Review* 62(2): 123–154.

Lacan, J. 1977. *Écrits: A Selection*, trans. A. Sheridan. New York: Norton.

———. 1988. *The Seminar of Jacques Lacan: Book II, The Ego in Freud's Theory and in the Technique of Psychoanalysis*, trans. Sylvia Tomaselli, ed. Jacques-Alain Miller. New York: Norton.

———. 1993. *The Seminar of Jacques Lacan: Book III, The Psychoses, 1955–1956*, ed. J.-A. Miller, trans. R. Grigg. New York: Norton.

———. 1997. *The Seminar of Jacques Lacan: Book VII, The Ethics of Psychoanalysis, 1959–1960*, ed. J.-A. Miller, trans. D. Porter. New York: Norton.

Laclau, E., and Mouffe, C. 1985. *Hegemony and Socialist Strategy: Towards a Radical Democratic Politics*. London: Verso.

Pinar, William, ed. 1975. *Curriculum Theorizing: The Reconceptualists*. Berkeley, Calif: McCutchan.

Schwab, J. J. 1977. The Practical: A Language for Curriculum. In *Curriculum and Evaluation*, ed. A. Bellack and H. Kliebard (pp. 26–45). Berkeley, Calif.: McCutchan. (Original work published in 1969, *School Review* 78: 1–24.)

Thorndike, Edward L. 1906. *The Principles of Teaching, Based on Psychology.* New York: A.G. Seiler.

———. 1965. The Contribution of Psychology to Education. In *Teacher Education in America: A Documentary History*, ed. S. Borrowman (pp. 172–183). New York: Teachers College Press. (Original work published in 1910, *The Journal of Educational Psychology* 1: 5–12.)

Warwick, D. 1974. Ideologies, Integration and Conflicts of Meaning. In *Educability, Schools, and Ideology*, ed. M. Flude, and J. Ahier (pp. 86–111). London: Halstead Press.

Wilson, J. 1975. *Educational Theory and the Preparation of Teachers.* Slough: NFER.

Winch, P. 1958. *The Idea of a Social Science and Its Relation to Philosophy.* London: Routledge.

Žižek, S. 1989. *The Sublime Object of Ideology.* London: Verso.

———. 1991. *For They Know Not What They Do: Enjoyment as a Political Factor.* London: Verso.

———. 1992. *Enjoy Your Symptom: Jacques Lacan in Hollywood and Out.* New York: Routledge.

———. 1993. *Tarrying with the Negative: Kant, Hegel, and the Critique of Ideology.* Durham, N.C.: Duke University Press.

———. 1994. *The Metastases of Enjoyment: Six Essays on Woman and Causality.* London: Verso.

Part II

The Question of Authority

Chapter 3

The Teacher Is a Prick

Douglas Sadao Aoki

BAD PRICKS

This chapter and its title began as a presentation at the meeting of the American Educational Research Association (AERA). Actually, both article and title necessarily began before that, in a piece solicited by Derek Briton for a symposium on Lacanian curricular theory that he was proposing for that conference. He accepted the abstract that I sent him, but only after he had made some judicious revisions, including a substantial renaming. His version was "Teaching and Transference: 'Making a Big Stink about Teaching'." When I read that, I imagined him turning pale on seeing the title that I had sent him. As he sat down to rewrite it, forced into labor he never expected he would have to do, he must have regretted ever inviting me to participate. In my mind's ear, I can hear him muttering to himself, "That Aoki, he's such a prick."

By saying this, I do not mean to retroactively critique Derek's edition, nor to mock his linguistic sensibilities. Quite the opposite: I heartily endorse what he did, despite the fact that I have now restored the original title. He did the right thing, not only for his purposes—his version of the proposal was subsequently accepted by the conference—but also for mine. Derek accurately judged the prick as manifestly too vulgar for the professional discourse of the AERA, or at least for a proposal that had to pass blind review by serious-minded AERA scholars. From my perspective, the whole process of writing, rewriting, and restoration of the title, the obligatory discursive circuit through Derek and myself, away from the prick and back again, both incarnates and illuminates the significance of the prick in teaching much better than if Derek had left the original title and abstract intact.

Lacan (1977, 288) insists that the phallus only operates when veiled; I propose that in education, the prick is made most present in its effect by its direct absence. The exemplary work of the prick is best accomplished when the word itself is neither spoken nor written nor read. Because my title entered and escaped the machinery of gentrification regulating good discourses of education, it is an analytical lever that can open up that machinery and its related apparatuses.

It may come as a surprise that the most obvious and familiar effect of the prick in teaching is quintessentially Lacanian. It is a pedagogical truism that good teaching eschews bad language. The imaginary scene of a young student writing, "I will not use bad words in class," over and over again on a blackboard, supervised by a stern teacher, seems quite Norman Rockwell–like in its traditional exemplification of classroom discipline. And yet the essence of the scene, if not its particulars, cannot be disregarded as simply quaint, out-of-date, or of no contemporary currency. Bart Simpson is the 1990s/twenty-first-century update of that student, still chained to his school's disciplinary blackboard discourse. Of course, the very fact that both of these examples are icons of an already thoroughly gentrified pop culture means that they must exclude precisely the object that constitutes them: the bad language that is forbidden in the classroom. In this sense, the category of "bad object" that subsumes the prick effectively levels a whole set of prohibited words. This does not mean that every instance of offensive language is equally bad. Students and teachers share an awareness of at least a rough scale of the offensiveness of terms. Still, bad language as such—or vulgarity or obscenity as such—is defined by the line between the acceptable and the unacceptable, not by how much the standards of acceptability have been violated. In this sense, any bad word is equivalent to *prick*.

To put this in more Lacanian terms, *prick* is a metonymy for not just the phallus, but every thinkable vulgarity. A metonymy, because *prick* locates the intersection of two fields of terms, the phallic and the obscene, so that *prick* is related, in an enchained and even spatial way, to every other term in those fields. The logic is similar to that structuring the word-maps of Saussure (1979, 175), in which *enseignment* leads on to *enseigner* and *enseignons* in one direction, and *apprentissage* and *éducation* in another. These terms are not substitutions for one another, and are therefore not related by any metaphoric logic. In this case, the distinction between metonymy and metaphor is more than a linguistic nicety, for terms related metonymically are made present, or nearly present, when any one of them is articulated, as if they collectively haunt each other. The phallus is therefore always accompanied by its obscene specter, the prick.

Yet *prick* is a peculiar term, albeit hardly unique, in that its obscenity is neither immanent to it nor given by historical context. Like "shifters"— pronouns like "I" or "you"—whose meaning and referents are only established by the momentary circumstances of their articulation, the obscenity of the prick is generated by the synchronic and syntagmatic circumstances of its usage. *Prick* is obviously a perfectly respectable verb, with a perfectly respectable substantive form. Moreover, even when *prick* is offensive, it isn't strictly because of its meaning. Naming its signification of the penis or the phallus is not nearly as scandalous, regardless of one's suspicion of phallocentrism, as the material pronouncement of the word *prick* itself. This is elementary Lacan, in its shift from the signified to the signifier, or, rather, the enchainment of signifiers. The paradigmatic instance of the vulgarity of the prick is not the word/concept in itself, but the sentence "X is a prick," with X being a specific subject—such as the teacher. We could say that the prick becomes obscene exactly when it articulates a subject. In the pedagogical case, it is actually the teacher who makes the prick vulgar (and sometimes the student: "that little prick . . .").

Concentrating on these rhetorical niceties may appear to be making much of very little, but that seeming exaggeration is itself pertinent to the prick. First, measured against the rough scales of obscenity invoked above, *prick* surely registers as very mild. If it is obscene, it is rather trivially so. Second, the teacher as a prick is one of the most common and mundane denigrations of teachers, and perhaps the most common and mundane contemporary one. For example, a character on the high school television series *Freaks and Geeks* is referred to as a "sadistic-prick-math-teacher," one who takes entirely too much pleasure from the prospect of one of his students failing.[1] Can any of us look back at our own schooling and fail to remember at least one teacher who vividly fit that description, even if we are too genteel to ever put it that way? And how many of us can be utterly confident that none of our own students have used exactly such words to describe us? One of my cherished colleagues, seeing the title of this chapter, brightly and sincerely asked me, "Is that a quote from one of your teaching evaluations?" But then, if "the teacher is a prick" is both so gentle in its obscenity and so general in our experience, why must it be excluded from the AERA discourse? Although the AERA has obvious pertinence in education, I am not singling it out as a special case of an institutional regulatory authority. Even the U.S. Supreme Court ruled against a high school senior whose crime was to tell a friend off-campus that his teacher was a prick: "The court said that the student's conduct involved an invasion of the right of the teacher to be free from being loudly insulted in a public place. The judge concluded that the use of fighting words is not protected by the constitutional guarantee of freedom of speech."[2] How can such a trivial prick become so serious?

JANE GALLOP'S PRICK

One possible explanation returns to metonymy. Perhaps the problem with "the teacher is a prick" is not so much the phrase itself, but rather its implications—what it leads to. A fundamental Lacanianism (1977b,

154), after all, is that every signifier slides to another, and then another, and another, with no ultimately enforceable limit. As Jane Gallop (1985) puts it, "Not just *Écrits* [Lacan's magnum opus] but all writings lead elsewhere" (p. 34). And it is Gallop who simultaneously proves and refutes the worst fears of my erstwhile organizer Derek. In the book that established Gallop's reputation as a psychoanalytic critic, *The Daughter's Seduction* (1992), she argues that Derrida errs when he condemns Lacan as phallocentric.[3] Lacan, she says, is much worse and better than that. In reality, "he is a prick" (p. 36). She goes on to carefully work through the consequences. Her analysis is acute, in large part because it begins by recognizing the gap between the phallus and the prick, one whose material significance cannot be reduced to either signification or reference. The prick, rather than being just a schoolboy's naughty word or an academic's vulgar demand for attention, turns out to be a key concept for Lacanian psychoanalytic theory. The prick, Gallop argues, is "beyond the phallus," even "beyond good and evil" (1992, 37). Yet just when the prick seems to achieve this unexpected exaltation, Gallop's logic suddenly takes a twist, for she notes that it was exactly when Lacan historically manifests as the prick, "at the very moment in Lacan's text when phallic privilege is asserted, [that] the cunt clamors for recognition, makes a big stink" (1992, 32). Of course, I could not resist quoting Gallop on this point in the abstract I sent Derek, and that's where he no doubt started to go pale. It appears that if we admit the trivial vulgarity of the prick, where we slide is directly into the grossly obscene and the utterly unacceptable.

Yet Gallop's extravagant transgressiveness recalls the ordinary fact that there is a large and obvious class of teachers who are unlikely to have been condemned as pricks: women. The *OED* categorically declares that *prick* is a "vulgar term of abuse for *men*" (emphasis added). Gallop herself is a little less sure; she says that this epithet is "usually" restricted to men (1992, 37), although she does not specify the unusual circumstances in which a woman can be a prick. She does give a hint, though, in a revealing theoretical distinction: "The phallic role demands impassivity; the prick obviously gets pleasure from *his* cruelty" (1992, 38; emphasis added). Sadism, which is at least coherent with the aforementioned math-teacher-as-prick, isn't necessarily gendered in itself, even though Gallop's pronoun makes it so.[4] But even highly sadistic female teachers aren't customarily condemned as pricks, although they might well be called by other familiarly awful names. One possibility, to follow Gallop's own audacious lead, is *cunt*. But something goes awry immediately in this calculus of obscenity, for while there may be historically a rhetorical equivalence between phallus/penis and vagina, *prick* and *cunt* are by no means level in their obscenity. The latter is much worse in ordinary contemporary discourse, even if Gallop elevates the cunt into an incisive analytical device for deconstructing Lacan himself (Gallop 1992, 15–32). The reasons for this acute difference are beyond the scope of this chapter. Here, I merely want to note that these casual vulgarities embody an acute asymmetry of the sexes. In other words, it's not simply that the prick denotes a male teacher; it's that there is no direct female equivalent for him at all.

Yet neither the derogation nor the sexing of the prick is as straightforward as it seems. Gallop makes the crucial move by proposing that "the prick, in some crazy way, is feminine" (1992, 37). She begins by noting that "unlike ... phallocentrism, which women resent on principle, the prick is both resented by and attractive to women. . . . [The prick is] someone whom women (or men who feel the 'prick' of his man's power, men in a non-phallic position), despite themselves, find irresistible" (1992, 36–37). Her proposition might be disputed, but its cogency is evident in how an expression like, "he's a charming prick," is by no means oxymoronic. As Gallop perceptively recognizes, the prick has its seductiveness. This is another reason that she nominates Lacan as a prick: He was lionized in Paris despite what she identifies as his gratuitous nastiness—or, more precisely, *because* of his gratuitous nastiness. Paris flocked to his famous seminar, year after year, in large part *because* he was a prick. Gallop describes his seminar this way: "Lacan, who in his seminars continuously belittles and insults his audience, has no trouble filling a huge hall with people who adoringly write his pronouncements down word for word" (1992, 37). And from one of those who attended:

Lacan, after having slowly laid out on the chair papers he never consulted, books he didn't open, after having wiped the lenses of his spectacles for several minutes and having cast over the assembly a gaze that he endeavoured to make as gloomy as possible—as if it were really beyond his powers to address such a collection . . . as if despairing of ever waking us up to what he was addressing; sometimes he would apostrophize us directly: "So, are you ever going to open them up now, your brain-boxes! When will you begin to understand the first thing about what I've been working myself into the ground to teach you all these years?" (Pontalis 1993, 114–115)

So Lacan was the exemplary charming prick when he was a *teacher*. But more than that, he was a prick because he was a flirt, a "ladies' man" in both senses of the term, for he was "always embroiled in coquetry" (1992, 35). The prick does not play by the rules; he (she) is a narcissistic tease who persuades by means of attraction and resistance, not by orderly systematic discourse. The prick, which as male organ might be able to epitomize masculinity, lays bare its desire. Since the phallic order demands that the law rather than desire issue from the paternal position, an exposure of the father as desiring, a view of the father as prick, a view of the father's prick, feminizes him (Gallop 1992, 37–38).

So despite the authority of the *OED*'s definition, the prick slides across both masculinity and femininity, just as it slides across the despicable and the seductive. Yet the prick is not merely ambivalent through these registers. Just as the prick can be charming *because* he is obnoxious, he becomes feminine through precisely the epitomization of his masculinity. The prick is that peculiar nexus of the body, the image, and the word where male and female turn out to be neither simple binary categories nor polar opposites. Instead, it is where emphasizing masculinity—displaying or exposing the prick—feminizes the teaching subject, where femininity is revealed as an exaggeration of the masculine. If this proposition seems outrageous, one need only consider the parallel and material example of male body-building, in which the hypermuscular, hyperbolically male body, in its voluptuous curves, hairless smooth skin, seemingly dainty joints and slender waist, fastidious attention to hairstyle and body-image, aesthetic posturing, and constitution as an object displayed for an authoritatively assessing gaze, is strangely but very conventionally, feminine. This curious turn in Gallop's argument is actually faithful to Lacan (1977), who notes, "the curious consequence of making virile display in the human being itself seem feminine" (p. 291). For both, the complication of sex and the prick turns on the exposure of desire.

THE TEACHER'S PRICK

John Glavin (1997) retells an anecdote about a rather distinguished teacher:

When W. H. Auden was a schoolmaster, he "threatened to 'cut [his] prick off' if the boys continued to fool about . . . next time a hullabaloo broke out in class, [he] opened his fly, brought out this [piece of butcher's] meat, and appeared to be actually carrying out the threat with a sharp knife." Of course the immediately pliant, teachable boys cried out: "No sir! Don't do it!" (p. 18)

I'm not sure which aspect of this story seems more improbable today: the teacher pulling down his fly in front of his class, or his pupils earnestly begging him to not cut his prick off. Yet even in its far-fetchedness, the anecdote turns on an issue that is very real.

Glavin goes on to blithely observe that "Auden, with his usual directness, had got clearly to the center, if not the heart, of the male pedagogic matter. The male teacher's sexuality is virtually the precondition of his success." Glavin goes on to argue that teaching by a woman "heads in exactly the opposite direction" (p. 18). That is, the female teacher also seduces, but her teaching only succeeds insofar as that seduction is resisted. This version of the asymmetry of sex is debatable, but it does open the way to understand how the classroom is ordered to be exactly the opposite of what Glavin contends it is.

Are we not in thrall to a sexual/pedagogical politics that demands the annihilation of the teacher's sexuality as the precondition of her/his survival as a teacher, much less her/his success? That is, isn't there an institutional demand that teachers be castrated even before they set foot in the classroom? The lurid media attention to the stories of teachers Mary Kay LeTourneau and Heather Ingram demonstrate the severity of that demand (and those particular examples demonstrate that our social institutions demand that female teachers be castrated, too).[5] Today, castration is the very condition of the teaching subject. In other words, the teacher can be a prick; s/he just isn't allowed to *have* one. The good teacher must be a eunuch, since his/her sexuality must be barred from the classroom, in the strongest of all possible senses. This pedagogical regulation of being and having the prick returns to the Lacanian analysis of sex, in which being the phallus is characterized, at least at the first level, as a female position, while having it is characterized as male (Lacan 1977b, 289). Gallop's identification of the femininity of the prick is therefore merely an orthodox Lacanianism. Yet the systematicity of the sexed distinction between being and having cannot be sustained, as Judith Butler astutely recognizes. Both being and having the phallus are pretensions doomed to farcical failure. "Both positions of 'having' and 'being' are, in Lacan's terms, finally to be understood as comedic failures that are nevertheless compelled to articulate and enact these repeated impossibilities" (Butler 1990, 46). No one really has the phallus, and no one really is the phallus.

Within this framework, the prick becomes a rather iffy concept, treacherously constituted through layers of failure, slippage, impossibility, masquerade, and difference. The prick is a kind of vulgar distortion of the phallus, a not-quite-phallus stripped of any dignity, but the phallus itself turns out to be a comedic failure. The phallus even fails to sex. The conventional categorization of being the phallus as the female position is immediately complicated by the fact that for Lacan, it is prototypically the young boy, in the Oedipus complex, who seeks to be the phallus—that is, he seeks to be what he perceives is desired by his mother. Then the institutional apparatus that regulates the prick, whose name is the Law, must also be somewhat ridiculous, regardless of the presumption of its authority or the ferocity of its enforcement. One definition of the prick is exactly the paternal figure, whose indisputable power cannot prevent him from being regarded with contempt. The comedic failure that defines the prick thus also manifests the severe limit of his authority. "The paternal law ought to be understood not as a deterministic divine will, but as a perpetual bumbler, preparing the ground for the insurrections against him" (Butler 1990, 28).

The bumbling of the institutional apparatus regulating the teaching prick is obvious in its most stringent demand. The mandatory castration of teachers is imaginary in the purest sense, despite its symbolic (that is, linguistic

and juridical articulation), because it is immediately ludicrous, an arche-
typal instance of *méconnaissance*. The good teacher, of course, is never
really castrated; s/he only agrees to sustain the professional farce of pricklessness that allows the classroom to operate. S/he maintains the image of
pricklessness. In accordance with this illusory image, s/he and her/his institution agree to act as if sexuality has been evicted from the classroom,
when both sides know very well that such eviction is impossible. This is
an instance of what Slavoj Žižek (1992) refers to as the quintessential articulation of ideology: "I know very well, but nonetheless. . . ."

The prick in the classroom is classical Foucault on sex, with a Lacanian
twist. Foucault (1980) famously asserts that the discursive "repression" of
sex actually sustains and disseminates it; Lacan maintains that anything
repressed in the symbolic must return in the Real. The imaginary castration
of teachers is a symbolic demand, codified by schools and government, but
the real prick evades symbolic regulation. In an infamous *Harper's* forum,
the distinguished John Boswell, the A. Whitney Griswold Professor of History at Yale University, confesses his keen awareness of beautiful students
in his school (Hitt et al. 1993). That admission doesn't make Boswell a
prick, but just the opposite: He is much more honest and therefore more
ethical than most professors, since he is at least open about the untenability
of grounding of pedagogy in castration. Concern about the sexual harassment of students on campus is, of course, utterly necessary and mostly
genuine. Nonetheless, those concerns are problematized by the fact that the
university structurally sexualizes the relation between professor and student. That is, it is not just that the teacher–student relationship maintains
its prohibited sexual aspect, but it is the institution of school that engenders
and sustains the sexualization that it prohibits. Every turn of the school
year means one more parade of young, lithe bodies before the aging professorial gaze. The lesson is not that we should therefore mark every professor as a potential sexual predator, nor that we should surrender our
concerns about sexual harassment of students. Instead, the lesson is that if
we pried open the skulls of absolutely "safe" professors and discovered the
thoughts that s/he would never either openly reveal or directly act upon,
we should expect to discover very "unsafe" desires (which is exactly why
they are locked away).

Besides, regardless of the proliferation of university prohibitions of consensual sexual relations between student and professor—the specific topic
of the *Harper's* forum—such liaisons continue unabated, and only the ter-
minally naïve or ideologically hamstrung could believe that they will ever
be eliminated. The rock of pedagogical castration is its material, ubiqui-
tous, and continuing failure. To put it another way, the structures, practices, and experience of teaching castrates pedagogical castration.
Moreover, it is important to recognize how the institutionalized sexualization of teaching so effectively subverts itself. Just this year, I had a couple

of young women approach me after a first-year sociology class in which we discussed race and dating. One told me that I was her "second-best-looking professor," which is rather like being nominated the second-best Lacanian theorist on your hockey team. The best-looking one, she added, without any prodding on my part, was her chemistry prof—whereupon the student accompanying her asked brightly (and accurately), "You mean Dr. X?" They both cooed over Dr. X's good looks for a minute, then the first added nonchalantly, "But sometimes he has a hygiene problem." Debates about sex in the academy generally miss this crucial aspect of how romantic student identification with professors is characteristically constituted through a simultaneous disidentification. That is, having a crush on a professor with a hygiene problem is not some bizarre, exceptional version of the sexualized pedagogical relationship, but instead so realistic as to be paradigmatic.

Consider the general aesthetic status of professors. Not very many supported themselves through graduate school, or could have supported themselves, as, say, underwear models. And how many professorial faces show up in *People* magazine's annual survey of the world's most beautiful people? The sexualization of the pedagogical relationship, at least in universities, obviously turns on something other than the immanent and transcendental beauty of professors. Yet because sexual attraction is such a scopic function, if a professor is to be attractive, s/he must *appear* to be attractive. In other words, pedagogical sexualization is that function that operates to make professors look much better than, well, professors. In Lacanian terms, it must be an *imaginary* function. There is the illustrative story of the graduate student who falls in love with her professor, whom she idealizes as the wise man, the very embodiment of *le sujet supposé savoir*. They move in together, and the relationship survives until that moment when she looks over at him watching television and sees, not a sage, but an old man in his undershorts, scratching his testicles with a fork. This is the acuity of Butler: The problem with accusations of phallocentrism is that they don't take into account how the evident possession of the phallus so easily makes someone ridiculous. The problem is that phallus is always shadowed by its metonymic spectre, the prick.

The prick as an obscene shadow or specter, together with its feminizing energy, converges with another of Žižek's (1992) readings of Lacan:

This is the way psychoanalysis subverts the usual opposition of the paternal and the maternal: it brings out what this opposition has to repress, to exclude, in order to establish itself, namely the *reverse* of the father, the "anal father" who lurks behind the Name of the Father *qua* bearer of the symbolic law. This "anal father" is the third element which disturbs the familiar narrative of the gradual prevalence of the paternal over the maternal in history as well as the subject's ontogenesis. . . . The mad "anal father" is the nauseous debauchee, threatening yet ridiculously impotent, who simply does not fit the frame of the "complementary relationship between *yin* and *yang*" and the like. A new light is thus shed on the Cartesian *cogito*. . . . The Cartesian God—the correlate of the *cogito*—is, of course, nothing other than Lacan's "big Other," the place of the supposed symbolic knowledge (*le sujet supposé savoir*). (p. 127; emphasis in original)

The phallus is the ultimate *point de capiton* for Lacan, that center which stabilizes and knits together a specific symbolic order—a systematic, institutionalized body of knowledge, emblematized by a curriculum. In other words, the phallus *qua point de caption* works to stop the incessant glissade of signifiers, so that a field of knowledge and the institutions that it underwrites can be established. So, insofar as the teacher embodies the Name of the Father as the bearer of symbolic law—the conflation of disciplinary knowledge, in all its senses, with the authority of assessment—the teacher purports to have the phallus. Yet the Lacanian lesson is that no one can really have the phallus, that everyone who presumes to possess it is an imposter and a fraud. When the imposture falls apart, when the veil of teaching is stripped away, what is revealed is not the phallus, but the prick, the "ridiculously impotent" *poseur* is all the more laughable for her/his claim to the phallus. In Žižek's terms, the "anal father" is just another name for the prick.

From this point of view, the teacher is ultimately *always* a prick. Lacan maintains that every subject faces a forced choice between being and meaning. Equivalently, it could be said that the teacher is given a forced choice between having the phallus and being the prick—except that it turns out to be no choice at all, since it is impossible to have the phallus. Or, on the other side, in Butler's terms, being the prick is the inevitable result of the comedic failure to be the phallus. Then the banal derogation of the teacher as a prick is something more than a casual slur. To invoke another bodybuilding parallel, Alphonso Lingus (1994) suggests that the loud mainstream revulsion for the bodybuilder derives from the dim but accurate sense that s/he has "desecrated the ritual structures with which we maintain dignity in and conjure ridicule from our physical nature" (p. 36). The obscenity that attends on the prick, the vulgarity that good teaching discourses forbid, reveals that the symbolic order of pedagogy is more than a body of teachable knowledge, more than the systemization of human wisdom, more than even the politicized regulation of the discourses it animates and disciplines. It is a set of ritual structures with which teachers (and students, parent, administrators, government, etc.) maintain their dignity as pedagogical subjects, and conjure ridicule from their pedagogical natures. The prick is simply that abiding portent of the ongoing desecration of those structures.

NOTES

1. Maggie, "Tests and Breasts," *Mighty Big TV: Freaks and Geeks.* http://www.dawsonswrap.com/index.html?/freaks_and_geeks/01-04.asp&0.
2. Beate Baltes, "The U.S. Supreme Court Would . . .", *CLD 615: Educational Foundations: The Study of the American Mosaic.* http://nunic.nu.edu/~bbaltes/syllabi/615_laws.html.
3. Derrida (1979, 58–61) and (1987, 479–481).
4. Obviously, arguments can be made about the historical gendering of sadism and masochism, but the issues under consideration here do not turn on that kind of distinction.
5. LeTourneau was convicted of having sex with a 13-year-old former student, who fathered two of her children. Ingram had an affair with a 17-year-old student, and pled guilty to having sex with an under-aged student.

REFERENCES

Baltes, Beate. The U.S. Supreme Court Would . . .". *CLD 615: Educational Foundations: The Study of the American Mosaic.* http://nunic.nu.edu/~bbaltes/syllabi/615_laws.html.

Butler, Judith. 1990. *Gender Trouble: Feminism and the Subversion of Identity.* New York: Routledge.

Derrida, Jacques. 1979. *Spurs.* Chicago: University of Chicago Press.

———. 1987. *The Post Card: From Socrates to Freud and Beyond.* Chicago: University of Chicago Press.

Foucault, Michel. 1980. *The History of Sexuality, Volume I: An Introduction.* New York: Vintage Books.

Gallop, Jane. 1985. *Reading Lacan.* Ithaca, N.Y.: Cornell University Press.

———. 1992. *The Daughter's Seduction.* Ithaca, N.Y.: Cornell University Press.

Glavin, John. 1997. The Intimacies of Instruction. In *The Erotics of Instruction,* ed. Regina Barreca and Deborah Denenholz Morse (pp. 12–27). Hanover, N.H.: University Press of New England.

Hitt, Jack, Blythe, Joan, Boswell, John, Botstein, Leon, and Kerrigan, William. 1993. New Rules about Sex on Campus. *Harper's* (September): 33–42.

Lacan, Jacques. 1977a. The Signification of the Phallus. In *Écrits: A Selection,* trans. Alan Sheridan. New York: Norton.

———. 1977b. Agency of the Letter in the Unconscious or Reason Since Freud. In *Écrits: A Selection,* trans. Alan Sheridan. New York: Norton.

Lingus, Alphonso. 1994. *Foreign Bodies.* New York: Routledge.

Maggie. Tests and Breasts. *Mighty Big TV: Freaks and Geeks.* http://www.dawsonswrap.com/index.html?/freaks_and_geeks/01-04.asp&0.

Pontalis, J.-B. 1993. *Love of Beginnings,* trans. James Greene with Marie-Christine Réguis. London: Free Association Books. (Originally published as *L'amour des commencements.* Paris: Gallimards, 1986.)

Saussure, Ferdinand de. 1979. *Cours de Linguistique Générale.* Paris: Payot.

Žižek, Slavoj. 1992. *Enjoy Your Symptom! Jacques Lacan in Hollywood and Out.* New York: Routledge.

Chapter 4

Being Outside the Circle: Postmodern Composition, Pedagogy, and Psychoanalytic Theory

Robert Samuels

As an experiment in a composition course, I decided to explore the role of my authority in the classroom by temporarily removing myself from its structure. What I did was to come into class and ask my students to form a circle. I told them that they should discuss the reading assignment for the day and that I would take notes on what they said, but I would not participate in the conversation. I then took my seat outside of the circle, and I waited for the class to begin. After some nervous moments, the students slowly began to talk about the subject matter. I wrote notes on what they said and after 20 minutes, I announced to the class that I would be leaving the room for an unspecified amount of time and that the only rules were that they must remain in the classroom. After waiting outside of the class for 10 minutes, I returned and asked them to take out some paper and respond to the following questions:

1. How did you experience today's class?
2. What did you like and dislike about it?
3. What did the class discuss when I was out of the room?

My rationale for these questions was that I wanted the students to examine the role of the teacher in the classroom, and I also wanted to see how they represented what they did when I left the room. The inspiration for this assignment came from the psychoanalytic idea that the analyst plays his or her role by removing him or herself from the expected place of authority and knowledge. In other terms, the neutrality of the analyst forces the subject to address both the usual role of authority figures and to see what happens when this role is not fulfilled.[1]

In fact, most of the student responses that I received did indeed concern these questions of authority. Several students wrote that they did not know what to say without me leading the class discussion. Other students added that they didn't know if what they were saying was right or wrong without a teacher being present. The lack of my presence thus brought them into contact with their expectations and desires regarding educational authority. One of the major things that the students learned from this exercise was that they are taught to be reliant on external authority figures in order to determine the worthiness of their own ideas. In other terms, their relation to knowledge is mediated by their need for an idealized master or authority figure.

Another interesting aspect of their responses was that many students in the same class wrote that when I left the room, they continued to discuss the assigned subject; however, other students wrote that they began to talk about the local bar scene. Some of them therefore decided to keep up the pretense of doing what they thought they should be doing, while others decided to be more accurate. The students in this sense showed multiple strategies in dealing with not only what they wanted from me but also what they supposed I wanted from them.

In order to further explore the relationship between my presence and the students' desires, I later handed back to the them a transcript of both the class conversation and many of the responses. We then read these aloud together and discussed some of their implications. Many students became almost giddy over seeing their conversation turned into a written document. They said it became more real and formal by being typed out and presented to them by their teacher. They also stated that they were surprised at how well the conversation went without me. They even asked me if I was offended because they did not seem to need me as much as they thought.

In relation to their responses to the class transcript, I discussed with them the idea that their discourses all centered around questions of authority, dependency, and legitimization. One student brought up the idea that they are out of their parents' houses for the first time, and so the teachers are now their substitute parents. I then talked about the psychoanalytic theory of transference as partially based on the reenactment of one's relationship with one's parents through the person of the analyst. I added that one of the roles of an analyst is to encourage the patient's independence and help her/him become less reliant on external authority figures.[2] One of my students responded to this by claiming that he pays good money to have an authority in the classroom and that I am here because I am supposed to have a great deal of knowledge in this particular area. I then asked him what would happen if there was no such authority in the classroom. His response was that nothing would be learned and it would be a waste of everyone's time. I replied that his argument assumes that what students think and write has no inherent value. He agreed with this and I thought that would be a good time to have students write about their ideas of the role of the teacher and the value of a truly democratic classroom.

I was a little taken aback when many of my students wrote that they did not think that the class should be democratic and that they do expect the teacher to give them knowledge and to represent a role model. In fact, many of the students returned to the idea that they pay the teacher so that he or she will be an authority. One student even wrote that she realized through this class how bad an idea democracy really is, because "you have to let idiots tell you what to do and think." Other students also showed a similar contempt for their fellow students and the general concept of democracy. The responses of my students forced me to rethink some of the pedagogical strategies that I had been employing in the classroom. I came to the realization that in my eager desire to have a student-centered classroom, I neglected to see how the students were already part of the academic discourse of the university and that they would often resist any mode of knowledge production that did not follow their cultural expectations.

Some of my students' expectations centered on a capitalist definition of knowledge production. For example, the most common complaints that they wrote about it in regard to my use of group work and other decentering practices were that (1) they were not getting their money's worth, (2) it was a waste of time and (3) I was not performing my role as the provider of specialized knowledge. If we look at the relationship between all of these modes of resistance, we find the foundations of a capitalist logic that sees time and knowledge in relation to money. Thus, if I am not delivering to them the expected product of knowledge, I am wasting their time and thus they are losing money. This may be common sense but I believe that we need to openly discuss with our students the way that this capitalist logic interferes and colludes with the writing process.

POSTMODERN STUDENTS AND THE DISCOURSE OF HYSTERIA

One way of approaching this question of the relationship between student-centered classrooms and the ideology of postmodern capitalism is to explore the multiple ways that students resist our efforts to democratize the university. In a series of articles in *Rhetoric Review*, one can trace a strong concern over the divergence between new teaching strategies and the expectations of students who have grown up in a postmodern culture. For example, in her article "Pedagogies of Decentering and a Discourse of Failure," Judy Segal (1997) argues that the resistance to new teaching methods often results in blaming the student, blaming the teacher, blaming the institution, or blaming the theory (p. 175). These different targets of blame relate to the ways that one understands the fundamental relationship between teachers and students. For instance, Segal posits that many teachers become frustrated when their efforts to put power in the hands of the students results in student passivity and/or verbalized resistance. We can find this sense of failure and frustration in Henry Ottinger's statement to his students: "[You] had the opportunity to be free . . . and you succeeded in proving to me that freedom is slavery" (quoted in Segal, p. 178). In this attempt to blame the students, Ottinger equates student passivity with a desire for enslavement. However, what he appears to neglect are the larger cultural forces and educational histories that help to create the situation where students expect to be told what to do.

Ottinger's desire to see the relationship between himself and his students as a master and slave relationship has a long history in pedagogical circles. In fact, Paulo Freire's (1970) influential theories of radical pedagogy often interpret the student–teacher relationship to be one of pure dominance and subjection:

The teacher presents himself to his students as their necessary opposite; by considering their ignorance absolute, he justifies his existence. The students, alienated like the slave in the Hegelian dialectic, accept their ignorance as justifying the teacher's existence. (pp. 58–59)

Following Lacan's (1991) theories of discourse, I would like to argue that this Discourse of the Master does not determine the postmodern Discourse of the University and thus Freire's model fails to account for the types of student–teacher relationships that are predominant today.[3] In other terms, radical pedagogy is often misleading because it critiques a mode of education that has very little power in our current culture.

Instead of seeing our students as locked into a system where they have no authority and the teacher has total power, we must see how the discourse of the postmodern university undermines the authority and power of every subject, including the professors. In Lacan's formulation of this type of discourse, he stresses the ways that symbolic knowledge is distanced from most past systems of mastery and subjective control:

$$(1)\ \text{Discourse of the Master} \qquad (2)\ \text{Discourse of the University}$$

$$\frac{S_1 \rightarrow S_2}{\rlap{/}{S} \leftarrow a} \qquad\qquad\qquad \frac{S_2 \rightarrow a}{S_1 \leftarrow \rlap{/}{S}}$$

In the older Discourse of the Master, the person in power controls the enslaved Other by taking control of the master signifiers (S_1) that order the symbolic realms of knowledge (S_2), language, and work. Lacan posits that within this structure, the social system is controlled by the person who subjects (S) him or herself to the role of being the master signifier (S_1) of the signifying chain (S_2). The hidden truth of this discourse is that the master is himself or herself subjected (S) to the Symbolic Order and thus barred ($\cancel{S}$) from total linguistic control.[4]

In opposition to this desire and attempt to control the symbolic, the Discourse of the University places the master signifier (S_1) below the pure production of symbolic knowledge (S_2). In many ways, Lacan follows Hegel here by showing what happens when the slave realizes that the master is dependent on the slave's production of knowledge and work. However, in Lacan's account, the slave's realization of the importance of knowledge does not result in an increase in personal power, but rather the very idea of personal empowerment is effaced by the dominance of abstract systems of symbolic knowledge. The strong example of this new Discourse of the University that Lacan gives is the bureaucracy of the former Soviet Union. In this mode of Discourse, symbolic codes and rituals supercede the power of the individual, and instead of knowledge being used to help empower individual subjects, it results in an increased sense of alienation. It is in turn this combination of the dominance of symbolic forms and the loss of the illusion of subjective power that, for Lacan, helps to define our current postmodern Discourse of the University.

According to this theory of academic discourse, we must think of the current teacher–student relationship in terms of bureaucracy and absent mastery. Yet, we should not ignore the ways that students and teachers react to this situation by trying to recreate the lost system of the Discourse of the Master. For example, when Ottinger's students demand to be enslaved or my students refuse to engage in group work, what might be going on is a desperate attempt to reinstate a sense of authority and power in relation to the production of knowledge. Moreover, as Segal (1997) points out, teachers may also desire to establish authority in a cultural context that constantly undermines authority (p. 179). This contradiction between the decentering of the class and a return to the teacher's authority thus results in a constant struggle with "issues of love and power" in the postmodern classroom (p. 179).

Segal's emphasis on the question of the teacher's love and authority points us to the Lacanian concept of the idealizing transference, which states that we love those people whom we suppose have great knowledge. In this secondary form of narcissism, the fantasy of the perfect knowledge of the Other allows us to maintain a fantasy that we are also all-knowing. In this sense, if the teacher can maintain a position as the one who knows, the students can continue the illusion that there really is a master of knowledge.

In order to define the intersubjectivity of the student, who is caught in the alienating Discourse of the University, Lacan develops his theory of the discourse of the Hysteric:

(1) Discourse of the Hysteric

$$\frac{\$}{a} \quad \overset{\rightarrow}{\leftarrow} \quad \frac{S_1}{S_2}$$

We can read this structure as indicating that students display their subjectivity by both affirming their subjective difference ($\$$) and calling for a new master signifier (S_1). This attempt to place the Other in a position of mastery is coupled with an insistence that the master knows nothing about the true nature of the object (a) of the student's desire (a) and experience.[5] In other terms, the hysterical student places the teacher in the ideal position of the one who knows only to show that this knowledge (S_2) is impotent in the face of real-life personal experience. Moreover, the truth of the students' discourse is defined by their unconscious awareness that they represent only an object within the dominant Discourse of the University. The Discourse of the Hysteric thus traces the structure of student resistance and protest by placing knowledge and objectification in the positions of loss and repression below the celebration of subjective differences and ideal mastery.

By stressing their own subjectivity and resistance to diverse modes of symbolic objectification, students protest against the ways that they are positioned as the objects and products of academic discourse. According to Segal, instructors who tend to blame the theories of decentered pedagogies for the failures in their classrooms, also tend to reduce students to being objectified stereotypes. Mimi Orner (1992) has echoed this point by arguing that "Those who would 'read' student silence simply as resistance or ideological impairment replicate forms of vanguardism which construct students as knowable, malleable objects, rather than as complex, contradictory subjects" (p. 181). Orner's insistence that pedagogical theories tend to objectify the students and remove their subjective differences can be tied to Lacan's argument that the main goal and role of the Discourse of the University is the transformation of students into objects of knowledge and social value. This objectification of students can also be related to the need for postmodern culture to produce mass-mediated and stereotypical images of the Other in order to overcome subjective feelings of fragmentation and the loss of identity. According to this logic, if my culture undermines my own sense of identity, I can find a stable mode of self-representation through the objectification of others.

In response to these different ways of blaming the teacher, the student, or the theory for the failures of a decentered pedagogy, Segal (1997) posits that we must begin to see the classroom as a rhetorical situation and the lecture format as a game of social action (p. 186). However, doesn't this stress on the symbolic aspects of teaching and learning only serve to reinforce the postmodern dominance of the Discourse of the University? What seems to be missing from this account is an extended analysis of what academic discourse is and how it is related to the larger general culture. Through Lacan's theory of the Discourse of the University, we can address this lack of analysis by positing that the four major components of academic discourse are: (1) a loss of authority (the master signifier); (2) a dominance of abstract systems of knowledge; (3) the objectification of Others; and (4) a repression of subjective difference. I believe that teachers and students must be constantly aware of these four components of discourse in their analysis of the university and of postmodern culture, for a failure to recognize these structures most often results in either the student's call for enslavement or the teacher's desire to be the master of language.

THE MASTER OF LANGUAGE AND ACADEMIC DISCOURSE

A central point of Lacan's theory of the postmodern Discourse of the University is thus centered on the constant dialectic between the undermining of language mastery and the call for a stable form of social authority. This question of the loss and desire for power has been recently articulated by Dennis Lynch and Stephen Jukuri (1997), who claim that the problem with new theories of radical pedagogy is that they often fail to take into account the power that they derive from their own academic institutions (p. 271). Thus, even if teachers announce that they will give up all of their authority in the classroom, students will place them in a position of power because that is how the university is structured. Once again, this theory fails to take into account the ways that students in a postmodern context tend to place teachers in the position of the disempowered authority of the lost master signifier. In other terms, teachers are expected to rule over the students, but the students also expect to resist the teachers. This double role of submission and resistance complicates both the traditional and the radical ways of seeing pedagogical relationships as pure master-and-slave dialectics, for in the Discourse of the Hysteric, the students place the teacher in the ideal position of mastery only to then question the teacher's mastery and power.

Another way that Lacan's theory of the Discourse of the University problematizes the construction of radical pedagogies is by its insistence that we can no longer speak about a ruling ideology or a dominant class whose values are merely reproduced by the academic system. In opposition to James Berlin's (1992) claim that "Ruling classes . . . are adept at the signifying practices that ensure the continuance of their power" (p. 116), we must affirm that no one can control the production of the multiple signifying ideologies in our postmodern universities. Thus, as Lynch and Jukuri show, radical pedagogical theories often draw their strength by connecting the university to the power and control of the dominant class, and thus their theories tend to feed into an older Discourse of the Master (p. 276).

In order to counter these notions of monolithic power, Lynch and Jukuri turn to Foucault's (1984) descriptions of the multiple and diffuse forms of power, discourse, and ideology:

Foucault argued on many occasions that our tendency to see power as monolithic, sovereign and repressive does not prepare us to grapple with the effects of a form of power that works its way into the little things we do: administer an exam, judge an essay contest, assign a research paper. (p. 279)

Power in the postmodern university has therefore not gone away; rather it has spread itself out in all directions and into all relations.[6] The questions still remain as to who benefits from this power and who tends to control it. Lacan's response to these questions appears to be that language itself is the master, but this master is hidden in the Discourse of the University with the double stress on symbolic knowledges and the objectification of all subjects.

In many ways, Lynch and Jukuri support Lacan's claims by analyzing the ways that universities tend to objectify subjects and teachers through the constant effort to produce more specialized symbolic knowledges:

Thus, subjectivity catches us in circular, circulating processes that separate us from others, trains and prepares us for institutional roles (teacher, student, doctor, patient, etc.), reconnects us to others (but only though those institutionally taught and sanctioned roles), defines any excess as one's "private life," and stands always ready to retrain or reshape what is private into a safer, more productive institutional role. (p. 280)

In this description of how academic discourse structures the subjectivity of everyone it encounters, we see that the symbolic processes of differentiation, linkage, and exclusion are directed toward the objectification of all aspects of human life. However, the question still remains of determining who or what controls these systems and who profits from their reproduction.

Lynch and Jukuri posit that one way of countering this constant transformation of subjectivity into discourses of power and control is to help students to develop the ability to "act and invent through language" (p. 281). The problem with this strategy is that it does not question the ways that language is itself responsible for the Discourse of the University's concentration on predictability and uniformity. In other terms, these authors call for more discourse in order to undermine the effects of academic discourse. It thus appears that the solution that most composition and rhetoric theorists see to the destructive aspects of academic discourse and postmodern culture is the production of more knowledge. In fact, this call for more symbolic production defines what Lacan has determined to be the hidden truth of the Discourse of the University, which is the constant demand for more knowledge and work. It is almost as if the signifier has a hunger to consume everything through the transformation of lived experiences into symbolic discourses.

For Lacan, the best hope in countering the signifier's constant demand for more symbolic knowledge is to first highlight the way that the unconscious (hysterical) subject resists the knowledge of the Other and then to use the Discourse of the Analyst to undermine the power of the signifier itself. We have already seen how the Discourse of the Hysteric challenges the production of symbolic knowledge; the question now is, how does the Discourse of the Analyst help us to produce a radical critique of language itself?

UTILIZING THE DISCOURSE OF THE ANALYST IN COMPOSITION AND RHETORIC

Just as I tried in my class to locate a position for myself outside of the class's discussion circle, Lacan posits that the analyst becomes the object (a) that has been rejected by the imposition of symbolic discourse:

Discourse of the Analyst

$$\frac{a}{S_2} \begin{array}{c} \rightarrow \\ \leftarrow \end{array} \frac{\$}{S_1}$$

We can read this discourse as arguing that the analyst (a) uses his or her objectivity in order to produce subjectivity (S) in the place of the Other. One of the results of this process is that knowledge (S_2) is placed below the presence of the object (a) and that the master signifier (S_1) of discourse is located underneath the subjectivity of the Other. This abstract structure can be explored through the concrete example of my classroom. For example, by refusing to participate in the students' discussion, I removed myself from the class's discourse and allowed my presence to be a pure object for their essays and unconscious projections. In turn, my lack (a) of discourse forced them to reflect on their own subjective (S) desires and their need to re-create a place for the master (S_1) of language. Once they saw that there was no immediate external controlling force regulating their production of knowledge, they were given the opportunity to acknowledge the limits of academic discourse. However, their ability to examine the Discourse of the University was greatly restricted by their hysterical desire to reinstate a master of language and their submersion in a postmodern cultural context. In order to overcome these resistances, the Discourse of the Analyst needs to help students to reconstruct their subjective relationships and histories to the very fact of language. In other terms, language itself must become an object of analysis within the classroom.

I believe that it is this attention to the fundamental relationship between language and subjectivity that is most sorely lacking in composition and rhetorical studies. While it is often the goal in these fields to help students enter into academic discourse and other modes of language production, what has been lost sight of is the ways that the abstract and distancing effects of language and discourse alienate every subject. Not only does language help us to objectify and stereotype Others, but it also serves to separate us from our own bodies, feelings, and enjoyments. However, I do not believe that we need to stop writing or communicating; rather, what we have to develop is a careful attentiveness to both the benefits and costs of being subjects to discourse.

A composition or rhetoric class that concentrates on the analysis of the Discourse of the University represents one of the best ways to help students enter into academic discourse without being completely alienated in it. In order to provide for this type of learning experience it is first necessary to develop a theory of the Discourse of the University that takes into account its own limitations and subjective structures. This entails that students and teachers must be constantly self-reflective at the same time that they realize that there is a limit to what one should represent and subject to discourse.

According to Lacan, this need to acknowledge the limits of knowledge and language are essential to the acceptance of the radical Otherness of both other subjects and one's own subjective difference. In order for us to resist the constant pressures to objectify ourselves and those around us, we must accept the impossibility of fully symbolizing the real. Since our postmodern Discourse of the University is centered on the production of symbolic knowledges directed toward the objectification of Others, we need to turn to the Discourse of the Analyst in order to articulate the logic of radical Otherness. This notion of radical Otherness, which has been developed by both Lacan and Jean Baudrillard (1993, 113–174), is founded on the critique of the Symbolic Order's reliance on a logic of binary difference. Radical Otherness implies that we cannot reduce our difference from Others to a purely oppositional conjunction of signifiers. For example, instead of seeing academic discourse as structured by the binary difference of student and teacher, we must see how Real learning relationships counter an "Us versus Them" logic. Thus, in my attempts to remove myself from the center of authority in my class's discussions, I was not only trying to upset the usual ways that my teaching role is objectified; I was also trying to allow for my Real presence to emerge beyond its symbolic and imaginary representations.[7]

This logic of absence can be related to Heidegger's claim that we only truly come into contact with something when it no longer works for us. For instance, if I have a hammer that I use every day, I never think about its multiple usage and the value it has for me. I treat my hammer as a pure tool or means until it breaks and then I am stuck with its brute presence in my hand. Once the hammer no longer works for me, I begin to reflect on all of the times that I used it in the past and all of the diverse functions that is has played in my life. Therefore, once the hammer no longer functions as a pure tool, I can begin to respect its presence and value.

Lacan takes this same logic of the hammer and applies it to language. He posits that normally we use language as a tool and we don't think about its presence or value in our lives. However, once language fails us or we see that we cannot control it, we enter into a different relationship with it. Lacan posits that while psychoanalysis is based on the method of free association, where the subject is supposed to commit everything to language and discourse, what happens over the course of an analysis is that one encounters resistances and limits to the production of symbolic knowledge. For example, a patient may have a traumatic experience that cannot be articulated or someone makes a slip of the tongue that shows that the "speaking person" is not in control of his/her own language. It is these encounters with the failure of language to act as a pure tool that pushes people to reflect on the very fact of language itself.

By thinking about the foundations of language and discourse we can thus begin to challenge the postmodern Discourse of the University that is dependent on the pure production of more symbolic knowledge. As teachers and students, we must refuse to present ourselves as the pure masters of language and allow for the radical Otherness of our own subjectivities to emerge. In fact, Lacan defines the subject of the unconscious as the presence of the radical Other within our own psyches and he posits that without an acceptance of this internal Other, we will remain unable to accept the radical difference of all external Others. Psychoanalytic theory and the practice of composition are therefore linked together in this shared need to explore the alterity of language, subjectivity, and Otherness. Perhaps the best way to resist our students' desires for us to enslave them or subject them to the abstract symbolic knowledge of academic discourse is to start from a position of absolute difference and then motivate them to analyze their own relationships to knowledge, power, authority, and discourse legitimacy. By placing our being outside of the circle of postmodern discourse, we allow ourselves and our students to explore the very foundations of language and knowledge.

NOTES

1. Freud (1963) claimed that he could not stand being looked at all of the time and so he had his patients lie down and not face him. One of the effects of this transition from the face-to-face encounter to a structure of blocked vision was that patients often became less aware of the analyst and felt more free to express themselves. Lacan adds that by moving away from a face-to-face encounter, the analyst is able to remove him- or herself from a purely imaginary relation of visual reflec-

tion. The analyst thus takes on a more neutral position in relation to vision and the imaginary world of rivalry and identification. This neutrality is also reinforced by the analyst's refusal to answer the questions and demands of the patient. In fact, the silences of the analyst can be seen as representing a purely neutral position in the symbolic realm of language and law.

2. I do not want to give the impression here that I tried to position myself as the analyst of my students. I think there is a great deal of difference between the analytic setting and the teaching situation. What I am articulating here are some of the ways that analytic insights and techniques can be employed within an academic setting.

3. For Lacan (1991), a discourse represents a series of fundamental social relationships that are mediated by different symbolic and linguistic codes (p. 11). In order to clarify the central structures that affect psychoanalysis and education, Lacan posits that there are four main forms of discourse (the Discourse of the University, of the Hysteric, of the Master, and of the Analyst), which contain four central elements (authority, knowledge, subjectivity, and objectification):

(1) Discourse of the Master $$\frac{S_1}{\cancel{S}} \quad \overset{\rightarrow}{\leftarrow} \quad \frac{S_2}{a}$$

(2) Discourse of the University $$\frac{S_2}{S_1} \quad \overset{\rightarrow}{\leftarrow} \quad \frac{a}{\cancel{S}}$$

(1) Discourse of the Hysteric $$\frac{\cancel{S}}{a} \quad \overset{\rightarrow}{\leftarrow} \quad \frac{S_1}{S_2}$$

(2) Discourse of the Analyst $$\frac{a}{S_2} \quad \overset{\rightarrow}{\leftarrow} \quad \frac{\cancel{S}}{S_1}$$

In each of these structures, the components above the bar represent manifest elements, while the elements below the bar refer to hidden or repressed aspects. For example, we can read the Discourse of the Master as formalizing the ways that authority commands knowledge and produces objects and a loss of subjectivity. In this structure, someone occupies the place of authority and uses this power to produce knowledge concerning objects. In turn, this knowledge of objects hides the truth about the authority's own subjectivity. A master is thus a subject who uses language in order to control knowledge and to objectify the world through the denial of subjectivity. On the other hand, the Discourse of the University points to an anti-foundational system, where knowledge is placed above authority. In this postmodern structure of academic discourse, universities concentrate on the circulation of knowledge and not the production of authority. This entails that academic structures are inherently postmodern because they undermine any attempt at establishing a single authority or source of knowledge.

4. In order to flesh out Lacan's theory of the Discourse of the University, I want to list several of the elements of this discourse as they are presented in his *Seminar XVII*:

1. knowledge is placed in the position of dominance (p. 34);

2. there is a movement away from the Discourse of the Master (p. 34);

3. humans become the object of knowledge (p. 35);

4. knowledge connects up with capitalism in order to turn subjects into consumable products (p. 35);

5. the absolute signifier underwriting the university is the transcendental "I" (p. 70);

Postmodern Composition, Pedagogy, and Psychoanalytic Theory 57

6. the disjointed knowledge of the unconscious is rejected (p. 104);

7. the Father no longer is a master, he works for the Other (p. 114);

8. science places abstract knowledge in the position of dominance (p. 119);

9. the hidden master demands that we create more knowledge (p. 119);

10. the subject of science is barred from discourse (p. 120):

11. science is based on a strict combination of signifiers in a signifying chain (p. 185);

12. the hidden truth of the university is the pure fact of language (p. 103);

13. knowledge becomes separated from its origins (p. 21);

14. knowledge is directed toward an impossible object (p. 112);

15. the barred subject is the product of the university system (p. 119).

These diverse statements all relate to the fact that in the Discourse of the University, the symbolic structures of science, technology, and capitalism become dominant and are directed toward the objectification of human beings and the world around them. Moreover, this ascendancy of symbolic knowledge is tied to a loss of older forms of cultural mastery. However, these masters do not disappear; rather, Lacan insists that they continue to play their role but in a more hidden and repressed way.

The central master of all discourses for Lacan is the pure fact of language and it is the power of language that is paradoxically repressed in the Discourse of the University. In other words, academic discourse is dependent on the imposition of language in human subjectivity; however, the Discourse of the University rejects all origins and foundations of knowledge. Most forms of education therefore cannot account for their own production of knowledge and this helps to feed into a cynical culture of lost authority. Yet, Lacan does not argue for a return to the past Discourses of the Master; rather, he attempts to combine a radical critique of all forms of mastery with an analysis of the alienating effects of the Discourse of the University.

As one can see from my list of elements concerning the Discourse of the University, Lacan's theory of academic discourse is not limited to an analysis of questions concerning education. Just as knowledge circulates in the university without a sense of mastery or authority, the social structure itself combines the production of symbolic systems of information with a loss of patriarchal and social control. Thus, when Lacan affirms that the Father now works for the Other, he is describing the ways that language overcomes every subject's power and sense of subjective control. The end result of our increased dependence on abstract symbolic systems (computers, postindustrial capitalism, mass media, etc.) is the production of a subject who is barred from mastering and controlling the discourses that surround him or her. In fact, Lacan argues that this barred subject of discourse and science is the subject of the unconscious.

5. One of the confusing aspects of Lacan's theory of discourse is that each of the central elements takes on a slightly different meaning, according to what discourse it is contained within. For example, the object (a) in the Discourse of the University represents the objectification of the Other, while in the Discourse of the Master, this object represents the surplus-value that the master steals from the worker. Moreover, this same object in the Discourse of the Hysteric represents the subject's sense of his or her own unknowable desire.

6. While Foucault (1984) tends to subvert the power of the subject to resist these processes of symbolic power and control, Lacan argues that the subject of the unconscious represents a whole in the symbolic discourse of the Other. In other words, the subject of psychoanalysis clings to a Real that is effaced by social constructionist thinkers like Foucault.

7. Lacan's notion of the Real stems from his argument that the Real is the presence of an experience that is impossible to symbolize or imagine. In this sense, the unconscious subject is Real because it resists being represented in the Symbolic and Imaginary Orders.

REFERENCES

Baudrillard, Jean. 1993. *The Transparency of Evil*. New York: Verso.

Berlin, James. 1992. Poststructuralism, Cultural Studies, and the Composition Classroom: Postmodern Theory in Practice. *Rhetoric Review* 11: 16–33.

Foucault, Michel. 1984. Space, Knowledge, and Power. In *The Foucault Reader*, ed. Paul Rabinow (pp. 329–356). New York: Pantheon.

Freire, Paulo. 1970. *Pedagogy of the Oppressed*, trans. Myra Bergman Ramos. New York: Continuum.

Freud, Sigmund. 1963. On Narcissism: An Introduction. In *General Psychological Theory*. New York: Collier.

Lacan, Jacques. 1991. *Le Séminaire: Livre XVII, L'envers de la psychanalyse, 1969–1970*, ed. Jacques-Alain Miller. Paris: Seuil.

Lynch, Dennis, and Jukuri, Stephen. 1997. Beyond Master and Slave: Reconciling Our Fears of Power in the Writing Classroom. *Rhetoric Review* 15: 271–288.

Orner, Mimi. 1992. Interrupting the Calls for Student Voice in "Liberatory" Education: A Feminist Poststructuralist Perspective. In *Feminisms and Critical Pedagogy*, ed. Carmen Luke and Jennifer Gore (pp. 74–89). New York: Routledge.

Segal, Judy. 1997. Pedagogies of Decentering and a Discourse of Failure. *Rhetoric Review* 15: 174–191.

Part III

The Ethics of Transference

Chapter 5

Toward a Pedagogy of Symptoms, Anxiety, and Mourned Objects

Marshall Alcorn

In Chapter 2 of *The Psychic Life of Power*, Judith Butler (1997) explains the difficulty of political resistance as an effect of irrational and inexplicable forms of psychic attachment. Integrating Freud within the political vocabulary of Foucault, Butler seeks to understand these mysterious attachments that determine so much of psychic life. She asks: "How are we to understand not merely the disciplinary production of the subject, but the disciplinary cultivation of an attachment to subjection?" (p. 102). In the final chapter of her book, Butler's reading of Freud leads her away from the language of Foucault, with its emphasis on law and discipline, to a psychoanalytic vocabulary, which represents problems of attachment as difficulties in mourning and identification. Following Freud, she declares, "there can be no severing of this attachment to the object without a direct declaration of loss and the desanctification of the object by externalizing aggression against it" (p. 192).

Butler's conceptual shift from the theme of discipline to the theme of mourning is apt. It offers an important contribution to a theory of teaching because it shifts the dynamics of teaching from a practice that constructs knowledge to a practice that works on desire and emotional subjection. If Butler, following Freud, is right in locating the difficulty of resistance at the level of pure dumb, irrational attachment, then we would do well to explore this dimension of human experience in considerable depth.

WHAT IS A SYMPTOM?

In analytic circles, dumb irrational attachments can be conceptualized in various ways. In this chapter, I will discuss attachments as symptoms and mourned objects and the anxiety these structures contain. One does not need to know anything about psychoanalysis to see how some individuals, "fixated" on certain beliefs, deny all rational evidence that contradicts their beliefs. We see evidence of anxious and irrational forms of attachments every day; we need only look more closely at what we commonly see to understand some of its properties. Joseph Conrad's (1988) fictional narrator, Marlow, offers an apt description of a clearly symptomatic belief:

I knew once a Scotch sailmaker who was certain, dead sure, there were people in Mars. If you asked him for some idea how they looked and behaved he would get shy and mutter something about "walking on all-fours." If you as much as smiled he would—though a man of sixty—offer to fight you. (p. 29)

There are two bits of evidence here to suggest that this sailmaker's belief is more than a reasonable deduction derived from a preponderance of evidence. First, the sailmaker is remarkably, even aggressively certain of a fact he is unable to support by means of concrete evidence. Second, he is extremely anxious and defensive in regard to this claim he seems unable to support. "Though a man of sixty," he is quick to fight to support a certainty that apparently lacks other means for support. He is particularly sensitive to personal insult, and he recognizes, when questioned, that his claims need support in order to be held as certain; but he is unable to make any defense of his position other than that of pure bodily aggression. These two qualities, lack of rational support, and hostile bodily defensiveness, are characteristic of symptomatic thinking. If we are to make progress as teachers in dealing with these forms of defense, we must better understand their structure.

If we consider that many if not all irrational beliefs have the literal structure of the symptom, we can better understand how such beliefs function in relation to a wider field of knowledge, discipline, and discourse. In "Inhibitions, Symptoms, and Anxiety" (1926 [1925]), Freud describes symptoms as produced by defensive processes that generate repression. Symptoms, and the repressive material they hide, are necessary to defend the ego from anxiety. Two factors are worth remembering here.

First, we must see the symptom as having its ground, not in language and rational meaning, but in anxiety. The symptom is a response to anxiety. It is an irrational response because it does nothing to truly protect the bodily self from danger; yet while it does not protect the biological body, it does protect the ego. But this relation between the symptom and anxiety becomes particularly important for the teacher because it means that any attempt to undo a symptom has the effect of releasing anxiety. This suggests that whenever teachers attempt to "prove" the falsehood of a belief that is purely symptomatic, the proof will function as nothing more than a pure release of often unbearable anxiety. The old sailmaker threatens to fight, the student may remain silent but will certainly generate feelings of hostility to hold in check whatever logical or evidentiary material the teacher tries to introduce.

A second factor here involves the relation between ordinary language and the symptom. If the symptom generates repression, then the ground of the symptom is not integrated within the laws of language that normally determine how language functions in a social field. Freud (1926 [1925]), for example, observes that repressed material is an "outlaw" independent of social demand: "The repressed is . . . as it were, an outlaw; it is excluded from the great organization of the ego and is subject only to the laws which govern the realm of the unconscious" (p. 79).

As teachers we commonly resist the idea that many beliefs have the literal structure of symptoms, and yet it should be obvious that this is the case. We frequently encounter situations where students insist on believing something that is demonstrably false. When we try to talk to them we find that we somehow cannot "reach" them. It is as if our talk has no effect. Often, to be more effective, we become simply more insistent. But this insistence also will not work, although it may force a student to give some sign of submission. We cannot reach the student, Freud suggests, because the core of the belief is "subject only to the laws which govern the realm of the unconscious."

In teaching we encounter two rather different kinds of mental acts that support knowledge. We encounter both rational truth claims and symptomatic beliefs. A symptomatic belief is not the same thing as a verbal truth claim. Truth claims respond effortlessly to the pressure of demonstration and logical argument. Symptoms do not.

Consider the example of a person who chooses, through a phobia, to avoid public swimming pools because he is afraid he may be eaten by sharks. Imagine telling this person that there is really nothing to fear in the pool. It may be obviously true that there are no sharks or crocodiles hiding in public swimming pools. Nonetheless, phobic swimmers may imagine these animals present. A symptomatic belief is not banished easily by what we consider "proof." A person with a symptom can believe that there are sharks in a public pool, and feel compelled to act on that belief, even though he/she also "knows," in some sense, that there are no sharks in the pool. Psychoanalytic practice repeatedly demonstrates that knowledge does not easily change the symptoms expressed by people in therapy.

I once had a student who wrote about her fear that she would be eaten by sharks if she stepped on the wooden floor of her bedroom. She had gone to see the movie *Jaws*, and after she came home she developed an unbearable fear of her bedroom floor. She knew, of course, that there were no sharks hidden in the wood of her floor. But even though she "knew" this to be true, she still feared sharks might eat her if she stepped on the floor of her room. She told this story in my classroom, and when she tried to explain what happened, some students laughed. But she herself was very tense and serious. She described how she had moved her bed as close to the door of her room as possible and had filled her floor with her stuffed animals; but she still could not move from the bed to the door without walking over some floor, and this move terrified her. In time her parents took her to a therapist and her fear slowly disappeared.

This story indicates complex relations existing between knowledge and irrational fears or desires we see in symptoms. Truth claims, no matter how true, no matter how well supported by established facts, do not change symptomatic behavior. Thus if a student claims, "I am against paying taxes to feed the poor," we might imagine this position to be something like a symptomatic expression. No amount of proof that the poor do not easily find work and success will change this student's mind. What is at stake in this belief is not a judgment about facts, but anxiety and irrational fears that resolve themselves in a compromise formation that analysts call symptoms. The symptom is an expression of desire and that supports a "knowledge" in a tenaciously non-dialectical manner. The student "knows" that everyone in America can be successful, but this knowledge is not supported by evidence.

In the example of Conrad's Scotch sailmaker, the features of the symptom are obvious and perhaps exaggerated. It will be useful, now, to consider the symptom as having a more subtle structure; as part of any irrational identification that a subject defends with hostility, as opposed to a defense that relies on reason and patient exploration of evidence.

Let me offer, as a more complex example of symptomatic thinking, an example from a student diary discussed by Jeffrey Berman (1994) in *Diaries to an English Professor*. This example comes from Berman's chapter "Sexual Disclosures," where he introduces some statistics about male abuse of women:

In a recent survey of 114 undergraduates, a large majority agree with the following statements: "I prefer relatively small women" (93.7 percent agreement); "I like to dominate a woman" (91.3 percent); "I enjoy the conquest part of sex" (86.1 percent); "Some women look like they're just asking to be raped" (83.5 percent). (p. 200)

Berman observes that generally the men in his class do not write on these issues. Part of his policy is that he does not require students to write about anything. They have complete freedom to explore what they want. Nonetheless, Berman finds that, on the average, 30 percent of his students write about sexual experiences or feelings which they find problematic. Many of these entries are about harassment, homosexual identities, or homophobia. In the example I want to examine, a student writes an entry about sexual abuse:

A few days ago my friend told me a story about what he and his fraternity brothers did to some innocent, unsuspecting female. While one of their friends was in a room with this girl, they all decided to hide in the closet. After the friend was engaged in coitus with this girl, the fraternity brothers slowly revealed themselves and drew nearer to the bed. They were all naked. When at last she saw them, she struggled to get her clothes on, but her partner for the night held her in the rear-entry position and stayed inside her, until she was finally able to break free and run out of the room. This, as I discovered, was called a "rodeo." It seems that while the girl struggles, the audience would holler out like they were watching a cowboy ride a bull.

Honestly, at first I laughed, I really thought it was funny. I mean, my friends aren't rapists. In fact, the word "rape" didn't come to mind until I thought of all the implications of their actions. This girl was humiliated in front of them, and they loved it. This "rodeo" was purely acting out desires. Just thinking about it now makes me sick. These aren't lowlife degenerates; these were all wealthy, middle-class boys. I guess their drives are just the same as everyone's. But it is hard for me to understand why people need to make someone else suffer in the process. I wish they would have never told me that story. (Berman, 1994, p. 201)

It is difficult to determine from this entry where this student stands in relation to sexual politics. On the one hand, there is an overt attempt to "be on the right side," when the writer says, "it is hard for me to understand why people need to make someone else suffer." And yet the entry never fully charges the friends with rape. The closest the student comes to thinking this thought is in the passive sentence, "the word 'rape' didn't come to mind until I thought of all the implications." This sentence shows that the thought of "rape" does come to mind, but the context of the entry suggests that while the term comes to mind it is never actually thought. It is as if some irrational force holds the thought at arm's length.

I would argue that this slowness to think is something symptomatic. The "game" played by these middle-class boys is rape. The writer is aware of this judgment, but cannot quite think it in a direct and responsible way. The word "rape" is introduced by a defensive sentence, "I mean, my friends aren't rapists." And the sentence that suggests rape is concluded by another defensive and problematic claim, "I guess their drives are just the same as everyone's." What we see stated is an irrational belief, "my friends aren't rapists," that is defended by a set of shy assertions, "I guess their drives are just the same," that never focus on the central moral issues of the story.

Berman (1994) writes that he was himself "horrified" by the diary entry, but unsure about how to handle it in the class. As a scholar trained in psychoanalysis, Berman understands the need to control anxiety as he seeks to increase moral accountability. He says:

As a rule I do not read a diary aloud if it might make either the diarist or another student in the class to feel defensive. Scott was honest enough to admit that his first response upon hearing his friend's story was laughter—and he was sensitive enough to realize later that his amusement was inappropriate. (p. 201)

Berman argues that he does not judge his students when they make journal entries. And even in writing the book, he tries to be careful with judgmental terms. While he earlier described his response to the event with a feeling of "horror," he is very careful in the paragraph after the quote to control his judgment of his student's initial amusement. It is, Berman says, "inappropriate." Berman did not offer a strong moral judgment of this man's diary entry, but another student in the class, a woman, did. She wrote:

In my diary for this week, I'd like to comment on a diary read last week about a bunch of frat guys who cheered on one of their so-called brothers as he raped a girl. When I heard that diary, I thought I'd be sick. I was so repulsed that this actually happened. It's not as though I don't know that rape is a common occurrence, especially on college campuses, but since I've been in school, I haven't heard of that many.

The person who wrote that diary, if I can remember clearly, didn't use the word "rape." Why? In my opinion, that girl was raped in every sense of the word, and what's worse is that a bunch of guys cheered it on! The thought makes me want to throw up! I don't care if the girl went willingly to that guy's dorm or apartment. I don't know of many girls, or guys, for that matter, who haven't gone back willingly to someone's room for whatever the reason. That's no explanation to rape someone. This sadist obviously had the whole escapade planned for the sole reason of humiliating the poor girl. (p. 202)

This example brings into focus key issues I want to develop from this focus on symptomatic beliefs. If some beliefs held by students are in fact symptoms, how might teaching address these beliefs in a fruitful manner? If rational discussion is ineffective, what are other possibilities for interaction?

Our most common response to the kind of entry above is a quick rational response. In Berman's class a woman who heard the entry was able to quickly make the judgment that the male could not make: "The person who wrote that diary, if I can remember clearly, didn't use the word 'rape.' Why? In my opinion, that girl was raped in every sense of the word, and what's worse is that a bunch of guys cheered it on!" (Ibid.)

Consider the emotions that are brought into play by the interchange between these two students. The male writer says that he first laughed when he heard the story from a friend. He really, he says, thought the story was funny. His laughter makes him a member of a particular social group that does not make careful observations about rape. Some might argue that his laughter is "instinctive" because it reveals how he "really" feels about the event as opposed to what he will say when he is called to speak in front of people who might be uneasy with his friends' behavior.

Most of us who are not part of fraternity culture find it difficult to imagine how anyone could laugh at being told this story, and the writer's record of laughter immediately triggers our anger. The male behavior described is clearly sadistic, and for many of us, our first response as teachers would be to confront the student exactly as the woman confronts the student later. How could anyone admit such a response in a journal without also showing a greater sense of guilt? What is wrong?

It seems to me that if these two students were simply to argue about what happened, it is very likely we might see very little change in the male writer. Even though he himself provides plentiful evidence to charge his friends with rape, he himself does not do so. He is anxious and defensive in writing the entry, and he is likely to be even more anxious and defensive if he finds himself and his friends attacked by a woman. Our most common response to being attacked is to defend ourselves from such attack. This is especially true when the attack seeks to separate us from a social group with which we have strong ties.

Having read Berman's book carefully and with some skepticism, I have become persuaded that Berman's journal-writing dramatically helps students develop moral sensibility. His quotations from the entries of students suggest that they develop in a manner that makes them less likely to show race and gender prejudices. It seems to me that Berman shows a variety of skills that make it easier for his students to manage their symptoms. Let me summarize Berman's practice as a teacher and try to emphasize how it usefully engages the symptomatic attachments that Butler finds central to ideological subjection.

First, Berman's use of the diary allows for students to speak their inner feelings, their "instinctive" or "symptomatic" responses. There is a guarantee, early in the course, that the writer can say however he or she feels, and he or she will not be attacked. The journal, as Berman remarks, offers a space where such defensive and symptomatic behavior can be expressed and examined. Students are encouraged to express their feelings and this means that symptomatic thinking that might otherwise be self-censored (and thus lost to meaningful engagement) is able to be examined.

Second, the diary readings also offer a situation where symptomatic responses can be reworked. The kind of reworking which Berman offers is, I believe, far more effective than the political training offered by many politically progressive teachers. Rather than engaging in argument or debate with his students, Berman simply allows powerful feelings to be spoken and heard in a social space that is charged with different kinds of strong feeling. I would argue for example, that in the entry about rape we can already see the writer beginning to shift his identity from his friends to the class. He admits his laughter, but he also wonders why people do such things. This shift in identification is an extremely delicate procedure. Attempts to rush such feelings, such as forceful appeals to simple logic, often backfire. Students are free to make adjustments in identification on their own terms and in their own time. The teacher does provide a moral perspective on student behavior, and this judgment obviously plays a role in shifting perspectives. But this shift is not forced; it is allowed to develop in its own time.

Berman's classroom allows for the development of identifications that complicate the subject's relationship to the symptom. This theme of identification is extremely important to the activity of teaching. I want to discuss its complexity, and its relation to symptomatic thought, at some length.

LEADERSHIP, IDENTIFICATION, AND THE SYMPTOM

The most common understanding of Freudian symptoms describes symptoms as arising from early trauma. In his discussion, for example, of "Little Hans" in "Inhibitions, Symptoms, and Anxiety" (1926 [1925]), Freud argues that Hans develops a phobia of horses as the result of a reaction formation against his hostile feelings for his father. "The instinctual impulse which underwent repression in 'little Hans' was a hostile one against his father." In his discussion of group psychology, however, Freud (1921) argues that some symptoms develop, somewhat mysteriously, from identifications with others who show symptoms. In a suggestive example, Freud tells of a number of girls in a boarding school who develop hysterical symptoms when another girl shows hysterical symptoms after getting a letter from a secret lover:

Supposing, for instance, that one of the girls in a boarding school has had a letter from someone with whom she is secretly in love which arouses her jealousy, and that she reacts to it with a fit of hysterics; then some of her friends who know about it will catch the fit, as we say, by mental infection. The mechanism is that of identification based upon the possibility or desire of putting one self in the same situation. The other girls would like to have a secret love affair too, and under the influence of a sense of guilt they also accept the suffering involved in it. (p. 49)

In this example, the symptom is not an effect of some personal and private history located in an infantile past. Instead, the symptom is triggered by an identification. This link between symptom formation and social interaction is something I want to stress. Lacanian theory argues that leaders reproduce their symptoms through their discourse. In his analysis of the Discourse of the Master, Lacan suggests that whenever leaders seek to control cultural value by means of fixed labels of criticism or support, human desire is fixated by means of symptomatic signification.

Lacan represents the Discourse of the Master in terms of the notation:

$$\frac{S_1}{\$} \rightarrow \frac{S_2}{a}$$

This notation offers complex possibilities for interpretation. But for my purposes I want to call attention to the S_1 or master signifier which sits atop of the $\$$, or divided subject. Mark Bracher (1993) explains that the Discourse of the Master "promotes consciousness" by "instituting the dominance of master signifiers, which order knowledge according to their own values and keep fantasy in a subordinate and repressed position" (p. 59). This ordering of knowledge which fixes fantasy in a subordinate position is the work of an S_1 which operates as a symptom. Desire is in effect held captive in repetitive performances that replay the Discourse of the Master. This happy repetition of the master's discourse is the key element that makes the master's discourse operate across a social field. Followers, as we all know, enjoy repeating the pronouncements, aphorisms, and asides of the master. They are happy to tell, as a follower, others about the words of the master's truth. Repetition of the master's ideology is not the work of a discipline, but the work of enjoyment. "Thought is *jouissance*," Lacan says in *Seminar XX*.

Ellie Ragland (1994) describes the master's discourse as the "foundation of the social link" because it "masters the subject's division" and resides "at the place of hysteria" (p. 69). When the master's discourse "masters" division, this means that it functions precisely as an expression of desire that represses the truth of self-division. Thus, while it serves as "truth" (S_2) for the master and his followers, it is, in fact, a denial of the free movement of desire (the *objet a* is under the bar in the graph) and logic in discourse. Ragland describes this insistence as "nothing more or less than a libidinal consistency in thoughts, actions and events, that (mis)takes itself for the truth, be it an ideology or a system of knowledge" (p. 70).

This "libidinal consistency in thought" is precisely what we see in the male writer of Berman's diary entry. He has an emotional tie to his friends. His friends, in terms of this tie, are good people; they do not do bad things like rape women. And so consistency in "libidinal ties" makes negative judgments very difficult. There is a symptomatic pull that warps language in relation to friends that one laughs with.

In order to perform the action we call "real" thinking, significant emotional elasticity must be available to a thinking subject. Symptomatic thinking is always a failure in the possibility of fully flexible thought. Symptomatic thinking displays "consistency" that is determined by nothing more than a kind of loyalty to a master discourse, an emotional loyalty to friends and leaders. To liberate thinking from such consistency, a classroom has to make available new forms of identification, but this experiment in identification is not as easy as it might seem.

We might imagine that teaching operates according to a process like a process of addition. Every class offers every student new possibilities for the expansion of his or her identity as he or she finds new teachers with which to identify. Such an assumption, however, fails to appreciate what is so hard for the male writer in Berman's class. The key difficulty is not to entertain a new identity, but to give up or abandon an old identity. It is in terms of this last observation that I want to finish this argument.

TOWARD A PEDAGOGY OF MOURNED OBJECTS

I began this chapter with Butler's (1997) claim: "there can be no severing of this attachment to the object without a direct declaration of loss and the desanctification of the object by externalizing aggression against it" (p. 192). With all due respect to Butler, I think that she misrepresents the real process of giving up attachments. She is right to suggest that politics requires in its most essential form "a severing of attachment to the object." She is right to insist that this severing of attachment requires a "declaration of loss and the desanctification of the object." But her own thinking is a bit too hasty, too much determined by a certain "consistency in libidinal ties" when she wants to simply declare loss and mobilize anger at the lost object. No one mourns an attachment by a simple process of declaration and angry rejection of an object.

Confronted with the fact of death, no one can complete the work of mourning by a simple thought. No one can simply say, for example, "OK, I understand, Dad is dead." Perhaps something significant does take place in this simple act of thought. But this simple act will never accomplish all the work necessary to reprocess the internal representations that make "Dad" an abiding presence in the unconscious. I remember that when my children were young and one of their guinea pigs died, I suggested that we go to the pet store to find a replacement. They were insulted. I then remembered how I felt when I was four and my pet dog "Jock" was killed by a car. My uncle informed me of his death, and when I cried he suggested that we could get a new dog. His answer to my grief made me angry. Jock, in my mind, could not be replaced. He was special. All mourned objects are special, and that is why changes in identification in the classroom often operate according to a principle of subtraction, the loss of an object, rather than addition, the gain of an object.

This curious fact of human grief is important in the classroom. Lost objects must be mourned to be given up, but the giving up of an object is not a simple act of thought. The process of mourning is complicated, and to the extent it is significant, it is also, as Freud describes it, absorbing. Freud (1917) describes the mourner as one who "abrogates" interest in the outside world as he or she attends to the painful demands of a mourned internal world. The internal task of mourning is both exhausting and painful because it is a process that takes time and requires a prolonged experience of pain, and this time is used in the mourning process. This is the case because mourned objects are not present to subjectivity as simple signifiers to be abandoned. They are instead dense and complex networks of memories that are experienced in some almost bodily manner as part of the self.

Erich Lindemann (1994) observes that the "picture shown by persons in acute grief is remarkably uniform":

Common to all is the following syndrome: sensation of somatic distress occurring in waves lasting from twenty minutes to an hour at a time, a feeling of tightness in the throat, choking with shortness of breath, need for sighing, and an empty feeling in the abdomen, lack of muscular power, and an intense subjective distress described as tension or mental pain. The patient soon learns that these waves of discomfort can be precipitated by visits, by mentioning the deceased, and by receiving sympathy. (p. 19)

Mourning requires adjustments of thought, but these adjustments also require painful emotional readjustments. If both teachers and students pay attention to acts of thought only, they may fail to recognize important processes that take place in the bodies of those who mourn. If Freud is right about the grief process, a failure to recognize and process pain in the body will impede the fluidity with which ideas can be entertained.

Freud (1917) observes that mourning requires a reprocessing of multitudinous images and memories. Discussing the absorbing work of mourning, Freud observes that "Reality passes its verdict—that the object no longer exists—upon each single one of the memories and hopes through which the libido was attached to the lost object" (p. 166). For a person to be mourned, each of the elements of memory must be brought forward and its attachment given up. Freud describes these attachments to elements as cathexes of libido. Libido is, in effect, a kind of glue that holds various elements in relation. As I have argued in an earlier essay (Alcorn 1991), the *work* of mourning consists in bringing all these various and sundry elements, memories, images, hopes, into consciousness to undo this glue, to sever the attachment of libido. We might imagine this multiplicity of elements involved in the work of mourning as similar to Saussure's (1966) description of a synchronic dimension of language. These multiple elements are part of a system or gridwork that simultaneously links many elements in relation.

The *work* of mourning, Freud (1917) says, consists in *withdrawing* libido from its attachment to an object. Such work, Freud points out, is hard and painful work because the self "never willingly abandons a libido position, even when a substitute is already beckoning" (p. 126). Freud's point here is worth emphasis: What is painful is not the *fact* of not having something, but the *effort* required to "withdraw libido" from something that you have *already* (in some "imaginary" sense) had. In this sense, people and beliefs can have the same status in the mind, both are internal constructions; both are cathected and subject to de-cathexis. Both people and beliefs are not simple signifiers, but part of a network of signifiers that form a system that supports the sense of self.

Mourning, however, is more than an adjustment in elements within a system of representation. Mourning is a time of pain. Mourning is painful because memories and hopes must be abandoned. Grief then is not a thought to be thought; it is a feeling to be felt. It is frequently an unmistakable bodily feeling often experienced in the chest or stomach. This pain, researchers claim, must be experienced in order for the process of mourning to make progress. Lindemann's (1994) now classic paper, "Symptomatology and Management of Acute Grief," observes:

The duration of a grief reaction seems to depend upon the success with which a person does the grief work, namely emancipation from the bondage to the deceased, readjustment to the environment in which the deceased is missing, and the formation of new relationships. One of the big obstacles to this work seems to be the fact that many patients try to avoid the intense distress connected with the grief experience and to avoid the expression of emotion necessary for it. (p. 21)

Everyone knows that mourning is painful, but most of us do not want to accept or acknowledge the degree to which it requires the experience of pain.

If much of the work of teaching involves helping students to experience the pain of loss, we should consider how this pain is managed by effective teachers. Why should students want to experience pain. At what point are classes too painful? I want to emphasize here that pain is necessary for mourning, but also that the teacher's role is to make sure that pain is not too much for students to manage. If mourning is to make progress the teacher must never simply inflict pain.

Berman (1994) makes it clear that he is not "practicing psychotherapy" in his classes. He is, he says, simply encouraging students to "engage in self-discovery" (p. 242). This adventure in "self-discovery" is not, however, a happy adventure. The second part of Berman's title, *Pain and Growth in the Classroom*, gives emphasis to the suffering that his writers must face if they are to grow. Indeed, many of the entries show that "self-discovery" is generally painful. One woman writes: "Seeing the truth about myself is very painful because I have lived in a fantasy life for so long. I was never able to deal with the pain of life from an early age, so to protect myself I made up an imaginary world in my head." (p. 173)

If mourning means the withdrawal of libido from a fantasy world and the feeling of the pain of this loss of self, this student, who "sees the truth" about herself, has learned to mourn.

CONCLUSION

Changes in subjectivity do not take place in the instant of a moment of thought. Changes in subjectivity take place in a temporal horizon where a play of thought can have structuring effects as an entire system of desire repression and *jouissance* is brought into new relationships. This prolonged temporal adjustment is, perhaps more than anything else, an exercise in pain and anxiety. Symptomatic beliefs supported by desires are a network of libidinal affects holding in place particular relations of language. In analysis these affects and their related networks must be talked through various nodes of resistance in a lengthy series of staged denials, defenses, protests. One cannot simply insist on a factual truth to change a symptomatic belief. Symptoms are primitive forms of subjectivity resistant to alteration through discourse.

Victor Vitanza (1999) has recently challenged classroom teachers to study the effects of cultural studies on their students. The primary questions in such a study would have to be, Vitanza observes:

Do the students ever stop thinking and practicing racism, sexism, classism, age-ism; do they ever stop thinking and practicing their homophobia and self-hatred, etc; or do they, in taking on an understanding of false consciousness . . . only become more cynical in their acts of violence against other human beings and themselves? (p. 700)

If teachers of cultural studies do not help their students mourn their attachments, their teaching will only, I fear, develop more cynical forms of consciousness. The changing of the symptom in analysis typically generates significant emotional affect. Often in this "talking cure" changes begin through what is termed the transference effect of love, but generally also these changes involve significant and diverse emotional turbulence. There is resentment, aggression, and not infrequently murderous rage. Teachers seeking to change the desires of their students should expect precisely these responses; and many teachers of cultural studies do encounter these responses daily.

The purpose of the symptom is to manage anxiety. When teachers seek then to remove the symptom, they often simply expose students to unmanageable anxiety. If the work of teaching is to succeed, it must manage anxiety through the process of mourning. The task of teaching resistance is not a practice of "discipline," nor the transmission of some content ("knowledge"), nor the social construction of some object ("knowledge"), but a labor of mourning that works on a dead or dying body that we might call a body of knowledge or a body of ideology. The essentially defensive nature of the ego makes change difficult. But a teacher sensitive to the need for mourning and responsive to the demands of the mourning process can, like Berman, help students develop more flexible powers of thought and greater opportunities for political engagement.

REFERENCES

Alcorn, Marshall. 1991. Loss and Figuration: Paradigms of Constructive and Deconstructive Mourning. *Centennial Review* 35: 501–518.

Berman, Jeffrey. 1994. *Diaries to an English Professor: Pain and Growth in the Classroom.* Amherst: University of Massachusetts Press.

Bracher, Mark. 1993. *Lacan, Discourse, and Social Change: A Psychoanalytic Cultural Criticism.* Ithaca, N.Y.: Cornell University Press.

Butler, Judith. 1997. *The Psychic Life of Power.* Stanford, Calif.: Stanford University Press.

Conrad, Joseph. 1988. *Heart of Darkness.* New York: Norton.

Freud, Sigmund. 1917. Mourning and Melancholia. In *The Standard Edition of the Complete Psychological Works of Sigmund Freud*, ed. and trans. James Strachey (vol. 14, pp. 237–260). London: Hogarth, 1953–1974.

———. 1926 [1925]. Inhibitions, Symptoms and Anxiety. *SE* 20: 77–179.

———. 1921. Group Psychology and the Analysis of the Ego. *SE* 18: 65–144.

Lacan, Jacques. 1998. *The Seminar of Jacques Lacan: Book XX, Encore: On Feminine Sexuality, the Limits of Love and Knowledge, 1972–1973*, ed. Jacques Alain-Miller, trans. Bruce Fink. New York: Norton.

Lindemann, Erich. 1994. Symptomatology and Management of Acute Grief. In *Essential Papers on Object Loss.* New York: New York University Press.

Ragland. Ellie. 1994. Psychoanalysis and Pedagogy: What Are Mastery and Love Doing in the Classroom? *PRE/TEXT* 15: 46–78.

Saussure, Ferdinand de. 1966. *Course in General Linguistics*, trans. Wade Baskin. New York: McGraw-Hill.

Vitanza, Victor. 1999. "The Wasteland Grows": Or, What Is "Cultural Studies for Composition" and Why Must We Always Speak Good of It? ParaResponse to Julie Drew. *Journal of Advanced Composition* 19: 699–703.

Chapter 6

The Pedagogical Is the Political: Reconfiguring Pedagogical Mastery

Kirstin Campbell

PSYCHOANALYSIS, EDUCATION, AND GOVERNMENT

In the field of psychoanalysis, Freud (1937) argues that analysis, government, and education are the three impossible professions. Throughout his work, Freud raises the question of the relationship between psychoanalysis, politics, and pedagogy, those impossible practices "in which one can be sure of achieving unsatisfactory results" (p. 248). In the field of feminism, consideration of this question of the relationship between the political, the pedagogical, and the psychoanalytic has become increasingly important.

This question forms a central thematic of an influential anthology in this field, *Pedagogy: The Question of Impersonation* (1995), edited by Jane Gallop. Gallop argues that "[i]f we take seriously the notion of feminist criticism as a collective movement, then critical anthologies, especially those which purport to represent the entirety of that movement, may be the best place to hear that collective subject" (1992, 8). By reading *Pedagogy* as a collective engagement with this key question in contemporary pedagogical theory, it is possible to trace the formation of theories of education which claim to be both psychoanalytic and political. Such a reading shows how political theories of the pedagogical have theorized the relationship between psychoanalytic, political, and pedagogical practice.

In *Pedagogy*, Gallop identifies a shift in contemporary feminist theories of education. In her own reading of the 1985 anthology of feminist writing by Culley and Portuges on pedagogy, *Gendered Subjects*, Gallop argues that these theories increasingly conceive pedagogy as an intersubjective relation between embodied subjects. These theories emphasize "classroom dynamics and teacher/student relations," conceiving "the teaching relation as enacted between persons" (1995, 79), and understanding the practice of education "as 'dynamic' " (ibid.). In this model of education, the pedagogical is the personal and the personal is the political. This particular feminist model of pedagogy does not understand education as simply being the transmission of knowledge. Rather, it conceives pedagogy as a relationship between subjects. For this reason, these theories frequently deploy psychoanalysis to understand the pedagogical relation. Whether implicitly or explicitly, they utilize psychoanalytic concepts such as identity, identification, affect, desire, and transference, or employ a psychoanalytic theoretical framework to describe the intersubjective effects of the pedagogical relation.

In the *Pedagogy* anthology, Scheman (1995) argues that "if the scene is pedagogical, the site of instruction, of knowledge and self-knowledge, the language of psychoanalysis presents itself, bidden or not" (p. 106). Bidden or not, the analogy between psychoanalysis and education recurs throughout *Pedagogy*. The comparisons move from the claim of "the basic analogy between the lecture and the psychoanalytic encounter" (Frank 1995, 31), to the positing of an "intersubjective affective force" of pedagogical desire (Simon 1995, 95); "the paradox of teacher/student identification" (Amirault 1995, 76); and the descriptions of the teacher as "object of desire" (Litvak 1995, 26); and of the feminist teacher as (good or bad) maternal breast (Gallop 1995, 87).[1] In this collection, the dominant model of the relation between teacher and student is the transferential relation between analyst and analysand.[2]

However, Scheman (1995) points out that "once you are on the terrain of transference and counter-transference, there it is: students in love with (or at least drawn to) teachers and vice-versa" (p. 106). In the *Pedagogy* collection, the question of the transferential pedagogical relationship becomes the question of the erotic pedagogical relationship, such that "teacher/student erotic encounters" assume an "unquestioned centrality in our discussions" (ibid.). Typical of this conceptual slide from transferential desire to pedagogical erotics is Roger Simon's (1995) characterization of Shoshana Felman's work, in which he argues that "[t]he substance of the eroticisation of faculty is, in part, articulated in Shoshana Felman's groundbreaking work on the importance of Lacan's theoretical writing for questions of pedagogy" (p. 99). However, Felman does not describe the pedagogical relation in terms of the erotic. Rather, it is Jane Gallop, the anthology's editor, who has most influentially formulated the description of the pedagogical relation as a transferential and hence "amorous" relation.

TRANSGRESSIVE TRANSFERENCE

Simon (1995) characterizes Gallop's pedagogical practice as the enactment of "desires which often eroticize students in the eyes of faculty," as it constitutes "teaching as an act of love, as a 'gift', structured by [a] desire to arouse and instruct the desire of others" (p. 96). This desire for desire is evident in Gallop's "dedication" of her 1992 volume of essays, *Around 1981*, to her students: "[t]he bright, hot, hip (young) women who fire my thoughts, my loins, my prose. I write this to move, to please, to shake you." For Gallop, the pedagogical relation *is* an erotic relation. For Gallop, "[a]t its most intense—and I would argue its most productive—the pedagogical relation between teacher and student is, in fact, a 'consensual amorous relation' " (1997, 57).

In *Thinking Through the Body* (1988), Gallop explicitly theorizes her position as both student and teacher through her erotic relations to her former teachers and her present students. As Gallop describes it, this erotic relationship is a transferential relationship. For Gallop, the transferential relation is integral to the pedagogical relation because:

[i]t is a nearly universal response to people whose opinions of us have great authority, in particular doctors *and teachers*. Since our feelings about our parents include an especially powerful form of love, transference is undoubtedly an "amorous relation." But the transference is also an inevitable part of any relationship we have to a teacher who really makes a difference. (1997, 56)

The transference between teacher and student produces their "amorous relation." In this way, Gallop conceives transference as an inevitable and integral part of the pedagogical relation. Just as the analysand necessarily falls in love with the analyst because of the transference created by the psychoanalytic scene, so too the student falls in love with the teacher because of the transference produced by the pedagogical scene.

However, for Gallop the importance of transference is not only that it forms an inevitable part of the pedagogical relation. Rather, the transference enables teaching to become a transgressive and hence political practice. From her earliest work, Gallop argues for a "feminist disturbance of the distinction masculine/feminine and the correlative privilege of the male, ideal sphere" (1981, 3–4). Kiti Carriker (1994) argues that Gallop's "body-centred criticism" aims "to acknowledge rather than censure the physical body as it affects both an author and the texts she creates" (p. 52). In this "body-centred criticism," Gallop privileges the feminine body as a feminist disruption of the masculine ideal. For this reason, Gallop rejects a model of pedagogy that insists that the teacher is the disembodied man of reason and that teaching is the neutral transmission of objective knowledge. Instead, Gallop argues that the teacher and student are embodied subjects and that teaching is a bodily practice. Therefore, teacher and student are desiring subjects and teaching is a practice of desire. To disclose the erotics of pedagogy is thereby to reconceive pedagogy as a transgressive practice.

This reconception of education is transgressive because it refuses masculine models of teachers and teaching.

However, importantly, the transference also provides a means of enacting pedagogy as a feminist practice. For Gallop, the "gift" of desire represents "access to learning and pleasure [which] will always be the root meaning, my most powerful personal sense of feminism" (1997, 5). For this reason Gallop contends that

[i]t is because of the sort of feminist that I am that I do not respect the line between the intellectual and the sexual. Central to my commitment as a feminist teacher is the wish to transmit the experience that brought me as a young woman out of my romantic paralysis and into the power of desire and knowledge, to bring the women I teach to their own power, to ignite them as feminism ignited me when I was a student. (1997, 13)

Pedagogical practice is a political practice because its transferential relations invoke desire and knowledge, learning and pleasure. The transferential relationship between teacher and student links learning and pleasure. It produces an identificatory desire for the teacher and hence her knowledge, and, in particular, an identificatory desire for the feminist teacher and her political knowledge.

In her most recent publication, *Feminist Accused of Sexual Harassment* (1997), Gallop writes that "[w]hen I call myself a feminist . . . I necessarily refer to that milieu where knowledge and sex bubble together. . . . Perhaps that makes me the kind of feminist who gets accused of sexual harassment" (p. 6). The book itself encircles the complaints of sexual harassment which were brought against Gallop by two of her students in 1992. Gallop comments that "[a] year before I was accused of sexual harassment, I began to organise a research conference on teacher-student sex" (1997, 59). Following the complaints of sexual harassment against her, Gallop shifted the theme of the conference to pedagogy and the personal. The collection of papers which came to form the *Pedagogy* anthology emerged from this conference, "Pedagogy: The Question of the Personal," organized by Gallop.

In her earlier book, *Intersections* (1981), Gallop defines an intertextual reading as "a reading which does not respect textual frontiers [and] assumes that a literary work is not a closed unity" (pp. 1–2). To read *Pedagogy* with *Feminist Accused of Sexual Harassment* is not to respect "textual frontiers" and not to assume that either text is "a closed unity." The importance of an intertextual reading of *Pedagogy* with *Feminist Accused of Sexual Harassment* is that it reveals another reading of the politics of Gallop's model of the transferential pedagogical relation.

THE DISCOURSE OF THE MASTER

In his later seminars, *L'envers de la psychanalyse* (1991) and *Encore* (1998), Lacan presents his theory of the four discourses. In his theory of the discourses of the master, the university, the hysteric, and the analyst, Lacan presents an account of knowledge as a symbolic and social network. Each discourse formalizes a position of the subject, its relation to that which is excluded by its discourse, to its master signifier, and to its knowledge. The structural relation of these key elements constitutes the operation of the discourse, so that the formulae represent stable structures of discourses of knowledge. In this theory, Lacan describes the different relations of the subject to other subjects, to its objects, and to the different forms of its knowledge. Lacan's theory of the four discourses focuses on the Imaginary and Symbolic economy that produces the subject and its knowledge.

In his later seminars, Lacan identifies the Discourse of the University as a dominant form of knowledge in the modern social order. He links this form of knowledge to the Discourse of the Master, which is both its condition and foundation. The function of the University, with the State, is the elucidation and justification of the Discourse of the Master (1991, 172). It makes manifest the master's discourse in the field of knowledge, positing knowing only in terms of authorization, justification, and completeness. The Discourse of the University installs the Discourse of the Master, such that the imaginary object of the discourse, "knowledge," dominates and produces an illusory *tout-savoir* (p. 34). The Discourse of the University attempts to know all, including that which is excluded from its discourse. A desire for mastery and control of its objects dominates this discourse, which at the same time operates to reproduce the exclusions of its knowledge (pp. 70–71)

Lacan (1991, 232) defines a master as a subject who intervenes in an order of knowledge. The knowing subject of the University is founded on the "myth of the ideal *Je*, the *Je* which masters": the "transcendental *Je*," the "*Je* which is identical to itself" (pp. 70–71). For example, philosophy, which is for Lacan the paradigmatic University knowledge, founds its knowledge on a conscious self—an "I" which believes that it can know itself and hence that it can master itself. The Discourse of the University thus supports the master's desire for omniscience, justifying its insistence on univocal conscious belief and the concomitant refusal of the unconscious. For this reason, the product of the Discourse of the University is the barred subject—the unconscious truth of the subject refused by that discourse. The *Je* of the conscious self masters and founds the knowing subject of the University.

In that illusion of conscious mastery, the subject misrecognizes itself as a subject which is whole and complete of itself. It is a subject position of masculine mastery. The subject produced in the university discourse is a masculine subject that masters itself and others. This subject claims presence in its being as subject, and in its mastery of itself and the universe (1998, 56). Lacan emphasizes the drive to mastery of its self and its universe that characterizes this subject of the conscious. Lacan describes the masculine subject "comme tout" (p. 79), and as a being where all succeeds. (p. 56). It is a position of presence, of the universal masculine subject which is "whole" and which does not suffer loss or lack. The Discourse of the University describes the production of the knowing master, a masculine subject that secures its identity through a repudiation of castration.

The Discourse of the University thus produces an imaginary subject, which is a fictional master. However, the subject that it supposes is a masculine subject. Reading Lacanian psychoanalysis with feminist theory, that normative subject reflects a modern Western ideal of white bourgeois masculinity. This ideal is "The Man of Reason"—with his attributes of individuality, autonomy, rationality, and universality—in short, of mastery.[3]

THE PEDAGOGY OF THE MASTER

It is the Discourse of the University that Gallop's model of pedagogy enacts. In this conception of teaching, the teacher assumes the position of the subject-supposed-to-know. Lacan first introduces this term "to designate the illusion of a self-consciousness which is transparent to itself in its act of knowing" (Evans 1996, 196). In this position, the teacher claims to be the transcendental, foundational, and illusory "I" who masters itself in its act of knowing. The teacher projects consciousness, self, and subjectivity as a unified identity. That unity of identity enables her to claim mastery and presence of self, and produces her relation to others as an aggressive relation of masterful ego to masterful ego. In this perceived act of mastery, the subject believes that indeed she does know all. This subject is attributed with a "a certain infallibility," as the possessor of knowledge (Lacan 1986, 234). In this conception of the pedagogical relation, the teacher is the "Absolute Master" of knowledge.

Paul Verhaeghe (1997) argues that "in the discourse of the university, the master functions as the formal guarantee of knowledge" (p. 116). The complainants in Gallop's sexual harassment case recognize the operation of this "formal guarantee." The complainants requested that Gallop (1997) not "make their complaints the subject of [her] research" because to do so "would constitute retaliation" (p. 78). Gallop vehemently objects to this possible bar upon her taking "the case as an object of intellectual inquiry. That is to say, I was not to study it nor to derive knowledge from it" (ibid.). Gallop's drive to derive knowledge from her case is similar to the master's drive to turn all into pure, mastering knowledge (p. 79). Gallop objects to being refused the position of the master of knowledge, and its formal guarantee. In this objection, it is possible to perceive that for Gallop, "knowledge justifies authority and justifies the position of the academic" (Grigg 1993, 39). Gallop thereby reproduces the Discourse of the University in which knowledge of the master discourse justifies the position of the academic as master. In this discourse, her knowledge of the master justifies her intellectual and institutional position of power.

This model of pedagogy conceives knowledge as a possession of the master teacher. Knowing is posited in terms of authorization, justification, and completeness. In this Discourse of the University, the relation between the knower and its object takes the form of mastery of the object. "Mastery" does not imply competence, proficiency, or reasoning; rather, it represents a discourse that produces knowledge as domination, as instrumentality, and as objectification, in which the subject seeks to master its object of knowledge.

Intellectual and institutional mastery subtends this model of pedagogical practice. Burt and Wallen (1999) argue that "Gallop's account reveals her own will to power: as the professor, she will be the one in authority, the one who will say whether French-kissing a student outside of class in a bar was a teaching performance or whether it was sexual harassment" (p. 77). The teacher's knowledge and power inextricably intertwine, such that the teacher "knows" the nature of the relationship between teacher and student, not the student. For Gallop, it is not just institutional knowledge and power which guarantee her position, but also her political knowledge. For example, Gallop argues that "I was construed as a sexual harasser because I sexualise the atmosphere in which I work" (1997, 11). For Gallop, the sexualization of the pedagogical relationship is a political act *of the teacher*. However, as Burt and Wallen (1999) point out, "Gallop, as the one who can transform 'erotic dynamics' into a 'teaching relation,' becomes the arbiter of consent" (p. 77). This model of pedagogical practice does not consider the relationship *of the student* to this sexualization of the pedagogical.

Instead, this discourse constitutes the student as an imaginary fantasy object. The teacher misrecognizes the identity of the objectified student as a specular reflection of herself. An example of this process can be seen in Gallop's (1997) characterization of the pedagogical relation, in which the "most intense relations involve students who take me very seriously as a teacher. These are students who want, in some way, to be intellectuals or academics like I am. And these are the students I care most about" (p. 20). In this discourse, the student's identification with the teacher reproduces the teacher's image of herself. However, the teacher is thus captured in the imaginary order, perceiving her self and her objects within the imaginary projections of the mirror of the ego (Lacan 1977, 17). The self and its others are posited in a relation of narcissistic and objectifying identification, in which they appear as objects to be controlled.

In this imaginary pedagogical relation, the teacher narcissistically perceives the student as a reflection of her own desires. For this reason, she perceives the transferential identification of the student *with her* as a sexual desire *for her*. For example, Gallop perceives the pedagogical act as the "gift" of desire for her intellectual knowledge embodied in her person. For Gallop (1997), in the exemplary learning experience, "my students love me and I'm crazy for them" (p. 20). A "good" student desires her teacher and hence her knowledge. Knowledge is thus conceived as a possession of the master teacher. The teacher is an omniscient knower, whom the student must love (and hence identify with) in order to incorporate her knowledge.

This model of pedagogy constitutes it in the imaginary register. It continually reproduces the teacher's phantasmic relationship to the student, constructing the student as a reflection of the master teacher's ego. This pedagogical practice acts out those imaginary relations, continually repeating their phantasmic support. That fantasy is, of course, a cover for the unconscious desires of the teacher and her fundamental lack. The Mistress refuses the possibility that she is also castrated, repressing in her discourse the analytic truth that all subjects suffer lack and loss.

Gallop's pedagogical practice thus reproduces the Discourse of the University and its foundational *Je* which masters itself and its Others. This university discourse produces a knowing master, a masculine subject that secures its identity through a repudiation of castration. Ironically, her model of pedagogy does not disturb "the distinction masculine/feminine," but instead reinstitutes the "privilege of the male, ideal sphere" (Gallop 1981, 3–4).

ACTING OUT

In *Pedagogy*, Scheman (1995) argues that "potential and actual abuses of power and trust . . . seem to be taken care of (in theory, at least) by the psychoanalytic model, since sex between analyst and analysand is more strictly forbidden than sex between teacher and student (in theory, at least)" (p. 106). In the psychoanalytic model, the analyst should not act on the analysand's transferential desire. For Freud (1905), transferential "love" is an acting out of the analysand's "impulses and phantasies which are aroused and made conscious during the progress of analysis [such that they] are revived, not as belonging in the past, but as applying to the person of the physician at the present moment" (p. 157). For this reason, the transference is a form of unconscious repetition, which forms a "resistance" to analytic treatment. Were the analyst to return the analysand's transference love, the analysand "would have succeeded in acting out, in repeating in real life what she ought to only have remembered, to have reproduced as psychical material and to have kept within sphere of psychical events" (Freud 1915 [1914], 166).

The analyst "must recognise that the patient's falling in love is induced by the analytic situation, and is not to be attributed to the charm of his own person; so that he has no grounds whatsoever for being proud of such a 'conquest' " (Freud (1915 [1914], 161). Rather, such a "conquest" is an acting out of the analyst's unconscious desires. Freud argues that the analyst must take a position of strict neutrality, of "abstinence" toward the patient. (p. 165). Because the analyst is offered the analysand's love only because of the analytic treatment, the analyst "must not derive any personal advantage from it. The patient's willingness makes no difference; it merely throws the whole responsibility on the analyst himself" (p. 169). In psychoanalysis, "ethical motives unite with the technical ones to restrain [the analyst] from giving the patient his love" (ibid.).

If Gallop (1997) is correct in her claim "that transference is an inevitable part of any relationship we have to a teacher" (p. 56), then according to the psychoanalytic model the teacher should never act on that transferential relation. To do so wilfully confuses the transferential identification of the student with the teacher and a sexual desire of the student for her teacher. It acts out unconscious fantasies that are themselves produced by the structure of the pedagogical relationship. To sexualize that relation is, at the very least, to act out the fantasies of the teacher. Like the analyst, the teacher "must not derive any personal advantage" from the pedagogical transference, for deriving such an advantage is contrary to ethical and technical principles.

While Gallop uses psychoanalysis to argue that an enactment of the erotics of pedagogy is a transgressive political practice, the Lacanian theory of the Discourse of the Master reveals that her pedagogical practice is not transgressive. Rather, it is a repetition of the Discourse of the University, with its symbolic and imaginary economy of mastery. The sexualization of the pedagogical relation by the teacher repeats this discourse. It does not disrupt or transform it, but rather continually reenacts it.

This practice reproduces the social relations of power which enable the teacher to enact her Real, symbolic, and imaginary mastery of her student. That reproduction leaves the operation of power within the pedagogical relation unchallenged. Gallop's claim that "feminist politics" somehow exempts her model from the operations of power is clearly untenable. A pedagogical practice is not exempt from the operations of power just because it is undertaken in the name of feminism. Power enables some subjects rather than others to insist that it is their self, and not another's, that decides whether a pedagogical practice is sexual harassment or feminist performance. In its refusal to recognize the politics of power within the pedagogical relation, this imaginary model of pedagogy is a reproduction of, rather than resistance to, those politics of power. Feminist pedagogy involves rethinking education as an "emancipatory feminist praxis" (Green 1992, x). For Carmen Luke and Jennifer Gore (1992), this praxis involves the creation of "pedagogical situations which 'empower' students, demystify canonical knowledges, and clarify how relations of subordinations of domination subordinate [disempowered] subjects" (p. 1). By these criteria, Gallop's pedagogical practice is not a feminist practice.

Gallop's conception of pedagogical practice is inadequate both as a viable psychoanalytic insight and as a feminist model of pedagogy. Because of the influence within feminism of the reconception of education as a relationship between two embodied subjects, psychoanalysis has been and is likely to remain an important model for understanding the pedagogical relationship. However, the political and theoretical problems of Gallop's deployment of psychoanalysis indicate that a feminist model of pedagogy requires a different conception of the transferential pedagogical relation from that proposed by Gallop.

RECONFIGURING PEDAGOGICAL MASTERY

An Other to the Master

For a theory of feminist pedagogy, the question is how to create an ethical and political model of pedagogy that does not reproduce the Discourse of the Master. For Lacan, the Discourse of the Analyst stands in opposition to that of the Master (1991, 99–100). It operates against the closure and rigidity of the master's discourse, since "it is opposed to all will of mastery, engaging in a continuous flight from meaning and closure" (Bracher 1994, 124). Analytic discourse disrupts and shifts structures of intrasubjectivity by reconfiguring those structures and changing the subject's relation to others. It unfurls the otherwise fixed structures of signification and intersubjectivity, making them less rigid and more mobile.

The Discourse of the Master is founded on a fundamental symbolic exclusion, which Lacan designates as the *a*. The *a* represents that which the discourse cannot represent in its symbolic economy. Analytic discourse acknowledges the lack of the subject and recognizes its subjection to the signifier. In the Discourse of the Analyst, the *a* which is the excluded part of discourse, puts the subject to work and is the cause of its desire. Through the process of analysis, the fixed structure of the analysand's discourse shifts because of the reinscription of the *a* into the analysand's signifying chain. Because the Discourse of the Master excludes that *a*, it is disrupted by the inscription of that excluded element. The reinscription of the excluded *a* permits the analysand to reconfigure its structure of signifiers, and with that reorganization of signification, to produce new meaning and knowledge. The knowledge of the analysand is *savoir*—symbolic knowledge (Lacan 1991, 32). *Savoir* implies a movement from the order of the Imaginary to the order of the Symbolic, from *méconnaissance* to *savoir* (Sheridan 1980, xi).

In his later work, Lacan does not conceive transference as the relation between subjects, but "as the relation of the subject of the analysand to the other as loved object" (Libbrecht 1998, 91). Thus the transference is an imaginary relation, "with its affective reactions of love and aggression" to the imagined Other (Evans 1996, 212). The analysand's relationship to the analyst is one of idealizing identification (Lacan 1986, 273). However, as Katrien Libbrecht (1998) argues, "[t]he analytic process is not directed towards a *re*stitution of the subject, completing it by means of identification, but towards a *de*stitution of the subject, in the form of the patient's acceptance of the fundamental lack" (p. 92). The aim of analysis is to traverse the fundamental fantasy which sustains the subject as subject, and to reveal the fundamental lack in the subject which that fantasy covers over (ibid.). The desire of the analyst "firstly directs the treatment away from identification, and secondly, conducts it towards the traversing of the fantasy and the laying bare of *jouissance*" (Libbrecht 1998, 93).

In this account, the psychoanalytic relation is not "a function of subjective desire" (ibid., p. 94). Rather, the desire of the analyst is psychoanalysis itself: "what the analyst desires, is psychoanalysis" (ibid.). The psychoanalyst desires "the psychoanalytic setting, i.e. analysis as a social bond" (ibid.) For this reason, the analyst does not desire that the patient be "cured," obtain "social goods," or enact the "social good" (Lacan 1992, 230). Instead, the analyst desires that the unconscious truth of the subject emerge in its absolute difference. The analyst does not constitute her relation to the analysand through the imaginary phantasms of identification. Instead, she constitutes that relationship through a symbolic relation to psychoanalysis that institutes the social bond of psychoanalysis. Lacan thus conceives the psychoanalytic relation as a discursive, symbolic relation, rather than as being an imaginary, affective relation. Deploying this conceptual shift from the imaginary to the symbolic permits a feminist reconception of pedagogical practice.

Feminist Pedagogies

In this practice, just as the task of the analyst is to enable the analysand to interpret more effectively, so too the task of the teacher is to enable the student to interpret more effectively. Like the analyst, the teacher's desire is not for the student's identification with her. Instead, the teacher should desire pedagogy as a social bond, as a symbolic relation to knowledge that forms the relation between them. Like the enigmatic desire of the analyst, the teacher has a desire for that x which is specific to each pedagogical relationship: learning.

The teacher accepts that while the pedagogical relationship may constitute her as the subject-supposed-to-know, she should not take up that position. That position is an imaginary position, constituted by her own fantasies of mastery. Instead, she should take up the position of the analyst, a subject who does not know the desire of the analysand. The analyst does not mistakenly misrecognize the analysand as an imaginary reflection of herself, but rather recognizes the analysand as a speaking subject. Like the analyst, the teacher must also engage in an ethical desire for the absolute difference of the other, allowing the student to constitute herself in difference (Lacan 1986, 276).

To take up the position of the analyst, the teacher must acknowledge both the lack in her field of knowledge and the lack in her own knowledge. This model of pedagogy does not conceive the knowledge of the teacher as the product of a universal method that guarantees all knowledge, but rather as a signifying practice which acknowledges its temporality and its intersubjectivity. The teacher accepts the radical finitude of her knowledge, recognizing its limit and its failure. With this acceptance, her knowledge can represent a relation other than aggressive mastery to its object and her Others.

Such an acknowledgment of lack permits the student to conceive a different relation to her teacher and to her knowledge. Her teacher's refusal of the pedagogical fantasy of mastery enables the student to identify her phantasmic desire for knowledge, and thereby to reveal her drive for knowledge. Psychoanalysis perceives the act of knowing as an act of desire such that "all knowledge is desire of knowledge, or knowledge of desire" (Braidotti 1991, 25). Freud argues that epistemophilia (the drive for knowledge) has its aetiology in the frustrations of the child who is unable to master its world. The desire for knowledge is the child's narcissistic attempt to cover its loss of perceived omnipotence. It is "a self-defeating drive for imaginary satisfaction" (Moi 1989, 202). By traversing the pedagogical fantasy, the student is able to consider her drive to knowledge and her pleasure in learning, as well as recognize the stakes of that drive and those pleasures for her, and thereby use those insights to reconsider her relation to knowledge.

This model of pedagogy does not conceive the student's desire as an imaginary identification with her teacher, but as a symbolic articulation of her relationship to knowledge as such. This desire for knowledge does not aim to produce an imaginary object, but instead to produce an act of signification. The aim of the pedagogical relation is not, therefore, to reproduce the knowledge and the person of the teacher. Rather, it aims to enable the student to articulate her relation to knowledge (her desire), and hence to change the imaginary configurations of her pedagogical discourse. With that change, instead of reproducing her teacher's discourses of knowledge, the student can produce new signifiers and hence new discourses.

This model does not found itself on the imaginary relations of ego-counterparts. Rather, it conceives the pedagogical relation as a relation between speaking subjects, formed in the symbolic tie of discourse. In this way, feminism can conceive pedagogy as a political practice that is not founded in the repetitions of mutual identification, but rather on an ethical relation between speaking subjects.

In Lacanian theory, the Discourse of the University enacts the Discourse of the Master in the field of knowledge. This discourse constitutes pedagogical practice as an act of mastery of the self and its Others, and the pedagogical relationship as a relationship of mastery. This discourse sustains that relationship through a phantasmic and imaginary *méconnaissance* of the Other. However, Lacan's theory also offers feminism a means of developing a political model of pedagogy that does not conceive pedagogy as mastery. That model conceives the pedagogical relationship as an ethical relationship, which entails the teacher's recognition of the difference of the Other and responsibility for the Other. It is a relationship between speaking subjects, a social bond in which those subjects share a desire, neither for teaching as mastery nor for learning as repetition, but for knowledge (*savoir*).

NOTES

I would like to thank David Bausor for his insightful and helpful comments on earlier drafts of this chapter.

1. In the three essays of the anthology that do not deploy psychoanalytic metaphors, two address the teacher as "cultural other" and the third rejects "the personal" as means of thinking the pedagogical.

2. This analogy has been made most influentially in the work of Barthes (1977) and Felman (1987).

3. For a further discussion of the relation between these tropes of the knower and the masculinity, see Genevieve Lloyd (1984).

REFERENCES

Amirault, Chris. 1995. The Good Teacher, the Good Student: Identifications of a Student Teacher. In *Pedagogy: The Question of Impersonation*, ed. Jane Gallop (pp. 64–78). Bloomington: Indiana University Press.

Barthes, Roland. 1977. Writers, Intellectuals, Teachers. In *Image, Music, Text*, trans. Stephen Heath (pp. 190–215). New York: Hill and Wang.

Bracher, Mark. 1994. On the Psychological and Social Functions of Language: Lacan's Theory of the Four Discourses. In *Lacanian Theory of Discourse: Subject, Structure and Society*, ed. Mark Bracher, Marshall W. Alcorn, Jr., Ronald J. Corthell, and Françoise Massardier-Kenney (pp. 107–128). New York: New York University Press.

Braidotti, Rosi. 1991. *Patterns of Dissonance: A Study of Women in Contemporary Philosophy*, trans. Elizabeth Guild. Cambridge: Polity Press.

Burt, Richard, and Wallen, Jeffrey. 1999. Knowing Better: Sex, Cultural Criticism, and the Pedagogical Imperative in the 1990s. *Diacritics* 29(1): 72–91.

Carriker, Kiti. 1994. The Student Body in the Text. *Frontiers* 24(3): 49–66.

Culley, Margo, and Portuges Catherine, eds. 1985. *Gendered Subjects: The Dynamics of Feminist Teaching*. Boston: Routledge.

Evans, Dylan. 1996. *An Introductory Dictionary of Lacanian Psychoanalysis*. New York: Routledge.

Felman, Shoshana. 1987. *Jacques Lacan and the Adventure of Insight: Psychoanalysis in Contemporary Culture*. Cambridge, Mass.: Harvard University Press.

Frank, Arthur. 1995. Lecturing and Transference: The Undercover Work of Pedagogy. In *Pedagogy: The Question of Impersonation*, ed. Jane Gallop (pp. 28–35). Bloomington: Indiana University Press.

Freud, Sigmund. 1905. Fragment of an Analysis of a Case of Hysteria ("Dora"). In *The Standard Edition of the Complete Psychological Works of Sigmund Freud*, ed. and trans. James Strachey (vol. 7, pp. 3–122). London: Hogarth, 1953–1974.

———. 1915 (1914). Observations on Transference-Love. In *The Standard Edition of the Complete Psychological Works of Sigmund Freud*, ed. and trans. James Strachey (vol. 12, pp. 157–171). London: Hogarth, 1953–1974.

———. 1937. Analysis Terminable and Interminable. In *The Standard Edition of the Complete Psychological Works of Sigmund Freud*, ed. and trans. James Strachey (vol. 23, pp. 209–254). London: Hogarth, 1953–1974.

Gallop, Jane. 1981. *Intersections: A Reading of Sade with Bataille, Blanchot, and Klossowski*. Lincoln: University of Nebraska Press.

———. 1988. *Thinking Through the Body*. New York: Columbia University Press.

———. 1992. *Around 1981: Academic Feminist Literary Criticism*. London: Routledge.

———. 1995. The Teacher's Breasts. In *Pedagogy: The Question of Impersonation*, ed. Jane Gallop (pp. 79–89). Bloomington: Indiana University Press.

———. 1997. *Feminist Accused of Sexual Harassment*. Durham, N.C.: Duke University Press.

Green, Maxine. 1992. Foreword. In *Feminisms and Critical Pedagogy*, ed. Carmen Luke and Jennifer Gore (pp. ix–xi). London: Routledge.

Grigg, Russell. 1993. Lacan's Four Discourses. *Analysis* 4: 33–39.

Lacan, Jacques. 1977. *Écrits: A Selection*, trans. Alan Sheridan. New York: Norton.

———. 1986. The *Four Fundamental Concepts of Psychoanalysis*, ed. Jacques Alain-Miller, trans. Alan Sheridan. London: Penguin.

———. 1991. *Le Séminaire: Livre XVII, L'envers de la psychanalyse, 1969–1970*, ed. Jacques-Alain Miller. Paris: Seuil.

———. 1992. *The Seminar of Jacques Lacan. Book VII, The Ethics of Psychoanalysis: 1959–1960*, ed. Jacques Alain-Miller, trans. Dennis Porter. New York: Norton.

———. 1998. *The Seminar of Jacques Lacan: Book XX, Encore: On Feminine Sexuality, the Limits of Love and Knowledge, 1972–1973*, ed. Jacques Alain-Miller, trans. Bruce Fink. New York: Norton.

Libbrecht, Katrien. 1998. The Desire of the Analyst. In *Key Concepts of Lacanian Psychoanalysis*, ed. Dany Nobus (pp. 75–100). London: Rebus.

Litvak, Joseph. 1995. Discipline, Spectacle, and Melancholia in and around the Gay Studies Classroom. In *Pedagogy: The Question of Impersonation*, ed. Jane Gallop (pp. 19–27). Bloomington: Indiana University Press.

Lloyd, Genevieve. 1984. *The Man of Reason: "Male" and "Female" in Western Philosophy.* London: Methuen.

Luke, Carmen, and Gore, Jennifer. 1992. Introduction. In *Feminisms and Critical Pedagogy,* ed. Carmen Luke and Jennifer Gore (pp. 1–14). London Routledge.

Moi, Toril. 1989. Patriarchal Thought and the Drive for Knowledge. In *Between Feminism and Psychoanalysis,* ed. Teresa Brennan (pp. 189–205). New York: Routledge.

Scheman, Naomi. 1995. On Waking Up One Morning and Discovering We Are Them. In *Pedagogy: The Question of Impersonation,* ed. Jane Gallop (pp. 106–116). Bloomington: Indiana University Press.

Sheridan, Alan. 1980. Translator's Note. In Jacques Lacan, *Écrits: A Selection,* trans. Alan Sheridan. London: Tavistock.

Simon, Roger. 1995. Face to Face with Alterity: Postmodern Jewish Identity and the Eros of Pedagogy. In *Pedagogy: The Question of Impersonation,* ed. Jane Gallop (pp. 90–105). Bloomington: Indiana University Press.

Verhaeghe, Paul. 1997. *Does the Woman Exist? From Freud's Hysteric to Lacan's Feminine,* trans. Marc du Ry. London: Rebus.

Part IV

The Pedagogy of Desire

Chapter 7

Identity and Desire in the Classroom

Mark Bracher

Education, like all other human enterprises, is a function of identity and desire: In order to have any success at all, it must engage the identities and desires of students, teachers, and the government and public who pay the bills; and it must direct these desires toward its fundamental aims, which are to produce collective benefits for society and personal benefits for students. The difficulty of education—what makes teaching one of the three "impossible professions"—is due first and foremost to the fact that engaging and directing identities and desires is fraught with multiple obstacles, most notably the presence, in all parties concerned, of identity components and desires contrary to those motivating and directing the educational enterprise. The fundamental challenge for educators, then, is to understand the multiple identity components and desires that pervade the educational field; and to variously recruit, redirect, reinforce, circumvent, or neutralize these forces in all parties, and particularly in themselves and their students, in such a way that the dominant vector of students' desire moves them toward the educational ends of social and personal benefits. Successful educators at all levels, from teachers to administrators to policy makers, are already doing this on a continuous basis. But they operate for the most part intuitively, with only a tacit and impressionistic understanding of the desires and identity components involved, rather than systematically, with an explicit and comprehensive understanding of identity and desire. An explicit and systematic mapping of the field of multiple and conflicting identity components and desires in which education occurs would thus provide educators with a valuable resource for improving education. I will attempt to sketch out such a map in this chapter.

IDENTITY AND THE DESIRE FOR RECOGNITION

The first and most important point that educators need to understand about identity and desire is that the most fundamental desire is the desire for a secure identity. By identity I mean the sense of oneself as a more or less coherent and continuous force that matters in the world. The most common manifestation of the basic desire for a secure identity is the desire for recognition—that is, the desire to have one's being appreciated and validated, or at least acknowledged, taken into account. The importance of recognition was noted by Lacan, who pronounced it to be the most basic desire, and it is indicated as well in the venerable sociological concept of the "looking-glass self," which holds that one's sense of oneself is largely a function of the feedback one gets about oneself from other people; in Erikson's observation that the first and most fundamental task for an infant is to establish a sense of basic trust, the conviction that other people and the world in general will provide for one's needs; and in Elisabeth Young-Bruehl and Faith Bethelard's (2000) account of the universal need to be cherished.

The desire for recognition can take multiple forms, depending on the aspect of oneself that one desires to be recognized and the type of recognition one desires, and each form of recognition can, in both teachers and students, either support or interfere with the aims of education. There are three basic dimensions of oneself that can be recognized, corresponding to the three registers of subjectivity identified by Lacan.[1] In the Symbolic register, we desire to be recognized as embodying certain signifiers. Students and teachers, for example, often desire recognition from each other as "intelligent," or "brilliant," or "an excellent teacher," or "excellent student," respectively. When these desires are not met, students and teachers may feel depressed, anxious, or angry, and as a result be less effective in their learning and teaching (Bracher 1993, chs. 1, 2). On the other hand, when such recognition is dispensed indiscriminately, it may either lose its credibility and hence its motivating force, or it may result in premature gratification and hence lose its power to compel action. These are dangers to which the emphasis on students' self-esteem can easily succumb. The motivational force of recognition is also frequently undercut by other sources—such as peers, family, and ethnic culture—providing recognition for attributes (such as anti-intellectualism) that oppose educational activities such as knowing, learning, reading, writing, and reflecting.

In the Imaginary register, the realm of visual-spatial images of self and world, we desire to be recognized for our bodily appearance or physical performance, or more generally for our agency, which is grounded in our body's effectivity. We manifest this desire in the often arduous, expensive, or time-consuming activities through which we attempt to shape our body image and agency: exercising, dieting, buying clothes and grooming supplies, grooming ourselves, and practicing and rehearsing various athletic and dance moves and skills. The desire for Imaginary-register recognition is the strongest desire operating in many students, especially in high school, as is evident in the prestige accorded students (especially girls) who are physically attractive and students (especially boys) with athletic prowess. Such desires obviously can interfere in multiple ways with the more educationally syntonic desires to be recognized as "intelligent" or "a good student." We need only consider the amount of time some students spend maintaining their appearance (hair, complexion, muscle tone, clothes), developing and performing their athletic abilities, and/or attending athletic events to realize what a serious competitor Imaginary recognition is to Symbolic recognition in general and education in particular.

The Real register also involves desire for recognition. This register is the dimension of experience and memory that escapes, transcends, and/or lies beneath the imagistic-perceptual (Imaginary) and linguistic-conceptual (Symbolic) codings of experience. Desire for recognition appears in this register first of all as the desire for emotional mirroring. Infants seek satisfaction of this desire in affective resonance with their caregivers, as provided by a mother's laughing, cooing, or frowning in concert with her child's feelings. Adults, too, seek such resonance, in various interpersonal, group, and mass experiences, such as rock concerts, sporting events, political rallies, and religious and civic ceremonies, where one can experience one's own emotions resonating with and amplified by those of hundreds or even thousands of other people. Teachers and students often seek emotional mirroring in the classroom in the form of shared attitudes toward, or responses to, a person, group, school of thought, idea, event, or social cultural phenomenon. Such a desire for emotional mirroring can be educationally productive, as when the enthusiastic desire of a teacher or student for a particular educational activity or subject matter elicits a similar desire in others in the class. It can also be problematic, as when the enthusiastic desire of the teacher or the majority deprives some students of the opportunity to voice, or even experience, their own desires. And the desire for emotional mirroring can also be counterproductive for learning and growth when it functions as an obstacle to thinking and reflecting about an issue, as when students resist thinking about the social and political significance of the cultural artifacts they enjoy, asserting that such phenomena are "just entertainment" and that it is illegitimate to seek any other significance in them.

Desire for recognition in the Real can also appear as the desire to be acknowledged as what Lacan calls the object *a*, the element of being that is excluded from the social Symbolic Order in general, or from a specific system (such as the education system, a knowledge system, the economic system, or the system of morality or propriety). Instances of this desire that are common in education include the desire to be recognized as one who resists, transgresses, undermines, or disrupts the classroom; disciplinary paradigms; professional protocols; or the social order in general. A well-known instance is the "trenchcoat mafia" of Columbine High School, which was composed of students who were excluded from the dominant system ruled by jocks and preppies. In teachers this desire can manifest itself in the wish to be recognized by students or peers as countercultural, resistant, rebellious, or revolutionary in relation to their role, school, or discipline.[2]

In addition to the desire to be recognized as a negative, disruptive force, there is also present in the Real register the desire to be recognized as an element that, while excluded by the system, is nonetheless extremely valuable for the system, or that is the core around which a new system can be constructed. Thus a teacher whose unorthodoxy makes her a pariah to her peers or administrators may fantasize that her methods will ultimately be recognized as superior to those of the current system. And a contrary student may desire to be recognized by his peers as a vital force that enlivens the classroom and rescues learning and thinking from a moribund system. While such desires can be an impediment to education, they can also provide a motive to teach and to learn in cases where the system does not engage these desires.

A third form of desire for recognition in the Real register is the desire to be recognized as having charm, charisma, sex appeal, or animal magnetism. This is the desire being engaged, for example, in perfume ads that promise to drive the Other wild with passion. Both students and teachers can have such desires as well, as is made evident when they dress or behave in sexually provocative ways. While such desires can support education by sparking greater mutual interest between students or between teachers and students, and while enacting these desires might in some cases provide an enabling recognition (as William Kerrigan [1993] infamously claimed several years ago concerning sexual relations with his female doctoral students), such desires can also be quite disruptive to both teachers and students, both socially and psychologically, as cases like those of Mary Kay Letourneau, Jane Gallop, and others variously demonstrate.

Besides the direct, voluntary, and explicit recognition from other people described so far, there is also desire for *indirect, tacit,* and/or *involuntary* recognition, including recognition from reality itself rather than from a person. Such a desire is sometimes preferred to direct, voluntary, explicit recognition because one realizes that the latter can be faked or unwarranted. Thus teachers who suspect that praise from a student is insincere may desire instead or in addition the tacit and involuntary recognition of being a "good teacher" that is provided by the reality of the student's learning and growth. And most teachers would prefer the tacit recognition of their worth in the form of respectable salaries to the express praise of politicians, who refuse to pay teachers what they are worth. Similarly, in addition to or instead of the teacher's explicit praise, students may desire the tacit, indirect recognition of being a "good student" or being "intelligent" that is provided by good grades or by the reality of enhanced knowledge, skills, performance, or well-being.

Where recognition for benign qualities is inadequate to a person's needs, he or she may resort to aggression to elicit involuntary recognition of malignant qualities. Such is often the dynamic behind the various forms of aggression that students (and teachers) manifest. As one homicidal youth remarked to a counselor, "I'd rather be wanted for murder than not wanted at all" (Garbarino 1999).

This does not mean, however, that being recognized for a negative quality is just as desirable as being recognized for a positive one. On the contrary, in addition to desiring recognition for possessing our identity components, we also desire recognition of the value of these components Hence we take pains not only to embody these components but also to protect and enhance their status. The desire to protect the master signifier "teacher," for example, can be seen in teachers' objections to statements or policies that denigrate or devalue teachers, as well as in their efforts to attain greater economic rewards for themselves and for education in general, a demand that is motivated by the desire to enhance their master signifiers in addition to the obvious wish to have more money. Similarly, the desire to maintain and enhance the status of systems of knowledge, belief, and organization manifests itself in battles between rival theories or systems of thought.

Students, too, desire to protect and defend the identity-bearing systems of knowledge/belief that they bring to the classroom. This desire often produces a resistance—sometimes overt and conscious, other times tacit and unconscious—to embracing, understanding, or even entertaining the systems of knowledge that their teachers are trying to impart to them. To give up their knowledge or to see it ignored or criticized involves relinquishing the identity-supporting mastery, agency, and significance provided by the knowledge.

A fundamental strategy for enhancing education would thus be to provide multiple opportunities for both teachers and students to obtain both direct and indirect forms of recognition of both their possession and the value of the various aspects of their identities that contribute to their teaching and their learning, respectively. This strategy has already been in wide use in the practices of positive and negative reinforcement and of providing incentives and disincentives. But reconceptualizing reinforcement and incentives in terms of the desire for identity-supporting recognition, which can take various forms and can be conferred on any of numerous identity components residing in one or more of the registers, provides a more precise understanding of how different sorts of reinforcements and incentives operate and reveals additional motivational possibilities that are not conjured up by the behaviorist concepts of reinforcement and incentives.

OTHER DESIRES SUPPORTING IDENTITY

The reason the desire for recognition is so basic is, as I have said, that it answers an even more fundamental desire, the desire for a secure identity. This desire for identity also underwrites other desires in each register that do not involve recognition but instead aim directly at an internally produced sense of continuity, coherence, and significance. In the conceptual-linguistic (Symbolic) register, identity is a function of signifiers, and the identity impetus manifests itself in our desire to maintain and enhance both the status and our possession of both the master signifiers and the systems of signifiers (systems of knowledge, belief, or social organization) that bear our identities. Thus teachers whose identity includes the master signifier "good teacher" will not only desire to be recognized by others as possessing this signifier, they will also desire to perform and embody it—that is, to actualize the signifiers of their ego idea, which elicits recognition and approval from their superego. Such a desire expresses itself as the wish to be a good teacher or do a good job regardless of recognition by others. Similarly, the identity-bearing function of systems of knowledge, belief, and social organization expresses itself in the desire to possess, master, and enact certain bodies of knowledge or systems of belief (e.g., through their application to and explanation of various phenomena). In students, this form of desire can be a powerful impetus to learning and growing, such as when it involves the master signifier "good student." But it can also interfere with learning, such as when the desire to enact the master signifier "man" conflicts with reading and enjoying poetry or art, or when the desire to enact the master signifier "woman" interferes with learning math or physics.

Similarly, identity in the Imaginary register is maintained not only through others' admiration of one's body image but also by the proprioceptive sense of agency one achieves through experiences of one's bodily strength, substantiality, agility, coordination, grace, or skill. Students involved in sports, dance, or crafts (making clothes, building things, working on cars, etc.) may thus desire to engage in such activities at the expense of their academic work, not simply because of the recognition such performances can command but because these activities provide them with a greater sense of agency than school work does. As Greenspan (1997) notes, some students, especially when they are children, can listen, learn, and think more effectively during or after large-motor activities such as walking, jumping, or swinging—activities that apparently establish and maintain their sense of bodily integrity, continuity, and agency—identity—more effectively than sitting or standing still.

A similar dynamic can operate in the Real register, involving the activation and regulation of affects. Students who feel anxious or depressed may desire to engage less in scholarly activities than in activities that they can use to reduce these affects and/or produce more positive, identity-supporting affects such as pleasure or anger. Such desire is often the primary motive for the chronic abuse of substances such as drugs, alcohol, and nicotine (Wurmser 1995), and it can be a prime impetus for producing and consuming music and for sexual promiscuity. There is also strong evidence that it is a major motive for violent acts (Glasser 1998; Katz 1988; Mitchell 1993). While some students' indulgence in substance-abusing, sexual, and aggressive activities may distract them from learning and reduce their need (and capacity) for the sublimated gratifications of libido and aggression that are present in thinking, learning, speaking, and writing, for other students sexual and motor-aggressive abstinence may produce an identity disruption in the affective-physiological (Real) register that interferes with their learning and development.

DESIRES FOR COHERENCE AND FOR DISSOCIATION

The fundamental need to establish and maintain an identity—that is, a sense of oneself as a relatively coherent, continuous, effective, significant presence in the world—also produces a desire to integrate, both within each register and across the registers, the various continuity-conferring components of each register (affects, percepts, and concepts, respectively). Thus there is an ongoing desire (pursued by what psychoanalysts call the synthetic function of the ego) to render one's ideals, values, and knowledge; one's body image, sense of agency, and perceptual paradigms; and one's affective and physiological states both mutually compatible and mutually supportive. This desire manifests itself in students' attempts to reconcile their newly acquired knowledge with their ideals and values, as well as with their sense of agency and their affective-physiological states. Students who revise their religious beliefs in light of scientific knowledge or who alter their prejudiced feelings and discriminatory behaviors in light of sociological or psychological knowledge do so in order to maintain or enhance their sense of coherence.

If one does not possess the opportunity or the capacity for such integration, however, the desire for coherence and continuity—identity—will manifest itself as the impetus to exclude (through projection, repression, denial, or disavowal) certain identity components. Thus, in order to maintain their sense of identity, students may reject new knowledge and values (denial); they may take in new knowledge and values but immediately forget them (repression); or they may embrace new knowledge and ideals but compartmentalize them (disavowal) in order to keep them from undermining certain identity components. In such cases a vertical split is established between two systems—such as scientific knowledge and religious beliefs, or sociological knowledge and prejudiced attitudes—which maintains both sides of the contradiction without allowing either side to undermine the other. The identity components students are refusing to relinquish may be certain ideals (such as those of white supremacy or patriarchy) or the indulgence in certain affects, such as the high of contempt or dominance or the rush of hatred and aggression.

Failure to achieve integration among the three registers results in deficiencies not only in knowledge but also in intelligence, social skills, moral responsibility, and, most crucially, affect regulation. When affective-physiological experiences are not represented by (i.e., translated into) images and, most important, words, they exist as discrete, isolated, private experiences that often conflict with other self-states and with the social order (Greenspan 1997). The desire to repeat these discrete affective-physiological identity components leads, most significantly, to rejection or divestment of identity components in the Symbolic register—which is the primary register in which education operates—and the investment instead in the desire for mind-altering substances, excessive food, danger, transgression, and even violence, all of which are antithetical to learning and developing, in addition to being socially and personally destructive.

THE UBIQUITY OF IDENTITY AND DESIRE IN THE CLASSROOM

The desire for a secure identity is continuous, the only question being what form of identity support a person will seek and what frequency and intensity of support are necessary to sustain the individual. While some people need almost continuous recognition from others, other people have the capacity to go for extended periods of time with no immediate influx of external identity support, because they have internalized mechanisms of recognition and other important processes of identity maintenance. Teachers and students, then, have a constant impetus to maintain their identity, and a constant, though widely varying (from one person to another and also within each individual), desire for recognition. Some teachers and students need frequent, explicit recognition from the Other in order to feel secure, while others can do without explicit recognition from the Other and can proceed with only the promise or hope of a recognition deferred far into the future. The desire for recognition, however, is constant, and it permeates teaching and learning.

The more fundamental desire to maintain identity through performing, defending, and consolidating its components and structures is also a constant force bearing on both teaching and learning. This means that optimum teaching and learning will occur within a system in which the greatest identity support, performance, and enhancement are available through those activities of the teachers that are pedagogically most effective. Likewise, the most effective pedagogical practices will be those in which the process of learning and developing brings to students the greatest identity benefits, whether in the form of recognition or increased agency, or the performance or defense of already acquired components.

THE ROLES OF DESIRE IN RELATION TO THE AIMS OF EDUCATION

On the basis of this general account of identity and desire, I want now to identify the most common forms taken by the dialectic between teachers' and students' desires and consider how they operate variously to promote or impede the realization of the fundamental aims of education. As noted above, there are two fundamental aims of education. One aim is to benefit students by helping them learn and develop. This aim involves:

1. Providing students with—and getting them to desire to acquire—the information, knowledge, and skills necessary to be fulfilled in the given social conditions.
2. Helping students develop, and thus desire to embody, the ideals and values—and perhaps also the desires, fantasies, enjoyments, drives, and defenses—necessary to survive and prosper in society.
3. Helping students develop the more complex psychological structures necessary for fulfillment in society—an aim that depends on students' desire to grow and to enhance their capacities.

The second aim is to educate students in such a way that they will benefit society as a whole. This aim entails:

1. Providing students with—and getting them to desire to acquire—the information, knowledge, and skills necessary for them to be productive members of society and, in some cases, to solve particular social problems or meet other collective needs.
2. Socializing students into—that is, fostering their desire to take on—the roles needed by society and its mode(s) of production, including the roles of critic, reformer, and even revolutionary.
3. Contributing to the "civilizing" process—that is, fostering students' desire to be more civil, circumspect, critical, self-critical, moral, and responsible—through the inculcation of particular values, ideals, desires, fantasies, drives, and defenses (e.g., sublimation,), and through the development of more complex structures of cognition, affect, relationship, and identity.

Ideally, the desires of both the teachers and the students would coincide with these fundamental educational aims, so that the only obstacles to their realization would be lack of knowledge or ability on the part of the students. And, in fact many teachers operate—and educational conditions, institutions, administrators, and policy makers often encourage or even force them to operate—as though this were indeed the case. Unfortunately, it is rare for all three factors—the teachers' desires, the students' desires, and the aims of education—to fully coincide, and often there are substantial discrepancies and even downright oppositions between two or even all three of these factors. This opposition between desire and the aims of education can take one of three forms.

Opposition between Teachers' and Students' Desires

The form most obvious to teachers is that in which their desires are in concert with the aims of education but the desires of their students conflict with these aims—when, that is, students are uninterested in or even downright hostile to pursuing the aims of education and engaging in the activities requested by their teachers. Teachers inevitably experience such recalcitrance and hostility, consciously or unconsciously, as a threat to their own identity, however subtle or insignificant the threat may be. As a result, teachers attempt in various ways to get students to embrace the teachers' ideals and desires, by either submitting to them or identifying with them. Either submission or identification on the part of students constitutes a powerful tacit recognition by the students of certain key identity components of the teachers.

A less frequently recognized impediment to learning occurs when students' desires are in concert with the aims of education but are met with contrary teachers' desires. Such teachers' desires are most easily detected when they lead teachers to act in ways that are clearly unproductive or even counterproductive for learning, such as when teachers berate or belittle students. Such aggression is itself the result of a desire for recognition and agency. As I have explained elsewhere (Bracher 2000), all aggression, including violence, is motivated by the need to protect or enhance a vulnerable identity, and in many cases, aggression aims to elicit recognition—from either the person(s) or institution that is the object of aggression or from observers whom the aggressor is trying to impress. Teachers who feel threatened or deprived of recognition that they believe is their due sometimes respond with unwarranted aggression toward their students. Such aggression can take the form of harsh or belittling comments, punitive grading practices, assignments that are excessively long or difficult, or spiteful withdrawal from one's students. While such action will not usually make teachers loved or admired by the students victimized by this aggression, it will elicit recognition from them, in the form of fear or resentment: whereas before the teachers' aggressive behavior these students may have ignored the teachers, now they at least have to take the teachers into account, a significant albeit minimal and negative form of recognition.

Teachers' aggression toward students may also elicit a more positive form of recognition—perhaps even in the form of admiration—from other students, administrators, parents, and the general public. Students often enjoy seeing their rivals reprimanded and punished, especially if they have themselves been victimized by these rivals, and they feel their stock rise when another student is put down. Administrators often appreciate—and show their appreciation for—teachers who force students to conform, and parents are also grateful, when their own children are not involved, to teachers who punish students who may be a threat to other children. And the general public admires teachers and principals who control their students with an iron fist, as witnessed by the publicity and acclaim accorded such individuals.

Complicity of Teachers' and Students' Desires

Opposition between teachers' and students' desires is thus a significant impediment to realizing the aims of education. Often, however, the main impediment to education is not the opposition but rather the complicity between the two desires, in which teachers and students engage in activities that both parties find gratifying but that do not contribute significantly to achieving the aims of education—activities such as the acquisition of trivial knowledge or relatively insignificant skills developed at the expense of acquiring more valuable knowledge or skills. As an example of the former, David Richter recalls that the professor of his eighteenth-century literature course distributed a 10-page list of dates in English literature from 1660 to 1800, a significant portion of which students were expected to commit to memory (Richter 2000, 121). An example of the latter would be the development of the ability to scan poetry and label the various metrical forms and devices employed. In such instances, performance of the knowledge or skill by both teacher and students elicits identity-supporting recognition, and provides other forms of identity support, such as a sense of participation in a meaning-giving system and an experience of mastery. Such complicity of desires is perhaps the major impediment to effective teaching and learning.

These various forms of opposition between desire and the aims of education can occur in virtually any pedagogical strategy. In what follows, I want to sketch out what I believe to be the four major pedagogical strategies available to teachers, and explore in each the various forms and the educational consequences of the dialectic between the teacher's desires and the students' desires. These four basic pedagogical strategies—authoritarian pedagogy, establishment pedagogy, resistance pedagogy, and critical pedagogy—correspond to Lacan's four discourses (those of the master, the university, the hysteric, and the analyst). Each strategy emerges out of a particular form of desire on the part of the teacher and attempts to elicit and direct a particular form of desire on the part of students. And each strategy can, in its own unique way, either advance the aims of education, fail to do so, and/or impede education.

AUTHORITARIAN PEDAGOGY

In authoritarian pedagogy, teachers desire students to identify with a particular authority's ideals or values—or in some cases, desire or *jouissance*. Authoritarian pedagogy engages students' desire for recognition, promising that if they can successfully embody the authority's ideals, values, desires, or enjoyments, they will merit recognition and validation by that authority or its avatars (e.g., the teacher). Despite the negative connotations of its label, authoritarian pedagogy is not necessarily all bad. Depending on its content, it can be quite beneficial, and in any case it is, in certain instances, unavoidable. It can be beneficial, for example, if, taking Jesus, Buddha, or Ghandi as one's authority, one embraces identity-defining ideals like love or non-violence, rather than the ideal of dominance and the feeling of hatred embraced by those who took Hitler as their authority. And authoritarian pedagogy is inevitable insofar as all infants must submit to the protective demands of their caregivers ("Don't bite the electrical cord!" "Don't touch the fire!") in order to survive. Authoritarian pedagogy, in fact, has its roots in our infantile experience with our caregivers, in which our well-being is totally dependent on their actions. From this situation in which our very survival depends on the actions of the Other, we learn that acceding to the Other's demands results in the provision of identity validation and support by the Other. This same desire—to protect and support one's identity by pleasing the Other—is at the heart of authoritarian pedagogy. The authority in such cases can be the teachers themselves functioning as masters, gurus, or mentors; or it can be great scientists, entrepreneurs, writers, thinkers, historical figures, or literary characters that the teachers idealize. Students who have already embraced the identity components embodied in these authorities identify with the authoritarian teacher more or less automatically. And students who do not already have these elements as components of their identities are coerced and/or cajoled to make them such by the powerful recognition that accrues to their presence and the lack of recognition that attends their absence. For such students, authoritarian pedagogy promises to satisfy the desire for recognition by supplying new identity components that will elicit greater recognition, and perhaps agency—at least in the immediate situation of the classroom and perhaps the academic community—than these students currently possess. Students who resist the summons of the teacher to assume the authority's identity components are often subject to exclusion from the teacher's recognition and interest and perhaps ultimately from the education system as well.

However, although it is impossible to completely avoid the authoritarian dynamic, and although the particular identity components one is coerced to embrace may be quite positive, acceding to the authoritarian teacher's desire and embracing his or her identity-defining master signifiers always comes at a price; in order to embody the authority's identity components, students must perform them—through their reading, their writing, or their thinking, and/or in their political and interpersonal actions. And this means that they must ignore other (especially Real) identity components that oppose those of the authority. The old components, of course, continue to insist that the subject (unconsciously) perform them, thus producing alienation, a split between the rejected (and still insistent) elements of their being and the identity components promoted by the authority.

In addition to alienating students and training them in authoritarianism, another problem with authoritarian pedagogy is that it encourages teachers to pursue their own desire for recognition and thus lose sight of the aims of education. This leads teachers to indulge in displays of their own learning and intelligence designed to elicit the admiration of their students. The simple rehearsal of knowledge can elicit admiration from many students, especially if it involves feats of memory, as in reciting poetry, quoting philosophers, or recalling numerous facts or dates. Performances that demonstrate significant skills—such as the ability to solve complex math problems quickly in one's head, or the capacity to speak extemporaneously in elaborate sentences with erudite diction—can be even more effective in eliciting student admiration.

Some teachers, desiring a more sincere form of flattery, seek to make their students desire to become like them; that is, they desire recognition from their students not (or not only) in the form of friendship, admiration, or sympathy but in the form of identification. Such teachers encourage their students, both overtly and covertly, to adopt the teachers' values, ideals, desires, fantasies, enjoyments, and aversions. One of the most pervasive manifestations of this desire is the attempt by literature teachers to bring students to love the literature that they themselves love. The most explicit and unabashed avowal of this desire can be found in Helen Vendler's 1981 presidential address to the Modern Language Association convention, where she declares, quoting Wordsworth: "What we have loved,/ Others will love, and we will teach them how" (Vendler 2000, 31). "We love," Vendler claims, "two things centrally: one is literature, but the other, equally powerful, is language" (p. 35). And from this fact it follows, for her, that our students *need* to love these same things: "Our students need to love, not just Shakespeare's characters but Shakespeare's language, not just Keats's sentiments but Keats's English" (p. 36). While it is certainly conceivable that such inculcation benefits some students, most teachers who engage in this practice have not considered its potentially negative ramifications, or conducted research to determine whether the practice does indeed benefit a significant number of their students; nor have they recognized that authoritarian pedagogy conditions students to take a fundamentalist approach to problem solving and inquiry.

In directing students to desire enlightenment from the teacher or from an authoritative thinker or text—whether that authority be the Bible or the Koran, or Marx, Mao, Freud, or Lacan—authoritarian pedagogy inculcates the assumption that the best way to understand a phenomenon or solve a problem is to devote oneself to reading and interpreting the writings of a master. This promotion of fundamentalism is evident in Vendler's authoritarian pedagogy, where the mode of reading that Vendler desires for both herself and her students is one of submission to the text:

In every true reading of literature in adult life we revert to that early attitude of entire *receptivity and plasticity and innocence before the text.* . . . The state of reading . . . is *a state in which the text works on us, not we on it.* . . . *It is this state of intense engagement and self-forgetfulness that we hope our students will come to know.* From that state, at least ideally, there issue equally the freshman essay, the senior thesis, the scholarly paper on prosody, the interdisciplinary paper on social thought and literature, the pedagogical paper on compositional structure, the variorum edition, and the theoretical argument. No matter how elementary or how specialized the written inquiry, it originated in problems raised by *human submission to, and interrogation of, a text.* . . . It is from that original vision—of the single, unduplicable, compelling literary object—that we must always take our final strength in university life and public life alike. (pp. 32, 37; emphasis added)

In this case, authoritarian pedagogy aims to perpetuate itself by establishing in students a desire for authority, teaching them that when they face practical problems in their jobs or difficulties in their lives, they should turn to authoritative texts. Such training in fundamentalism, here made plain, is produced by all teaching practices that, like those of New Criticism, emphasize reverential, devotional interpretation at the expense of critical analysis and encounter with and exploration of the things themselves. And this indoctrination into fundamentalism holds for authoritarian pedagogy whether it is reactionary or progressive (or even radical) in its aims.

ESTABLISHMENT PEDAGOGY

Although authoritarian pedagogy is by no means uncommon today, it is no longer the idealized and dominant practice that it was in previous decades and centuries. Today, in both theory and practice, the ideal teacher is often viewed as a servant of knowledge rather than a master. Thus, many teachers view their function as that of initiating students into the discourse of their particular discipline or into academic discourse in general, a process that they see as empowering students. In such cases, teachers desire that their students identify not with certain ideals or values but with an established system of knowledge, know-how, and/or practices. This pedagogy supports teachers' identities by allowing them to inhabit and perform systems the possession or mastery of which provides them with a sense of significance, agency, and continuity, and whose stature (in the profession, in the public mind, or in the eyes of one's students) confers a like stature on its servant, the teacher. In a like manner, this pedagogy appeals to students' desire for identity support by offering them a system that, when internalized, provides a sense of agency, and when inhabited, provides, like membership in a club, a sense of orientation, connection, and significance.

Mastering a field of knowledge and becoming fluent in a particular discourse can indeed produce agency and significance; and in any case, such mastery and fluency are practical necessities. The danger of establishment pedagogy is that it can meet the desire for agency and significance by providing knowledge and skills that are actually of little value. Teachers and students, and laypersons as well, can very easily get caught up in learning and performing a particular knowledge or discourse not because of its value for addressing human needs or solving problems, but simply because of its social currency in a particular sphere: Possessing it allows one to join the club or be a member of the gang. The knowledge itself may be completely trivial, the discourse utterly useless except as social currency within a narrow sphere, and yet teachers and students, and even laypersons will devote significant portions of their lives to acquiring, performing, and disseminating them.

This dynamic is quite common in the field of literary studies, where the Scholastic competitions between rival interpretations and theories are often enough to capture students' desire for agency, recognition, and other identity-supporting dynamics. Gerald Graff (2000), for example, reveals: "What first made literature, history, and other intellectual pursuits seem attractive to me was exposure to critical debates" (p. 42). It is evident from Graff's account of his conversion to literary study that the debates were attractive to him because they allowed him to satisfy the identity-supporting desires for stature, agency, aggression, and belonging. Explaining that he found the study of literature uninteresting until his class was informed that critics disagreed with each other concerning the merits of the ending of *Huckleberry Finn*, Graff recalls:

Reading the critics was like picking up where the class discussion had left off, and I gained confidence from recognizing that my classmates and I had had thoughts that, however stumbling our expression of them, were not too far from the thoughts of famous published critics. I went back to the novel again and to my surprise found myself rereading it with an excitement I had never felt before with a serious book. Having the controversy over the ending in mind, I now had some issues to watch out for as I read, issues that reshaped the way I read the earlier chapters as well as the later ones and focused my attention. And having issues to watch out for made it possible not only to concentrate, as I had not been able to do earlier, but to put myself into the text—to read it with a sense of personal engagement that I had not felt before. Reading the novel with the voices of the critics running through my mind, I found myself thinking things that I might say about what I was reading. . . . It was as if having a stock of things to look for and to say about a literary work had somehow made it possible to read one. (p. 43)

Graff goes on to observe that "reading books with comprehension, making arguments, writing papers, and making comments in a class discussion . . . involve entering into a cultural or disciplinary conversation, a process not unlike initiation into a social club"(p. 47), and he advocates that literature classes should therefore "teach the conflicts." This strategy for achieving recognition can thus easily lead, as it does in Graff's case, to what has been described as "a kind of perverse consummation of professionalism, the last refinement on the isolation and self-referentiality of academic studies: it makes what professionals do the subject of what professionals do" (Menand 2000, 109).

Thus, while helping students internalize and participate in academic controversies can be an effective strategy for helping students gain knowledge about phenomena that are important to them personally and to society as a whole, it can also get students to waste their energy and opportunities learning about and doing battle over controversies that are ultimately trivial. This is particularly the case in controversies over interpretations of particular literary works, the combined passion and insignificance of which should (but usually do not) remind their perpetrators of the bitter dispute between Jonathan Swift's Big Endians and Little Endians in *Gulliver's Travels* concerning which end of the egg is more valuable.

Moreover, while joining such an academic club or gang through mastering its discourse can, as its teachers maintain, be empowering (through the tacit recognition provided by membership), it can also be disempowering, even psychologically eviscerating, insofar as membership, like identification with an authority, entails renunciation of certain key components of one's identity. Thus students such as women, minorities, and others who have significant identity components that are devalued by, or incompatible with, the teacher's system, or with the more general educational or cultural system of which the teacher's system is a part, may resist learning because to learn would be to sacrifice crucial identity components. And if they do learn, one consequence is the sacrifice of certain identity components, as when female students who studied American literature in its patriarchal form "learned" that women and their accomplishments were less important (and hence less worth writing about) than men and their achievements (Fetterly 1978).

RESISTANCE PEDAGOGY

Resistance to authority and to establishment discourses and systems of knowledge has produced a third, increasingly prominent, pedagogical mode, that of resistance and protest. In such a pedagogy, teachers desire that their students identify with the teacher's own identity vulnerability or deprivation (or with that of a subaltern group with which the teacher has identified) and oppose the authorities and the establishment systems that are supposedly responsible for this lack. This pedagogy is most prominent in relation to various subaltern identity components, including those of gender, class, ethnicity, and sexual orientation, as frequently found in feminist, Marxist, postcolonialist, and queer pedagogies. Such a pedagogy can be wonderfully empowering for students in whom the subaltern identity is a significant component of their overall identity. And it can be empowering for others who are not themselves subalterns but who identify with the subaltern plight and thus strengthen their own identity through acquiring (1) the group membership and solidarity the identification provides, (2) the sense of agency produced through being an advocate for justice, and (3) the particular Symbolic Order identity components ("good," "just," "courageous," "caring") that such advocacy performs. Both subaltern students and those who identify with them have experienced by the thousands the identity support and development that such a pedagogy can provide. Moreover, the establishment or reinforcement of such identity components also contributes to social change, insofar as their identity vulnerability motivates students to take action to change the authorities and systems that are responsible for their lacks.

There is, however, a downside to protest pedagogy. The first problem is that for students who are not members of a subaltern group—and even for members of subaltern groups, such as women, African Americans, and gays and lesbians for whom these subaltern identities are not the dominant components—such a pedagogy can be restrictive; or worse, can seem like just another form of authoritarian or establishment pedagogy. And even for those students for whom the subaltern identity is central and who embrace and benefit from the pedagogy of resistance, such reinforcement of one identity component may have disempowering as well as empowering effects, such as when it encourages them to invest their identities almost exclusively in the subaltern categories and thus ignore other capacities and attributes the development of which might be of great value both personally and socially.

In addition, such a pedagogy can support socially destructive forms of identity politics that pit different groups against each other in a competition for recognition as the greatest victim (including the tacit recognition embodied in concessions from the establishment). Taken to its extreme, this logic can lead to disastrous results. As Richter points out, "In Rwanda and Kosovo, at least, 'identity politics' has already resulted in genocide" (Richter 2000, 130).

CRITICAL PEDAGOGY AND THE ANALYST'S DESIRE

The fourth prominent pedagogical mode is critical pedagogy, which might be described as resistance pedagogy combined with the Socratic method. Like resistance pedagogy, it aims at liberation from the oppressive forces and structures that constitute racism, classism, colonialism, and sexism. But in addition to liberating students (and others), it also aims to help them develop their full potentials, become empowered. A careful reading of critical pedagogical theory reveals that the central desire animating this pedagogy is the teachers' desire for identity itself—more specifically, their desire for a strong *identity for their students*, whose own desire for identity the teachers have identified with.

This desire is essentially the same as the psychoanalyst's desire, which Lacan called the desire for absolute difference. What Lacan's phrase means is, first of all, that the analyst desires not to clone herself or to replicate her own identity components in her analysands; rather, she desires that they develop and enhance their own identities, which will be fundamentally ("absolutely") different from hers in multiple ways, rather than just moderately different variations on the themes of her identity. And in order to enable her analysands to develop such an identity, the analyst desires a second absolute difference: those capacities and qualities in the analysand that remain undeveloped, repressed, or disowned because they are "absolutely different" from the analysand's dominant, socially sanctioned identity components, and which the analysand must recognize, own, and make peace with in order to find relief from suffering and to progress and develop in life. Thus what an analyst would desire in relation to an analysand struggling with his sexuality would be not that the analysand "become" heterosexual, homosexual, bisexual, transsexual, or any particular sexuality identity at all, but rather that he come to own all of his impulses, desires, ideals, and other identity components—many of them fundamentally different from the analyst's identity components—and arrive at an accommodation that he is satisfied with of these mutually "absolutely different" components.

Similarly, critical pedagogy, unlike the other three modes of teaching we have discussed, desires not that students embrace particular identity components but that they become aware of their present identity components, of repressed qualities that could become new aspects of identity, and of the consequences of both types of elements for themselves and for others. Such a pedagogy is like the discourse of the psychoanalyst in that it offers not prefabricated identity components but rather a process for discovering one's own potential identity components and developing them into an identity of one's own.

This desire for their students to enhance their identities is revealed by a careful reading of the writings of a number of the leading proponents and developers of critical pedagogy. Henry Giroux and Roger Simon (1992), for example, state:

Our project is the construction of an educational practice that expands human capacities in order *to enable people to intervene in the formation of their own subjectivities* and to be able to exercise power in the interest of transforming the ideological and material conditions of domination into social practices that promote social empowerment and demonstrate possibilities. (p. 189; emphasis added)

Another prominent advocate of critical pedagogy, Peter McLaren (1994), articulates a similar desire to enhance students' identities, emphasizing that "students especially need to be provided with opportunities to devise different assemblages of self" (p. 214). McLaren points out that such a project is not only an important end in itself but also a necessary component of any effort to achieve liberation and social justice: "The remaking of the social and the reinvention of the self must be understood as dialectically synchronous—that is, they cannot be conceived as unrelated or only marginally connected. They are mutually informing and constitutive processes" (p. 210). Likewise, Abdul JanMohamed (1994) describes the aim of critical pedagogy in terms of "the incipient constitution of a new identity" and the clarification of students' "nascent identities" (p. 245).

There is a profound difference between this desire for (one's students') identity and the identity-supporting desires animating the other three pedagogical modes. While in critical pedagogy, teachers identify with their students' desire for identity, in the other pedagogical modes teachers desire that their students identify with some aspect of the teacher's identity, such as the teacher's ideals, values, or enjoyments (authoritarian pedagogy), the teacher's knowledge or belief system (establishment pedagogy), or the teacher's lack of or desire for a particular identity (resistance pedagogy). Whereas the latter three desires involve practices that, in benefiting the teacher, may fail to help or may even harm the students, critical pedagogy's desire entails practices that are, strictly speaking, satisfying to the teacher only insofar as they benefit the students. Thus critical pedagogy's desire entails the importance of avoiding the imposition the teacher's ideals, values, beliefs, desires, or enjoyments on students. Rather than offering students new identity components, as the other three modes do in one way or another, critical pedagogy aims, like psychoanalysis, to help students understand (1) the nature and origins of their own identity components, (2) the consequences of these components for themselves and others, and (3) the nature, potential source, and likely consequences of alternative identity components that they might embrace or pursue. The aim is not to change students in any particular way but rather to provide them with the opportunities and resources to change and develop according to their own identity needs and desires. As Lawrence Grossberg (1994) puts it, critical pedagogy

aims not to predefine its outcome (even in terms of some imagined value of emancipation or democracy) but to empower its students to reconstruct their world in new ways and to rearticulate their future in unimagined and perhaps even unimaginable ways. It is a pedagogy which demands of students, not that they conform to some image of political liberation nor even that they resist, but simply that they gain some understanding of their own involvement in the world, and in the making of their own future. Consequently, it . . . deals with the formations of the popular, the Cartographies of taste, stability, and mobility within which students are located. (p. 18)

This same desire informs the political dimension of critical pedagogy, according to Grossberg:

If political struggles are won and lost . . . in the space where people and groups are articulated, both ideologically and affectively, to social identities, cultural practices, and political projects, then it is here that pedagogy must operate. The task of a politically engaged pedagogy is, after all, never to convince a predefined subject . . . to adopt a new position. Rather, the task is to win an already positioned, already invested individual or group to a different set of places, a different organization of the space of possibilities. . . . We cannot tell our students what ethics or politics . . . to embrace. Again, we must connect to the ethics and politics they already embrace and then struggle to rearticulate them to a different position (without necessarily knowing in advance that we will be successful, or even what that different position will actually be). (pp. 19–20)

The central process through which this desire is pursued is the mapping of students' identities, a process that is also central to psychoanalysis. McLaren (1994) states:

Educators need to stare boldly and unflinchingly into the historical present and assume a narrative space where conditions may be created where students can tell their own stories, listen closely to the stories of others, and dream the dream of liberation. Identity formation must be understood in terms of how subjectivity is contextually enacted within the tendential forces of history (Grossberg 1992). The exploration of identity should consist of mapping one's subject position in the field of multiple relationships. (p. 217)

This mapping can be pursued in several ways, including helping students identify and question their own individual and collective meanings, values, histories, cultural investments, desires, and affective responses (Giroux

1994, 47; Giroux and Simon 1992, 182, 195; and JanMohamed, passim). As in psychoanalysis, such mapping can help students become aware of their own intrapsychic conflicts. As Giroux (1994) puts it, in the form of critical pedagogy he advocates, "students would study their own ethnicities, histories, and gain some sense of those complex and diverse cultural locations that have provided them with a sense of voice, place, and identity. In this way, students could be made more attentive to . . . the struggles that inform their own identities" (p. 51). JanMohamed (1994) notes that overcoming hegemony requires engaging the internal division within oneself: "Denial of identity operates most effectively . . . through the construction of hegemonic rules and regulations that are 'internalized' as normal operating procedures. Thus, on the sociopolitical register antagonism exists on the 'inside': it cleaves the subject" (p. 247). An important step in critical pedagogy is thus for "students to develop relationships of nonidentity with their own subject positions . . . , [which] amounts to the development of an antagonism with oneself" (p. 246). By activating students' self-division, critical pedagogy can promote their development of new, alternative identities: "their new subject positions," JanMohamed explains, "begin to cathect around the project of excavating and reading their own social and physical bodies, which are in fact texts of the history of their oppression. Thus their new subjectivity emerges in the process of drawing borders around their old subject positions" (p. 248).

In this way, the key processes of critical pedagogy resemble those of psychoanalysis: Mapping one's identity leads to a recognition of oppositions and the experiencing of conflicts between different identity components, and working through these conflicts in relation to one's present realities and future possibilities promotes the alteration of one's identity, or the development of an alternative identity—a result that liberates subjects from a constricting identity and thus empowers them both personally and collectively.

FOR A PSYCHOANALYTIC CRITICAL PEDAGOGY

I have quoted extensively from its leading advocates to make the point that critical pedagogy is ultimately driven by the same desire as the psychoanalyst is and that (consequently) it enacts this desire through the same fundamental strategy—mapping identity and thus engaging with and working through intrapsychic conflict—that the psychoanalyst employs. But my selective quotation has made critical pedagogy seem to be a much more unified, coherent, and fully theorized practice than it actually is. And it has also made it seem more psychoanalytic and more effective than it really is; for while the core animating desire of critical pedagogy is that of psychoanalysis, its practice, and hence also its results often diverge significantly from those of psychoanalysis.

In the first place, critical pedagogy often equates identity with subject position, which is a function largely of the socially determined signifiers of group identity. By thus ignoring students' imagistic-perceptual identity components, their affective-physiological identity components, and their particular, individual (as opposed to collective) Symbolic identity components, critical pedagogy runs a significant risk of increasing their alienation rather than enhancing their empowerment. Such alienation is already quite familiar and well documented and criticized when it involves, for example, a feminist pedagogy that tries to help women own their identities as women but ignores differences of race, class, nationality, and sexual orientation among women, with the result that some female students feel that they are being pressured to own identity components that are not theirs at all. But even if one is sensitive to these multiple differences—distinguishing, for example, the subject position of black, lesbian, working-class, South African women from the subject position of black, lesbian, working-class American women—one still runs the risk of excluding key and even core identity components of the individuals occupying these subject positions, as well as the risk of imposing other identity components on them that they do not embody. A more adequately theorized notion of identity, such as I have sketched out above, helps avoid such exclusion and imposition by recognizing, first of all, that identity is a function not of one's *subject* position, but of one's *subjective* position. That is, one's identity and the desires that it entails, while multiply and powerfully influenced by one's social positioning, are not a direct reflection of that positioning, but are rather a function of the way one's social positioning has been internalized by the particular subjectivity one brings to this position (a subjectivity that is itself a function of a succession of previous similar encounters, all the way back to the first encounter of the zygote and its genetic givens with its uterine environment). The psychoanalytic model of identity I have presented further militates against reducing identity to subject position through its identification of three registers of identity, each incorporating multiple identity components. Armed with this model, critical pedagogy can thus avoid the alienating reduction of students to their subject positions.

The absence of an adequate theory of the nature of identity and of how it is developed and altered also leaves critical pedagogy with little indication of how it might best enable students to more fully own and develop their identities. More specifically, critical pedagogy lacks a theory of how to determine which identity components should be developed (and how) and which components should be subordinated, excluded, or eliminated (and how). Without such guidance, teachers easily fall into reinforcing components that mirror their own and undermining components that conflict with their own. An example is a politically correct classroom in which some students feel silenced.

As noted above, some practitioners of critical pedagogy appear to avoid this problem by recognizing the importance of helping students identify and explore their own internal conflicts. But critical pedagogy is largely silent about how to do this, saying little about the ways in which the transference and counter-transference desires that permeate classrooms can be most effectively and ethically negotiated. As a result, there is no safeguard against teachers simply following the desires of their own identity components when addressing their students' internal conflicts. And when critical pedagogy does articulate a strategy for operating with internal conflict, such as the strategy described by JanMohamed (1994), it reduces the internal conflict to being merely a reflection of, and a means to pursue, the external conflict between dominant and dominated groups. The problem, in the view of critical pedagogy, is not internal conflict per se; internal conflict appears to exist only because of external, social conflicts: the oppression of one group by another. The way to resolve the internal conflict as well as the external oppression, it is assumed, is thus to oppose oneself to the oppressive group and its culture, which cause internal conflicts by infiltrating the subjectivities of the dominated subjects (pp. 245–247). It is through such opposition that subjectivities are altered, according to JanMohamed. By reflecting on the (objective) "conditions of their existence," oppressed people in effect become archeologists of the site of their own social formation; their new subject positions begin to cathect around the project of excavating and reading their own social and physical bodies, which are in fact texts of the history of their oppression. Thus their new subjectivity emerges in the process of drawing borders around their old subject positions (p. 248).

Such a strategy overlooks the fact that precisely through the subjectivity-infiltrating hegemony of dominant culture, one's "own social and physical bodies" may include, as central components, elements of the dominant, oppressive culture. In such cases, opposing the dominant culture involves rejecting an integral part of oneself.

A psychoanalytic strategy, in contrast, does not define the qualities, ideals, values, desires, or enjoyments that are "one's own" in terms of their supposed correlation with or divergence from one's social position(s). In fact, psychoanalysis leaves open the very question of which elements are really "one's own" and which are hegemonic parasites, and this for two reasons. First, what seems most alien (both to observers and to subjects themselves) may in fact be most "one's own"—as in the case of virulently anti-gay people who unconsciously harbor powerful homosexual desires. And second, what one owns and what one disowns can change significantly as a result of working through one's internal conflicts.

As a result of its different and more fully theorized view of identity, psychoanalysis provides a very different strategy for working through internal conflicts. Instead of trying to resolve such conflicts by dissolving them into political conflicts and alliances, psychoanalysis aims to do precisely the opposite: to help the analysand or student remain focused on the conflict as his or her "own"—and not as an external, social or political, conflict in which one is simply caught up—and to explore the various manifestations, causes, and consequences of this conflict in the various domains and times of one's life, including one's social and political positions and actions. To the extent that this process of analysis, reflection, and working through is fully executed, certain ideals, values, desires, and enjoyments—and hence also certain behaviors, including social and political positions and actions—will emerge as more fundamentally one's own. Along with this emergence of certain identity components as central or dominant, other elements of oneself are altered (as in sublimation), subordinated, or, in some cases, disowned by renouncing (in contrast to repressing or projecting). The impetus beneath this process is the connecting, organizing, synthesizing function of the mind/brain—which is the function that produces, maintains, and develops identity.

Psychoanalytic theory thus provides a model of identity and an understanding of identity change and development that, when they inform the desire of the critical pedagogue for students to develop their identities, will enable critical pedagogy to more fully realize this animating desire and hence also its ideals of liberation, empowerment, and social justice. More specifically, psychoanalysis offers a strategy of identity development that can help critical pedagogy enable students to own and realize their identities through

1. identifying the various components of their identities, which operate in three different registers, which provides the basis for
2. throwing into relief central alliances and oppositions among identity components, both within and between registers;
3. identifying and assessing the manifestations, disguises, causes, and consequences of the various identity components, alliances, and conflicts; and
4. supporting the synthesizing, organizing function of the mind—that is, the identity-developing function.

This final function—supporting the synthesizing, organizing function of the mind—is particularly important, because it is what produces the more complex and capacious structures of identity (and hence of cognition, moral reasoning, and interpersonal relations) that constructive-developmental pedagogy emphasizes, and that are a prerequisite for living a productive and fulfilled life in the postmodern world (Kegan 1994).

In addition to adopting this general psychoanalytic strategy of identity development, critical pedagogy can also use this model of identity in conjunction with particular psychoanalytic techniques in order to foster in students the desire to acquire the knowledge, skills, and understanding of the subject matter being studied. The basic question asked by a psychoanalytically oriented teacher is, "Given the current identity contents and structures of my students, and given the educational aims of this lesson (or course, or curriculum), what issues, facts, questions, problems, or possibilities—and what mode of presentation of these by me and what activities by my students—will be most likely to engage key identity components of my students in such a way that the students will simultaneously achieve the desired understanding and further develop their own intellectual and emotional capacities?"

In cases where the subject matter is threatening to students—because either its content or its difficulty threatens students' identities—teachers will find it useful to employ techniques similar to those used in supportive and expressive therapy. Supportive techniques include reassuring students of their intelligence, ability, human worth, and eventual success as they are struggling with intellectually or emotionally difficult material—informing them, for example, that their struggle (or fear, or anger) is not abnormal, and/or providing a model (perhaps from one's own experience) of a successful struggle and an image of the benefits it brings. I find such support to be crucial for the theory courses I teach. Since most of my students in both undergraduate and graduate theory courses have had little prior exposure to the ideas and perspectives they encounter in these courses, they often find the material intellectually intimidating. By telling them of my own floundering when I first encountered this material, and describing how my perseverance was repaid with greater understanding and more critical tools, I reassure them that their present inability to understand the material doesn't mean they lack intelligence and that there are important benefits to be derived from this struggle.

I also find that expressive techniques are quite useful in these courses. Expressive techniques engage students in writing and speaking about their feelings concerning the task or subject matter at hand, giving voice in particular to their anxieties and resistances. In addition to its intellectual difficulty, theory often makes students anxious because it challenges fundamental assumptions they have about not only language and literature but also truth, reality, and human existence. Getting students to explore in personal journals the thoughts and feelings that these theories evoke can help them work through their own inner conflicts and anxieties concerning particular issues in ways that can have significant benefits beyond the course.[3] At the same time, by identifying points of resistance to learning or reflecting, such expressive writing can show teachers precisely where they need to direct their efforts in order to get the learning process moving.

Once students have expressed their anxiety, hostility, or lack of interest toward particular ideas or issues, teachers can then proceed, through clarifying and uncovering techniques, to help students identify their identity components that impede the educational process and those that support it.

Thus, in response to a student who expresses lack of interest in a particular course or topic on the grounds that it is irrelevant to his life, a teacher might remark, "So you feel that since you are going to become an engineer, studying philosophy (or literature, or history) will not be of any value to you?" and then proceed to engage the student in examining and clarifying just what he values and cares about. Through such an engagement students may come to see that a particular issue or subject matter is indeed relevant to things they care about, and they may also uncover things that they didn't realize they cared about (based, perhaps, on identity components that they were unaware of).

In those cases where the obstacle to learning and growing is not (overt) anxiety or lack of interest but rather students' complacency—their satisfaction with their current state of knowledge and mode of operation in a given field—the use of confrontive techniques is often productive. Such techniques involve bringing to students' attention facts, events, arguments, and perspectives that they have not considered and that appear to complicate, contradict, or even undermine the students' current position. I often have recourse to this technique in a course on the scholarship and pedagogy of literary study that I teach to first-year graduate students before they begin teaching. Many of these students, like Helen Vendler, approach their teaching of freshman English courses with the central aim of getting their students to love the literature that they love. In this class I often pose the question of whether we have a right to expect that others should love what we love and confront them with perspectives that question this aim on ethical and practical grounds. They are thus forced to grapple with such questions as, "What right do we have to expect our students to enjoy what we enjoy? What right do we have to expect that our freshman students— most of whom, unlike us, are not English majors—will benefit from the same texts and activities that we believe we benefited from? Why do I wish this for my students? Is my desire primarily a desire for their growth and development, or is it a desire to support my own affective and conceptual identity components by replicating them in others?" Such confrontation leads students to consider possible alternative practices that they will find productive and fulfilling, and also leads them to inquire into the ways in which their old assumptions support and defend particular identity components that they were not fully aware of and that have thus unnecessarily limited their activities and their growth.

Supportive, expressive, clarifying, and confrontive techniques also, in various ways, promote the integration of both identity components and understanding. This process is important educationally because it provides that grasp of an entire field, discipline, or problematic that is truly empowering. And it is important psychologically because it promotes both the coherence and the agency that are integral to identity. Teachers can promote both types of integration through additional techniques designed specifically for this end. Such techniques, similar to processes operating in reconstruction and working through in psychoanalysis, involve linking multiple and disparate issues and aspects together into a reasonably unified and coherent totality. The simplest such technique is to ask students to write a paper that integrates all the factors in a particular issue or problematic. Another way is to present a particular phenomenon and ask students to analyze and work through it from different perspectives, or using all the relevant conceptual tools at their disposal. Prompting students with a list of particular points to consider can ensure that the totality of the field is included.

Such integration can include one's own identity components as well as all the elements of the subject matter. For example, I sometimes ask students in the graduate class described above to articulate, at the end of the semester, their basic pedagogical desires with regard to their (future) students and to explain how these desires support their identities; and what sorts of texts, interpretive strategies, and pedagogical techniques will allow these desires to achieve the fullest realization. Such activity, in addition to whatever specific integration it achieves, also develops students' capacity and habituation for such integrative activity, which is the fundamental process through which both identity and understanding are generated. And once students experience and recognize the identity-enhancing benefits of such reflective, representational activities, they desire to pursue such activities and thus become lifelong learners (and developers), which is arguably the fundamental goal of education.

NOTES

1. The existence and function of these three registers have been implicitly verified by recent research in cognitive science, child development, and empirical clinical studies (see Bracher 1999).

2. Insofar as this excluded position to which one aspires is named or described, it can also involve a Symbolic Order desire for recognition as this signifier.

3. In addition, as the work of James Pennebaker (1997) has shown, writing about such stressful issues can produce both psychological and physical health benefits.

REFERENCES

Bracher, Mark. 1993. *Lacan, Discourse, and Social Change: A Psychoanalytic Cultural Criticism.* Ithaca, N.Y.: Cornell University Press.

——. 1999. *The Writing Cure: Psychoanalysis, Composition, and the Aims of Education.* Carbondale: Southern Illinois University Press.

——. 2000. Editor's Column: Adolescent Violence and Identity Vulnerability. *JPCS: Journal for the Psychoanalysis of Culture & Society* 5(2): 193–207.

Fetterly, Judith. 1978. *The Resisting Reader: A Feminist Approach to American Fiction*. Bloomington: Indiana University Press.

Garbarino, James. 1999. *Lost Boys: Why Our Sons Turn Violent and How We Can Save Them*. New York: Free Press.

Giroux, Henry. 1994. Living Dangerously: Identity Politics and the New Cultural Racism. In *Between Borders: Pedagogy and the Politics of Cultural Studies*, ed. Henry A. Giroux and Peter McLaren (pp. 29–55). New York: Routledge.

Giroux, Henry, and Simon, Roger. 1992. Popular Culture as a Pedagogy of Pleasure and Meaning: Decolonizing the Body. In Henry Giroux, *Border Crossings: Cultural Workers and the Politics of Education* (pp. 180–206) New York: Routledge.

Glasser, Mervin. 1998. On Violence: A Preliminary Communication. *International Journal of Psycho-Analysis* 79: 887–902.

Graff, Gerald. 2000. Disliking Books at an Early Age. In *Falling into Theory: Conflicting Views on Reading Literature* (2nd ed.), ed. David H. Richter (pp. 103–111). Boston: Bedford/St. Martin's.

Greenspan, Stanley. 1997. *Developmentally Based Psychotherapy*. Madison, Conn.: International Universities Press.

Grossberg, Lawrence. 1992. *We Gotta Get Out of This Place*. New York: Routledge.

Grossberg, Lawrence. 1994. Introduction: Bringin' It All Back Home—Pedagogy and Cultural Studies. In *Between Borders: Pedagogy and the Politics of Cultural Studies*, ed. Henry A. Giroux and Peter McLaren (pp. 1–28). New York: Routledge.

JanMohamed, Abdul R. 1994. Some Implications of Paulo Freire's Border Pedagogy. In *Between Borders: Pedagogy and the Politics of Cultural Studies*, ed. Henry A. Giroux and Peter McLaren (pp. 242–252). New York: Routledge.

Katz, Jack. 1988. *Seductions of Crime*. New York: Basic Books.

Kegan, Robert. 1994. *In Over Our Heads: The Mental Demands of Modern Life*. Cambridge, Mass.: Harvard University Press.

Kerrigan, William. 1993. New Rules about Sex on Campus. *Harper's* (September): 33–42.

McLaren, Peter. 1994. Multiculturalism and the Postmodern Critique: Toward a Pedagogy of Resistance and Transformation. In *Between Borders: Pedagogy and the Politics of Cultural Studies*, ed. Henry A. Giroux and Peter McLaren (pp. 192–224). New York: Routledge.

Menand, Louis. 2000. The Demise of Disciplinary Authority. In *Falling into Theory: Conflicting Views on Reading Literature* (2nd ed.), ed. David H. Richter. Boston: Bedford/St. Martin's.

Mitchell, Stephen A. 1993. Aggression and the Endangered Self. *Psychoanalytic Quarterly* 62: 351–382.

Pennebaker, James. 1997. *Opening Up: The Healing Power of Expressing Emotions* (rev. ed.). New York: Guilford.

Richter, David H. 2000. What We Read. In *Falling into Theory: Conflicting Views on Reading Literature* (2nd ed.), ed. David H. Richter. Boston: Bedford/St. Martin's.

Vendler, Helen. 2000. What We Have Loved, Others Will Love. In *Falling into*

Theory: Conflicting Views on Reading Literature (2nd ed.), ed. David H. Richter. Boston: Bedford/St. Martin's.

Wurmser, Leon. 1995. *The Hidden Dimension: Psychodynamics of Compulsive Drug Use*. Northvale, N.J.: Jason Aronson.

Young-Bruehl, Elisabeth, and Bethelard, Faith. 2000. *Cherishment: A Psychology of the Heart*. New York: Free Press.

Chapter 8

Sexual/Textual Encounters in the High School: "Beyond" Reader-Response Theories

Betty-Anne Schlender

WHAT'S SEX/GENDER GOT TO DO WITH IT?

"Alyssa" is a second-year high school student who carefully drew a red heart after her pseudonym each time she wrote it.[1] I asked Alyssa and her classmates to read and respond to Suniti Namjoshi's (1993, 303–305) "The Little Prince," a provokingly spare tale of just 290 words. (See Appendix 1 for the complete text of "The Little Prince.") The following is a portion of Alyssa's written response to the story:

> I don't think it's fair because she made her daughter powerful in her own way and made the prince shy and other stuff so he couldn't even have a chance to try to be a prince that could rule the kingdom.

If we look at her response closely, it reveals a great deal—not only about the sense that Alyssa made of the text, but about the meanings that she brought to it in order to do so. A prince who is shy "and other stuff" will clearly not be perceived as a fit ruler, and will not be given the opportunity to dispel this impression. It is not "fair" (right, just, equitable; offering an equal chance of success, in accordance with rules and standards of sportsmanship), in Alyssa's view, that the princess, whom the evil queen has made powerful in the same way as herself (apparently a threatening, emasculating power) should usurp the prince's rightful position and status. Alyssa's response appeals to patriarchal rules of competition and fair play, while at the same time it seems untroubled by, or unaware of, the injustice implicit in the traditional situation which places the princess at the same disadvantage that it protests on the prince's behalf.

Virtually every adolescent in our classrooms already "knows" what it means to be boy or girl. Each has constructed an identity in relation to various and often contradictory definitions of what it means to be "male" or "female," and each has a more or less fully developed image in her/his mind of the man or woman s/he might become. For most, this process is difficult, fraught with anxieties, precarious, and (possibly the worst news) unending. Problems arise when a reader meets a text that provokes tension and dissonance among conscious and unconscious knowledge/s, beliefs, attitudes, and/or feelings about sex/gender.[2] These problems are often obscured, ignored, or repressed, particularly in the classroom, but they may also create fruitful possibilities. I believe (as do many psychoanalytic theorists, including Shoshana Felman, Judith Butler, Mark Bracher, Elizabeth Ellsworth, and many others) that we need to meet our students at these sites of discomfort. The dissonance and anxiety evoked by a text may serve to prop up and reinforce hostilities and prejudices that manifest themselves in sexism, misogyny, homophobia, racism, and other expressions of fear, hatred, and intolerance, but they may also present opportunities for learning which result in the positive affective and attitudinal changes which we strive to promote.

HOW DO SEXED/GENDERED READERS READ SEX/GENDER? READER-RESPONSE AND FEMINIST THEORIES

I began my investigation of the relationship between sex/gender and reading by delving into literary critical theory—in particular, reader-response and feminist theories of reading. These theories have been influential in breaking the hold of the New Critics' perspective, and have generated discussions in the areas of literary theory, media studies, and pedagogy that differ markedly from those generated by the New Criticism. Very generally, reader-response and reception theories attempt to understand and describe the nature of the transaction between a reader and a text rather than the text itself. Largely because of these theories, it has become widely accepted by literary and film studies theorists that any reading of a text is a one-time *event* that takes place in the space between the reader and the text and is therefore impossible to replicate.

Reader-response theories have played an important role in reconfiguring the landscape of literary criticism, media studies, school curricula, and methods of classroom instruction. However, they also share an overarching tendency to imagine what they variously label an "ideal," "universal," "implied," "transcendent," or "androgynous" reader. While they implicitly recognize specificities such as race, class, and gender as determiners of individual psychology, they are virtually blind to the difficulties that may arise when an actual reader who is "Other" than white, of European descent, middle or upper class, heterosexual and male meets a specific text.

Umberto Eco (1994, 13–15), for example, argues that the model reader "should" cooperate with the author in the creation of the correct text—that is, the one that the author had in mind. By doing so, he dismisses as illegitimate and irrelevant any number of mis(sed)readings, and thereby readers, whose backgrounds and/or experiences differ in significant ways from the author's.

Feminist literary theories, on the other hand, have a long history of attempting to correct and compensate for the omissions, exclusions, and distortions of this disembodied view of literature by foregrounding the biological, material, and phenomenological realities which have meant that women's lives have been, and are, very different from men's. Elizabeth Wright (1998, 4) is among the many feminist theorists who remind us that the reader is necessarily an embodied reader who cannot receive or interpret a text except through filters determined by an almost limitless array of bodily specificities, such as race, class, sex/gender, and sexual orientation. From approximately the beginning of the twentieth century to the end of the 1970s, the quantity and the urgency of feminist writings increased exponentially and they have had a remarkable impact in redressing inequities in theories and practices surrounding the publication, consumption, criticism, and instruction of literature.

Reader-response and feminist theories, along with other influences in the twentieth century (such as postmodernism, postcolonialism, and poststructuralism) have prompted radical shifts in our thinking about the nature, the attributes, and the relative value of the literary contributions of sexed/gendered beings. They have not, however, had the revolutionary impact that one might reasonably or logically expect, given that so many of the most problematic and harmful attitudes and behaviors have long been widely judged to be indefensibly wrong by legal, ethical, logical, moral, and/or religious standards. I am troubled by this gap between logic and emotion, between what we know at an intellectual level to be true and what we know at a "gut-feeling" or somatic level to be true, and I am curious about the reasons that it persists so stubbornly.

These two schools of thought have shed some light on this question, and they have been the source of a great deal of productive and sometimes choleric dialogue. However, they share one basic assumption that I believe limits their explanatory potential if what we want to investigate is what (sexed/gendered) readers in our classrooms are actually doing with the texts that we offer them. This assumption is that the production/reception of a text is almost entirely an intellectual, conscious process. Theorists working within either of these theoretical frameworks generally conceive of a writer/reader who is more or less aware of the intentions, motives, and desires embodied in and produced by a text, and who possesses the ability to analyze, define, and control what it does for/to the reader and what the reader does with/to it.

ADD PSYCHOANALYTIC THEORY, SHAKE WELL

There is, however, another large body of writings around psychoanalytic theories, especially those written by Jacques Lacan and psychoanalytic theorists who have extended and emended his work, which tends to confound this view. These theorists share some common concerns and influences with post-structuralist theorists such as Jacques Derrida, including a radical re-definition of language and subjectivity. They mistrust the notion that either the author or the reader of a text can determine or state with any certainty what the text says or means, and they cast suspicion on what Lacan calls "the fancy of understanding" in a more general sense (in Felman 1987, 108).

These theorists view with skepticism any approach to literature which supposes that what an author intends to say corresponds neatly and trans-parently to the text itself or to any consequent reading. Regardless of dic-tums concerning "correct" textual analysis and interpretative practice, psychoanalytic theories suggest that in fact, our first encounter with a text (and for most of our students, any school-assigned reading is a first reading) does not normally (and indeed cannot) follow the rules of "good" (that is, rational and intellectual, objective, academic) criticism.

As much as our appreciation of a work of literature may be enhanced by this rational approach, the primary and often the most enduring reasons that a text grabs us, stays with us, or shifts our construction of ourselves and/or our world in minor or important ways often fall outside the domain of reason and cognition (Alcorn and Bracher 1985). Rather than asking us to simply describe and accept or reject our responses as "right" or "wrong," psychoanalytic theories provide us with a framework and a ter-minology to begin to retrace and analyze how we arrived at a particular interpretation of a text, which always involves attitudes, preconceptions, and intuitive agreement with or resistance to a text's representation of sex/gender.

One popularized conception of psychoanalysis holds that Freud at-tempted to explain all human motivation as the indirect expression of re-pressed infantile sexual impulses. Reading from a psychoanalytic perspective can, in this reductionist view, be taken as synonymous with indulging in a voyeuristic and somewhat lascivious hunt for phallic sym-bols, reenactments of the Oedipal drama, and incestuous imagery in a text. This approach too often leads to an emphasis on developing another body of knowledge about the "correct" way to interpret texts, and to arguing competing interpretations, rather *than a focus on the intrapsychic dimen-sions of the reader–text exchange.* Literary theorists and classroom teachers sometimes (quite reasonably) regard this approach to literary and film anal-ysis with a great deal of suspicion and/or distaste.

Unfortunately, this suspicion has also meant that the pedagogical potential of psychoanalytic theories has too often been overlooked. These theories do foreground some issues previously obscured because they fell outside the scope of the discourses that have defined the terms of the conversation. If we pay attention to some key principles of the various schools of psychoanalytic thought—for example, the trauma and the consequences of the original separation of infant from caregiver that inevitably necessitates and accompanies the construction of a sexed/gendered identity—and if we encourage students to explore and deconstruct their responses to the texts they meet, I am convinced that we can help them discover a great deal about themselves and each other. We can help them to recognize that these responses are always experienced as a simultaneous (con)fusion of intellectual, emotional, and physical activities, and that by attending to less intellectual as well as analytic and evaluative dimensions of a response, they can utilize these responses to develop and grow in important ways. In so doing, they might move away from the false and tired dualities and clichés surrounding masculinity and femininity that underscore everything they do, but that we seldom allow them to admit, identify, or discuss. Like the proverbial elephant in the drawing room that everybody assiduously pretends not to see, the "elephant" that is our students' (and our own) ongoing struggle with sex/gender and sexuality isn't going to disappear because we don't talk about it. Symptomatically, it will keep taking up space, taking up the energy that it costs to avoid mentioning its smelly presence, and "doing its business" on the carpet. The effect of the elephant's presence will be there whether or not we like it, are comfortable with it, or choose to deal with it.

It quickly became evident to me that there is much more going on in students' responses to these texts than conventional teaching practices and assessment measures take into account or reward. One of the ways that psychoanalytic theories have assisted my thinking about the nature and the purpose of these responses is through Lacan's formulation of the three psychic registers, which he terms the *Real*, the *Imaginary*, and the *Symbolic* Orders. Because these concepts have been instrumental in shaping my thinking about the struggles that appear to be going in these responses, it seems essential to briefly describe the three registers here before I begin my analysis of students' responses.

Lacan uses the term the *Real* to refer to the excess that preexists and cannot be encompassed in the Imaginary and Symbolic Orders. It is a subsymbolic order, founded out of the infant's original sense of completion and unity. It is an undifferentiated amalgam of feelings and impressions that cannot be symbolized in images or words, which is ruptured when the Symbolic and Imaginary Orders intervene with their insistence on difference, lack, and absence. The *Imaginary* Order is the realm of images and illusions, a product of what Lacan calls the "mirror stage," at which time the infant learns to recognize itself with reference to its image in a mirror.

This image and the infant's ego are consequently illusory and always split. The Imaginary Order embodies a sense of absence, lack, and alienation because the infant perceives itself only indirectly. Her/his perception and recognition of a "self" is necessarily a misperception and a misrecognition because the image the infant sees in a mirror and which s/he must identify with in order to construct a sense of self is not the "self" at all but a spectral image. The third order, the *Symbolic* Order, is the realm of language. It is the psychic register that is formed out of, and subject to, the interplay of presence and absence, the structures, dictates, and prohibitions of language, the Oedipal passage, the larger social order, the "Law of the Father," and the "Big Other." The Symbolic Order intrudes on and forever alters the infant's perception of, and relation to, the world. The subsymbolic order of the Real, into which the infant is born and in which there is nothing other than kinesthetic experience and affect, becomes a tripartite structure.

The three orders are interdependent and each is inextricably involved in a human being's perception and experience, barring the presence of psychosis by a foreclosure to the Law or other genetic or environmental factors which inhibit the infant's usual course of development. The conflict between these three registers seeks to reconcile the very different kinds of information that each processes. My research explores how students understand and read sex/gender in an unfamiliar text with reference to the strategies that their responses show for managing this uneasy and always provisional reconciliation.

READING AND THE RETURN OF THE REPRESSED

One of the more important functions of film and imaginative literature is that they also allow limited access to the unconscious. Psychoanalytic literary theories have interpreted Freudian concepts in various ways and explored their relationship to fiction since the 1920s. This view of literature acknowledges that the primary processes of the unconscious—substitution of one image, idea, action, or feeling for another through condensation, displacement, and symbolism—are always significant, if sometimes invisible, components of a reader–text exchange. Recognizing the enigmatic workings of the unconscious can help to unlock a text's richness and its depths, and can help to explain its attraction and its value to both an author and a reader. Reading can be regarded as a means by which we confront, manage, and/or negotiate our most basic impulses, desires, and fears (although these are often consciously inaccessible or largely incomprehensible) as if with hands protected by asbestos gloves.

On one very basic level of engagement, we look to literature and films to support and confirm our unconscious knowledges. But, as Marshall Alcorn and Mark Bracher (1985) argue, readers do more with literature than simply use it to affirm or replicate a preexisting and fixed construct of self.

It can also cause us to re-imagine and re-form this self and our view of the world in important ways:

Literary analysis engages students in activities that have the potential to re-form the self: by eliciting deep or unconsciously held primary values (introjects) and then bringing conscious reflection or competing values to bear on those values, the reading and interpretation of literature constitute an experience similar to that of confrontation and interpretation in psychoanalysis. (pp. 36–37)

Before we can take pedagogical advantage of this potential, we must first appreciate the power of such forces as desire, fantasy, pleasure, displeasure, disdain, anxiety, compliance, and resistance in shaping a reader–text exchange that is always unique. These forces can make the most carefully planned lesson and the most earnestly desired/desirable objectives of a literature lesson suddenly become elusive and even irrelevant in our classrooms when actual students encounter actual texts. We may have considered very carefully what we believe is "in" a particular text, what we want students to do to/with/because of it, what new insights or understandings we hope that they will come away with, and how we will measure whether they have done so. In fact, our students constantly remind us (if we pay attention to the messages they send) that we cannot predict or control what happens during or as a result of these encounters, and that we have only limited control over the new learning about/from a text that happens as a result of our selection of texts, our planning and teaching, and our assignments. This means that attempts to "teach" attitudes such as mutual respect, social justice, and harmony by exposing students to texts that embody exemplars of such ideals too often proves to be an ineffectual endeavor. We may mistakenly assume that because students can articulate the "theme" of a text to our satisfaction, their unconscious beliefs, biases, and prejudices have been altered.

I have become increasingly curious about the means by which unconscious anxieties, desires, and preoccupations color and shape any reading of a text, particularly with respect to issues that have their roots in the infant's primary family relationships (as any issue related to sex/gender necessarily does). We are often compelled to respond to a text less rationally and intellectually than we care to recognize, bringing to it powerful motivations to project onto it and take from it what we need to feel, imagine, and believe about sex/gender. Shoshana Felman argues very convincingly that ignore(ance) "is not a passive state of absence, a simple lack of information: it is an active dynamic of negation, an active refusal of information (Felman 1987, 79). It involves resistance to the text's potential to disturb what we already take to be true. Our students already know, both consciously and unconsciously, how gender works, what the "proper" roles and responsibilities of males and females are, and what to expect from relationships between males and females. A text does not simply "teach" new values and attitudes in an incremental sense, but must interfere, often in uncomfortable ways, with preexisting knowledges. We do our students a grave disservice when we make easy and unjustified assumptions about how they will create, understand, and respond to the multiple and contradictory meanings offered by a text. I hope to demonstrate that English Language Arts teachers are in a unique position to help students begin to recognize and confront the unconscious conflicts and anxieties surrounding sex/gender in texts, and thereby in their lives.

THE STUDY: HOW DO GENDERED READERS READ SEX/ GENDER?

Once I began to notice the pervasiveness of anxieties, hostilities, desires, pleasures, and rewards that surround sex/gender, identity, and relationships, I grew increasingly curious about them. I have been compelled to ask myself what it would mean if we were to acknowledge these unconscious forces as an integral part of what we do—and what we ask students to do—in schools. What might we say or do differently in our classrooms to help students surface, confront, and make sense (always provisionally) of the inevitable and powerful, but mostly unconscious and irrational, anxieties and hostilities surrounding cultural and personal definitions of sex/ gender, and their own experience of sex/gender in new ways? How might we help them to think outside of commonsense notions that have for so long structured and imposed the boundaries of the often emotionally volatile debates about sex/gender differences?

To explore these questions, I enlisted the help of 28 students in an English 23 class in a large city high school for six weeks and introduced them to seven short print texts and one movie.[3] My general procedure was to begin by reading the print selections aloud to the students as they listened and followed on their own copies. I then gave students a second copy of the text, which I had broken up into short sections interspersed with generous amounts of white space. I read the selection aloud once more, pausing at each break and asking them to respond by writing down any thoughts, questions, irritations, agreements, or associations that came to mind.[4]

PSYCHOANALYTIC INTERPRETATION

The students were receptive and cooperative. I came away with over 140 student responses that I have since attempted to interpret with the assistance of some fundamental psychoanalytic concepts. By interpret, I mean that I have tried to analyze them by interrogating the gaps, the silences, the elisions, and the contradictions within and among them, turning the responses that appeared at first glance to defy comprehension into questions.

As Shoshana Felman urges, I have attempted to heed Lacan's warning against trying to "understand" the meaning of a communication. He argues that it is a mistake to imagine that we can gain access to another person's meanings by way of intuition or empathy, or by trusting that the communicant has access to these meanings; and that all we need to do to ensure full understanding is to attend more closely to the meanings that s/he can already access and articulate (Felman 1987, 108). Rather, psychoanalysis teaches us that, because of the nature of the unconscious and the dynamics of repression, the author of a communication often has no more privileged access to its meaning than does the listener/reader. This does not mean, however, that we have no access at all to our own meanings or that we cannot help another person to gain a fuller access to their own. Mark Bracher outlines what interpretation means to him in the context of a writing classroom as follows:

Thus a properly psychoanalytic interpretation is any intervention, including silence, that advances the analysand toward articulating and assuming responsibility for his or her own desire. . . . It can take the form of helping the analysand make connections between different events or experiences, find patterns in them, or question what unconscious desire might be motivating these patterns. (1999, 135)

One way to partially circumvent the resistance to acknowledging and assuming responsibility for unconscious desire is to pay attention to the signifiers (the literal content of the message itself) rather than the signified (the meaning toward which the message is intended to point). Dylan Evans (1996) puts it this way:

Lacan argues that in order to interpret in this way, the analyst must take the analysand's speech absolutely literally (à la lettre). That is, the task of the analyst is not to achieve some imaginary intuitive grasp of the analysand's "hidden message," but simply to read the analysand's discourse as if it were a text, attending to the formal features of this discourse, the signifiers that repeat themselves (S2, 153). Hence Lacan's frequent warnings about the dangers of "understanding"; "the less you understand, the better you listen" (S2, 141). (Evans 1996, 89)

The kind of understanding that Lacan warns against is the kind of listening/ reading that seeks only to fit the Other's speech/writing into a pre-formed theory, which is a temptation that I have had to guard against continually.

I have been primarily interested in exploring the specificities of these responses, rather than formulating categories or typing male and female responses. In some cases the repetition of similar words, thoughts, or feelings has been important. However, for my purposes, it seems more important to look closely at specific student responses in an attempt to illustrate some valuable techniques for mining their truths and finding the sense in what might, at first glance, appear to be a nonsensical, thin, or indefensible

response. When I finished reading these responses in a fairly compressed
and intensive way, I was struck by several distinct and overarching impressions.

"IT IS JUST NOT AT ALL COMMON TO HAVE A PRINCESS RULE THE KINGDOM"

The most pervasive and insistent of these impressions is the degree to
which students' responses are suffused with sensitivity, discomfort, confusion, ambivalence, and denial about many issues that surround sexuation,
sexuality, and sex/gender. In general, they struck me as uncompromisingly
honest and uninhibited expressions of students' thoughts and feelings, as
the following comments in response to "The Little Prince" indicate (see
Appendix 1). Viper (m), for example, is confident that the stepmother is
indeed wicked:

> because she taught her son what he's not supposed to be taught so that
> he can't be ruler but she favored her daughter. It's like she'll do any-
> thing to arrive at her ambition, even favor one child more than the
> other. . . . She sounds like those kind of women that want everything
> to be equal when it comes to gender or more than equal. . . . In my
> opinion, she's a bad example of a mother.

His response communicates volumes about Viper's affective relationship to
feminism, "those kind of women," and mothers who stir up unnecessary
problems for everybody by teaching their daughters to resist the status
quo.[5]

Anxiety about the queen's efforts to destabilize the existing order and
resistance to her feminist notions is by no means limited to male readers.
Monica (f) is one of several female readers who resist the queen's efforts
to better her daughter's position. The underlying affect in this instance
seems to be passive resignation, while in other cases, opposition appears to
reflect a more active refusal of an alternative power structure:

> I think the wicked queen wasted her time trying to tutor her daughter
> and the prince in a different manner. It is just not at all common to
> have a princess rule the kingdom.

Doc's (m) reaction to "The Little Prince," on the other hand, emphatically defends and applauds the queen's plan and her motivation. His print-
ing for the last four words is larger and blacker, presumably to ensure that
I don't miss the emphasis:

> I don't think it right to call the queen "wicked" because she is looking
> out for her daughter. The prince is not a part of her. She does not care

about the prince. . . . She was trying to give her an advantage over the prince. I would do the same thing. Blood's thicker than water, and why should she care about the prince he is related by name alone. . . . I think the queen's a good mother and she is paving the way for her daughter to be successful. The queen used all her power **to help her daughter.**[6]

Mustang (f) takes another very different view of the queen. She introduces her conception of a mother's perfect and impartial love to help her interpret the queen's behavior, which she clearly finds unacceptable:

> Why would they be raised differently? I don't think its right to raise the children differently because it is saying you love one more than the other, in this piece the stepmother would rather see the daughter live a better life than the son. They should be equal.

The struggle to construct a sex/gendered identity, to perform it appropriately (Butler 1990) and with some degree of comfort, and to evaluate it in themselves and others plays a significant role in students' readings. Because parents, particularly mothers, are very powerful early models in this regard, characters such as the queen carry a potent affective charge. This is also true, however, of the king and the other fictional fathers they encounter in these texts. Alyssa's (f) response assesses the king not on his capabilities as a monarch, but on his deficiencies as a father, and judges him harshly for neglecting his children:

> Why did he rarely see them? He lives with them, doesn't he? Does he care about his son and stepdaughter. . . . What affairs are more important than his children. Does he forget he has children. Dealing with affairs is more important than his wife and two children. That's not right, what's the point of having a wife and children if you [don't?] see them often.

Raine's (f) response also makes it quite clear that she disapproves of the king's self-involvement and his neglect of his children. Quotation marks around key terms seem designed to ensure that a reader won't misunderstand the deliberately sarcastic tone of her comments:

> This is not unusual for a "important" father. Kids usually get neglected by these types. How come it is important in this story? It shows that the king is the "man." He supports the family & kingdom.

As with all of the selections that I asked them to read, "The Little Prince" apparently taps into unconscious structures and preoccupations about parental duty and parental love. Human beings inevitably come into the world as helpless infants with immature cognitive and perceptual systems. As a result, the affect evoked by the primary caregiver, and by characters who evoke this affect in subsequent textual encounters, is often more a product of fantasy and hallucination than it is a realistic image of the parent/caregiver. Lacking the perceptual acuity and the cognitive structures that later allow humans to process events and people in the world around them with less difficulty, infants are often overwhelmed by ambivalent feelings of love and hate toward the individuals who seem to arbitrarily refuse or deny satisfaction of primary physical and emotional needs. These people, who initially occupy a small circle around the infant, beginning with the mother/primary caregiver and moving outward to include the other parent and family members, are perceived through these filters of extreme helplessness and absolute dependence as larger-than-life and absolutely powerful. Reconciling these early impressions with the more mature and cognitively sophisticated images that we construct later in life is a very demanding and confusing task.

"THE REAL (SERIOUS) ISSUE ABOUT WOMEN AND MEN NOWADAYS"

"Behind Times" (Lautens, 1989) is another text that elicited a strong emotional reaction from students. Originally published as a newspaper humor column, Lautens' essay can fairly easily be read as a harmless, good-humored satire poking fun at popular culture, the generation gap, and aging "baby-boomer" parents. (See Appendix 2 for the complete text of "Behind Times.") The narrator relates that Stephen, his son, came home from a disco and told his parents that an attractive female stranger had pinched him on the behind as he danced. His horrified parents bewail the danger that he faced and give him advice about deterring such advances in the future.

A typical response to the story would likely involve amusement and pleasure, not anxiety and displeasure. Students offered a wide range of candid and impassioned reactions that often seem exaggerated when compared to the text itself. Theresa (f), for example, reads the story as a cautionary tale:

> I thought [the author] was using humor to get past the real (serious) issue about women and men nowadays. I think he wants us to think about the real issue that's happening instead of the humor behind it.

Mustang's (f) response clearly identifies the associations she drew on to construct her unique reading of Lautens' narrative and the emotional investments that made other readings inaccessible to her:

> When you are a victim of sexual advances it makes you feel like you are not important and that person sees you as an object. When I was

a victim it made me feel really guilty I don't know why but it was the worst.

"IT JUST PROVES THAT NO SEX/GENDER IS MORE SEX CRAVED THAN THE OTHER"

My second general observation concerns the paradoxically diversely uniform (uniformly diverse?) nature of the responses that surfaced. Students both "leaned into" and resisted stereotypical notions of sex/gender in a variety of ways, often at the same time. In almost all cases, when they drew on stereotypical images of masculinity and femininity to help them make sense of a text—whether they seemed to accept or to consciously reject these stereotypes—individual students put their own unique spin on them in ways that displaced and transformed them. It has become evident that every student's conception of sex/gender "stereotypes" that they bring to the reading of a text is a highly personalized construction, although the "fact" of their sex/gender is an extremely important determiner of these imaginary constructs.

Aaron's (f) response, for example, signals quite clearly that her reading is shaped by her preconceptions about the ways that adolescent girls, boys, and their parents (normally) behave. She uses her understandings about how "guys" and "chicks" relate to one another and how sex/gender operates in families and in adolescent dating/sexual encounters to analyze and critique "Behind Times." She is gratified that Stephen behaves differently than one might have anticipated:

> The one thing I liked about this story was that Stephen didn't drop his date for the chick that pinched him on the bum because some guys would drop there date and go to the chick that flirted with them. The thing I dislike is that he told his parents what happened. If it was someone else, I don't think they would tell there parents.

"Someone else," apparently the prototypical teenager, would not volunteer to share personal information with her/his parents.

Ninja (m) appears to have used similar images of "guy," "girl," "mother," "dad" and "family" to construct his reading and arrive at a similar understanding. However, the details and nuances of the images that he draws on to create adventurous, nonchalant males, a serious, concerned mother, and father–son jokiness and caring color his response in quite a different way than Aaron's:

> I found it unreal, in most cases he probably would have either liked it or if he didn't just kinda dance away. Also, even if he did I dought [doubt] he would make such a big deal about it and tell his parents to.

And whose dad would say any of those things about it anyway. . . . I think the author is trying to use humor to show how a girl & mother might react to the situation. Like if a girl would be touched by a guy she might freak out and take it like that but a guy wouldn't. In real life a father most likely would have been proud or just bugged his son if that happened to him. He wants us to think how different males & females think about sexual advances. . . . The thing that bothers me though is the fact that if a male makes a sexual advance to a girl its a big bad thing but if a female does it to a guy its no big deal. . . . The author's opinion is that guys should be able to take sexual harasement just the way girls do without it being a big weird thing. The thing that is stupid is that if a guy were to react like that people would think he's gay or stupid or something like that which I think is stereotypical. So, I would agree with the author's point of view.

Viper (m) is one student who sees the text as working to counter stereotypical representations of sex/gender and reinforcing his own liberal-humanist view:

It never changed my ideas. It just proves that no gender is more sex craved than the other.

"IN A MARRIAGE THE WIFE REALLY DOES PORTRAY A WOLF ALWAYS STALKING HER PREY"

A third conception that I was forced to recognize with a new clarity (as my conjectures and suppositions above undoubtedly illustrate) was that I could not know with any certainty when, or to what extent, the feelings that I sensed were "in" students' readings, and when I was mapping my own readings (of the text, of the student, of my world or myself) onto their responses. In order to read students' responses to "The Griesly Wife," a poem by John Manifold (1978), for example, I employed my knowledge of violent and gruesome, but fairly innocuous, fairy tales such as "Snow White" and "Little Red Riding Hood." I also drew on my familiarity with many print and Hollywood versions of werewolf legends. (See Appendix 3 for the complete text of "The Griesly Wife.")

I was intrigued by the poem's enigmatic quality and the novelty of visualizing the action set against my conception of the exotic Australian outback. I felt an instinctive aversion to the image of an older man attempting to convince his virginal, reluctant young bride to submit passively to her wifely duty. This aversion is at least partly an effect of my exposure to and sympathy with feminist readings of literature and popular culture, but it would undoubtedly be valuable for me to explore other possible reasons, more closely related to my own history, for my antipathy.

In my reading, the poem is a marvelous distillation of some primal and atavistic male anxieties. It encapsulates the fear of unleashing an insatiable, rapacious female sexuality; the desire to own, protect, and ultimately annul female innocence as embodied in a woman unsullied by sexual knowledge; and a powerful need to deny female subjectivity. I saw an ironic justice in the husband's fate that apparently did not enter into students' readings.

Ninja's (m) response suggests that, as an unmarried adolescent, he is having difficulty deciding what to think about the relationship depicted in the poem:

> The husband seems like he is either uncaring or just trying to make it easier for his wife the best way he knows how. I think the bride might have took him to seriously or what he said as such a bad thing. I feel the wife might be a little crazy. . . . You'd think if you were newly married you would want to have sex with your husband or wife and certainly not kill them.

To my ear, it seems that Ninja is ambivalent about the reading he has constructed. He begins by admitting that the husband might be uncaring, but immediately resists, negates, softens, and/or erases that suspicion by introducing another possibility. This reading ascribes a great deal of the responsibility for a nasty incident to the wife, largely based on Ninja's understanding that any sane bride would "naturally" welcome sex with her husband.

Cosmo's (m) reading is sympathetic to the husband and assumes that the woman has deliberately created the persona of an innocent bride to conceal her "real self." However, Cosmo seems uncertain of the extent of the wife's culpability and appears receptive to the possibility that her motives and feelings may be innocent. While it is "odd" and mystifying that a new bride would kill her husband, her guilt is apparently limited to her failure to disclose vital information:

> I felt that the husband should have been told about her real self, he seemed like a concerned loving person. The wife should have told her husband about the dingo, but I don't know why she killed him. . . . It did seem odd to me because she obviously loved him so why kill him?

In Cosmo's view, although the text provides few clues about the bride's feelings, "she obviously loved him." This statement may simply suggest that Cosmo's reading doesn't attend to details, but it also seems plausible to me that his fantasies surrounding marriage require that he refuse the image of an unloving or murderous wife.

In Viper's (m) reading, the husband is an aggressor rather than a victim:

> It [the poem] has a scary kind [of] atmosphere like he's hunting his wife as the dingoes would. . . . I think the poem was weird because it

> talks about her turning into a dingo and I feel he will turn into one
> too because he slept with her. . . . Maybe he [the author] was sug-
> gest[ing] watch what you're getting yourself into.

The man is "hunting his wife," not "searching for" or "following" her.
The word "hunting" does not appear in the original text, while "searching
for" and "following" are repeated several times. Viper notes that he found
the poem "weird," and adds an interesting intimation that sexual contact
can be a vehicle for the transmission of infectious diseases—not just of the
body, but of the mind and spirit as well. He adds a note of anxiety and a
warning about injudicious involvements.

Mercedes' (f) response avoids/ignores/resists suggestions of violence. It
appears not to recognize the influence of fantasy, the horror genre in literature and movies, and werewolf legends. Instead, it draws on the conventions of realism to understand the poem. In this reading, the relationship
between husband and wife seems to be dysfunctional and abusive, but almost pedestrian. Mercedes' matter-of-fact tone is reminiscent of a psychologist or marriage counselor:

> My first reaction is a newly wed couple and she is still not use to
> sleeping with someone by her side. . . . I feel the husband is cruel and
> has no feelings toward his wife. The bride got back at her husband for
> being mean and cruel. . . . It sounds as if they never should have been
> married in the first place if he was going to treat her that way. This
> poem seems to be suggesting sex and how she was nervous and he
> couldn't handle it.

The last sentence expresses a nebulous discomfort about the implied sexual
activity and the husband's vaguely threatening behavior. In Mercedes' reading, the wife did not attack her husband, as other students suggested;
rather, she "got back at her husband for being mean and cruel." Mercedes
seems to view the young wife's nervousness as natural, while the husband's
insensitivity, impatience, and inability to "handle" her misgivings are pathological, rather than the reverse.

CONCLUSION

I began this study with an interest in exploring how adolescent readers
approach and interpret representations of sex/gender when they meet them
in an unfamiliar text. I wanted to know more about the mysterious processes that cause student readers to accept, internalize, modify, resist, and/
or reject outright the attitudes, knowledges, beliefs, images, and emotions
that arise during such an encounter. My initial premise was that students
necessarily draw on preexisting cognitive, imagistic, and affective knowledges to interpret a new text.

I began with a strong focus on sex/gender issues as they affect girls and women in our Western, patriarchal culture, while also recognizing that the complex and rigid cultural norms surrounding sex/gender, sexuation, and sexuality present problems for all students in our schools, no matter what their sex/gender or sexual orientation. As my study progressed and I immersed myself in reading students' responses to the texts I offered, I found that it became increasingly more difficult to retain a feminist focus, particularly in one narrow sense of the term as it denotes a political project designed to enhance the power and prestige of women.

At the time I undertook this work, my understanding of what it means to read had been influenced by my exposure to feminist and reader-response critical theories. It quickly became apparent to me, however, that while the work done in both of these directions has made significant contributions to understanding what happens when a (sexed/gendered) reader meets a text, both also have some blind spots. Students' comments about the texts that I asked them to read convince me that feminist and reader-response theories, on their own, fall short in the task of helping us to recognize the desires and investments that can reveal themselves in our readings when we pay close attention to the linguistic choices that we make.

It was not until my study was well under way that I fully appreciated the contribution that psychoanalytic theories can make to illuminating these blind spots. During the course of my study, my conviction has grown that we need to do something very different if we want to reduce sexism, misogyny, homophobia, and other expressions of anxiety, hostility, and aggression among students in our schools. Providing students with more knowledge, more explicit instruction, and, in our English classes, with more fiction that presents exemplars of positive attitudes and values that we hope our students will embrace is not the only nor even the best solution. A superficial study of Western history is enough to convince me that these problems have been peculiarly resistant to solutions premised on philosophical ideals of justice and Judeo-Christian religious teachings about love.

I believe that much of what we have traditionally done in the name of promoting equity and harmony may in fact have an opposite effect. Psychoanalytic theories convince me that when we disavow and repress feelings and images that come to us through the Real and Imaginary registers, reshaping and distorting them according to the demands of the Symbolic Order, we give them more power to shape our behavior than they have once we recognize and own them as the good, bad, and ugly ingredients in the psychic stew that makes us unique.

This study is the first step in an effort to expand the definition and the scope of both reader-response and feminist theories of reading. It has laid the groundwork for an approach to literature and media texts in our classrooms that would radically alter the theoretical underpinnings of English Language Arts curriculum documents, evaluation strategies designed to measure the extent to which the outcomes recommended in those documents are being met, and the activities and assignments that a teacher plans on Sunday night for the upcoming week's lessons. Reader-response theories have become integral to the way we imagine our lessons proceeding and the way we evaluate students. Feminism, queer theory, and postcolonial theories have helped us to create and hold in our minds, as we plan and teach these lessons, a never-ending vision of achieving a just and caring society in which all members are encouraged and helped to reach their full potential, unhindered by racism, prejudice, and intolerance. Because there has been very little work done to this point exploring what English Language Arts instruction would look like, exactly, if we were to take advantage of the potential of psychoanalytic theories, it seemed to me that the present research is a necessary first step in exploring the viability of a psychoanalytic approach to English Language Arts classes. A crucial next step, I believe, would be to work with a smaller group of students and to talk to them about the value of viewing their own readings through a psychoanalytic lens. I would do this gently and carefully, by asking students first to respond to a new text in whatever manner it seemed to demand, and then spending some time with them helping them to re-read what they have written. I would not introduce psychoanalytic terminology at this point, but I would introduce them to what would be, for most of them, some new strategies for thinking about their responses. This would involve asking them to concentrate less on the text as an object of study and more on attempting to identify their own desires and resistances with respect to the text.

I strongly believe that adolescents are preoccupied with the work of constructing, reinforcing, and revising an identity, and that a crucial aspect of this process involves responding to and integrating information and feedback, from earliest infancy, about who they are as sex/gendered individuals, and striving for some degree of comfort around the Oedipal passage. This is a difficult and uncertain process which causes many of us to feel vulnerable, defensive, anxious, and sometimes hostile, but which becomes particularly problematic for an adolescent. It seems important to me to create the opportunity and the psychological safety in our classrooms that would support and promote students' efforts to negotiate these inescapable developmental tasks with reference to the new texts they meet.

APPENDIX 1: "THE LITTLE PRINCE" BY SUNITI NAMJOSHI

The wicked stepmother married a king who already had a son, and within a year she gave birth to a child, this time a daughter. / Both the children were healthy and affectionate, and good-natured and kind, and fond of one another. But this wicked woman had an extraordinary ambition: she herself had married a king, but she wanted her daughter to reign alone. / To this end she brought up the children. The princess was tutored to assume the sovereignty of her possible kingdom, while the prince was taught to be demure and shy, docile and gentle. / The king rarely saw them; he was immersed in the affairs of the kingdom. / One day, the wicked queen fell on her knees and begged the king for a small favor. "That depends," said the king, "What do you want?" "You have two children," she said, "Let the more capable rule the kingdom." "That's nonsense," said the king, but she was persistent. "Set the tests," she said. The king refused. But she kept on nagging until the king concurred. / It could do no harm, and it would teach her a lesson. They set the tests: hunting, tennis and mathematics, and a knowledge of the law. The princess won. The prince failed, or nearly failed, the entire set. The king was very angry, but he was also angry with his own son, so he kept his word. / Fortunately, the citizens had more sense. They all rose up as one man and yelled at the palace gates, "We will not be ruled by a woman." / They hauled out the prince and set him on the throne. The wicked queen and her unlucky daughter were exiled forever. And thus, order was restored, and justice done.

APPENDIX 2: "BEHIND TIMES" BY GARY LAUTENS

Our Stephen (who is eighteen) came home from a disco the other evening with distressing news: while minding his business on the dance floor, some girl he had never seen reached over and pinched him on the bum.

According to the account we received, the assaulter was about twenty, had a dynamite figure and gave Stephen a cheeky grin when he turned in total surprise.

Fortunately, Stephen was with a date, so the whole sordid business went no further, but Stephen's mother and I were seething, of course.

Can a young lad no longer boogie in safety on the hardwood surfaces of this city? Must he keep his wits about him and his vitals protected even during the intricacies of The Bump to make certain no lusting female, half-crazed by the sight of his Pierre Cardin loungewear, takes unwanted liberties with his person?

For someone of my generation, it's totally unthinkable. Why, when I was Stephen's age, a male person could fox trot, waltz and dip to his heart's content in the school gymnasium without fear of being womanhandled every time he box-stepped past a dark corner.

In all my years of swinging and swaying with Sammy Kaye, not once did I have to ward off the impudent grope or the lecherous pat. Women respected men for their minds then, and understood when we told them we were "saving" ourselves for marriage.

No more apparently.

Perhaps this young creature mistook you for somebody else," I suggested hopefully to my eldest. "Or else it was an accident."

"I don't think so," Stephen replied. "I think I can tell a deliberate pinch when I feel one, and she definitely smiled at me."

"You don't suppose she was in the middle of snapping her fingers to the music when your bottom happened to get in the way, do you?"

"No."

"Perhaps she works in a clothing store and was feeling the texture of your trousers. That's how they do it, you know, between the fingers."

"She pinched more than cloth," Stephen insisted.

"This is even worse than I suspected," I said. "If you eliminate the music and the cloth, it means she was interested in only—my God! Thank heaven you were with somebody. If you had been alone, it's anybody's guess what might have happened to you."

Stephen shot back an answering nod to indicate he had, indeed, thought about the possibilities.

Unlike other males his age who might have wept and made their complexions blotchy after such a harrowing experience at the hands of a female stranger, Stephen remained composed, and I was proud of him.

"I don't want this one unfortunate incident to change your attitude toward women," I cautioned. "There are lots of them out there who can control their hands at a dance and not get out of line. However, as a precaution, I think you should take some preventative steps to avoid similar pawings in the future."

"Like what?" he asked.

"First, I'd buy a pair of trousers that are a size or two too big. You're just asking for trouble if you wear form-fitting ones in front of some sexually liberated, twenty-year-old female who is only interested in a one-night stand.

"Next, for extra protection, put a thick hankie in the back pocket of the baggy trousers. Not only will it give a lumpy appearance that should be as good as a cold shower to any female out for a good time, it will provide protection in the event she still tries to get fresh during a Barry Manilow number.

"Finally, try not to turn your back on a female if she is pawing the floor with one foot, has steam coming out of both nostrils and spits in her hands as she walks in your direction. She's obviously up to no good."

Stephen said he would weigh my words carefully because, "I don't think any one in the country knows more about turning off women than you do."

It was difficult holding back the tears. It's not often an eighteen-year-old son pays his father such a glowing tribute.

APPENDIX 3: "THE GRIESLY WIFE" BY JOHN MANIFOLD

"Lie still, my newly married wife,
Lie easy as you can.
You're young and ill accustomed yet
To sleeping with a man."

The snow lay thick, the moon was full
And shone across the floor.
The young wife went with never a word
Barefooted to the door.

He up and followed sure and fast,
The moon shone clear and white.
But before his coat was on his back
His wife was out of sight.

He trod the trail wherever it turned
By many a mound and scree,
And still the barefoot track led on,
and an angry man was he.

He followed fast, he followed slow,
And still he called her name,
But only the dingoes of the hills
Yowled back at him again.

His hair stood up along his neck
His angry mind was gone,
For the track of the two bare feet gave out
And a four-foot track went on.

Her nightgown lay upon the snow
As it might upon the sheet,
But the track that led from where it lay
Was never of human feet.

His heart turned over in his chest,
He looked from side to side,
And he thought more of his gumwood fire
Than he did of his griesly bride.

And first he started walking back
And then began to run.
And his quarry wheeled at the end of her track
And hunted him in turn.

Oh, long the fire may burn for him
and open stand the door,
And long the bed may wait empty:
He'll not be back any more.

NOTES

1. All references to the students who participated in my study are self-selected pseudonyms.

2. At this point, I want to clarify my use of two terms, *text* and *sex/gender*. I use the word "text" in its most inclusive sense—for the purposes of this discussion, a text may be a novel, a film, a curriculum, or any communicative object, action, or event. A reader is a person who engages with a text regardless of its format. "Sex/gender" is a term that commingles all the meanings attached to both sex and gender. It recognizes that neither word on its own does justice to the complex of biological givens and social/cultural prescriptions and prohibitions that constitute sex/gender. I will continue to use the clumsy conjoined term to remind myself and readers of this paper of the complexities of what might at first glance appear to be two simple, discrete, and self-evident categories.

3. In Alberta, Canada, English 23 is designed primarily for second-year high school students who are not working toward university matriculation.

The eight texts I used include the following: *To Wong Foo, Thanks for Everything! Julie Newmar*, directed by Beeban Kidron (Willowdale, Ontario: MCA Universal Home Video Canada, 1995); Robert Browning, "Porphyria's Lover," in *Literary Experiences*, ed. John E. Oster, Margaret Iveson, and Jill McClay (Scarborough, Ontario: Prentice-Hall, 1989), 202–203; Rex Deverell, "Switching Places," in *Eureka!*, ed. Jacquie Johnston Lewis and Dianne Warren (Regina, Saskatchewan: Coteau Books, 1994), 95–128; Gary Lautens, "Behind Times," in *Literary Experiences*, ed. John E. Oster, Margaret L. Iveson, and Jill K. McClay (Scarborough, Ontario: Prentice-Hall, 1989), 303–305; John Manifold, "The Griesly Wife," in *Collected Verse* (St. Lucia, Queensland: University of Queensland Press, 1978); Suniti Namjoshi, "The Little Prince," in *Gender Issues*, ed. Greta Hoffman Nemiroff (Scarborough, Ontario: Prentice-Hall, 1993), 303–305; Alden Nowlan, "The Fall of a City," in *Gender Issues*, ed. Greta Hoffman Nemiroff (Toronto: McGraw-Hill Ryerson, 1993); Diane Wakoski, "Medea the Sorceress," in *The Norton Anthology of Literature by Women*, ed. Sandra M. Gilbert and Susan Gubar (New York: W.W. Norton and Co., 1996), 2150–2152.

4. This general procedure was modified slightly, however, particularly with respect to the feature-length movie *To Wong Foo, Thanks for Everything! Julie Newmar*.

5. Because students' sex/gender is significant in many ways, and because many of them (particularly the girls) chose pseudonyms that resist prevailing norms about "boys' " and "girls' " names, I will indicate the sex/gender of each participant by placing (f) or (m) immediately after their pseudonym.

6. In all cases, I have reproduced the students' responses as closely as possible to the way they were written. Because it would be unnecessarily intrusive, I have chosen not to indicate each time unusual spelling, punctuation, and so on is their own, but I will indicate any additions, deletions, or changes that I make.

REFERENCES

Alcorn, Marshall, Jr., and Bracher, Mark. 1985. Literature, Psychoanalysis, and the Re-Formation of the Self: A New Direction in Reader-Response Theory.

Publications of the Modern Language Association of America 100(3): 342–354.

Bracher, Mark. 1999. *The Writing Cure: Psychoanalysis, Composition, and the Aims of Education.* Carbondale: Southern Illinois University Press.

Butler, Judith. 1990. *Gender Trouble: Feminism and the Subversion of Identity.* New York: Routledge.

Eco, Umberto. 1994. *Six Walks in the Fictional Woods.* Cambridge, Mass.: Harvard University Press.

Evans, Dylan. 1996. *An Introductory Dictionary of Lacanian Psychoanalysis.* London: Routledge.

Felman, Shoshana. 1987. *Jacques Lacan and the Adventure of Insight: Psychoanalysis in Contemporary Culture.* Cambridge, Mass.: Harvard University Press.

Lautens, Gary. 1989. Behind Times (1978). In *Literary Experiences,* ed. John E. Oster, Margaret L. Iveson, and Jill K. McClay (pp. 303–305). Scarborough, Ontario: Prentice-Hall.

Manifold, John. 1978. The Griesly Wife. In *Collected Verse* (pp. 10–11). St. Lucia, Queensland: University of Queensland Press.

Namjoshi, Suniti. 1993. The Little Prince. In *Gender Issues,* ed. Greta Hoffman Nemiroff (p. 103). Scarborough, Ontario: Prentice-Hall.

Wright, Elizabeth. 1998. *Psychoanalytic Criticism: A Reappraisal* (2nd ed.). New York: Routledge.

Part V

Media Education

Chapter 9

Teaching Some Cruel Symptoms

J. C. Couture

The wager is . . . that helping subjects analyze their responses to cultural artifacts and discourses can provide an opportunity for them to begin to work through some of their more debilitating and destructive conflicts of identification and desire, and that such working through can open the way not only to greater *jouissance* for these subjects but also through the resulting changes in their attitudes and behavior, to benefit social change. (Bracher, 1993, 191–192)

For I know that nothing good dwells in me, that is, in my flesh; for the wishing is present in me, but the doing of the good is not. For the good that I wish, I do not do; but I practice the very evil that I do not wish. (Romans, 8: 18–20)

From the corporate boardroom to the public school classroom, suturing oneself into the project of "saving the Earth" has become *de rigueur*. Yet, the ironies and contradictions that weave the popular imaginary project of "being environmentally aware" are all too readily apparent. A recent television ad features a middle-aged male suburbanite, driving his four-by-four Sport Utility Vehicle (SUV). As he smiles into the camera, he beams that his truck is "my way of enjoying the outdoors and exposing my children to nature." With half of the arable land in Latin America now devoted to coffee production, pressure to open up marginal lands for agriculture is growing. To draw attention to this fact, the Seattle-based chain of specialty coffee shops, Starbucks, sponsored a coffee symposium at the annual meeting of the American Association for the Advancement of Science that examined the implications of increased coffee exports on Latin America's ecology (Haysom 1997).

One response to the psychic demand to "save the world" is the work of teachers to incorporate media literacy in the classroom. Configured as a modernist project of encouraging students to become "critical viewers," the idealized student is one who possesses "a skeptical eye," one who can see behind the naïve, subjective looking that we do. In specific curricular terms this involves developing strategies for students to "see" behind the camera, and for helping them fully understand how reality is constructed through codes of production that circulate particular ideologies and values.[1]

"DESIRABLE" TEXTS IN MEDIA LITERACY

Like many social studies teachers in Canada, I have explored environmental issues and the deforestation of the tropical rainforests for a number of years. A central difficulty in this work is obtaining learning resources that motivate students to engage environmentalism and ecology. The videos available to schools are careful to infuse teacherly values of "balance" and "objectivity." The result is the genre of the "educational video" that infantilizes students. As one student aptly put it, "the videos we watch in school are made to be watched only in school—nowhere else would you be caught dead watching this stuff." Clearly, the educational video limits the opportunity to engage students in visceral and immediate ways that appeal to their values and affective investments (Grossberg 1992).

For teachers committed to working in media literacy using artifacts of popular culture, two central questions emerge: *What is a legitimate text?* and *How can a text be engaged to render new meanings and possibilities?* Kellner argues that educators should draw on popular culture in an effort to create a new generation of students who are prepared to read and re-work everyday texts (print and digital) in order to repopulate them with meanings that promote critical thought and social justice: "Critical media pedagogy can thus serve as part of a process of social enlightenment, producing new roles for critical and public intellectuals" (Kellner 1995, 340).

Increasingly, my work with students is devoted to engaging them in the analysis of a medium that deploys a common genre they find so appealing: the music video. This chapter explores how a particular artifact of popular culture, the video *Supermodels in the Rainforest*, raises questions about the ways that I (m)ask myself in the classroom (jagodzinski 1996, 38) within the "impossible positionalities" that make up my teaching. I first stumbled on the video in late 1995 when I received an advertisement billing the program as a fund-raising effort to raise public awareness about the destruction of the rainforest. Marketed as a "celebration of music, beauty, and life," the video was a one-hour-long polysemic text that claimed to be a "video documentary."[2] But how could I justify buying such a video for my social studies classroom? The superego dictated my crime before I could commit it: "What are you thinking—you are a teacher—you can't possibly use this!" Yet, as Žižek (1994) draws from Lacan, "the art of looking for excuses is boundless"(p. 68). So here is one excuse. In 1995, the video received Gold Awards at both the Worldfest-Houston International Film Festival and the Worldfest-Charleston International Film Festival. The video is scaffolded around a series of eight "photo shoots" featuring each model. Interspersed in each "shoot" is a brief commentary by one of the models, a narrative dubbed by a commentator who describes a variety of threats to the globe because of the destruction of the rainforest. Each model is given three minutes of exposure (ex-posure), either dancing or being photographed for a calendar with the same name as the video.

Given my background in feminism and psychoanalysis, and my social position as a middle-class, heterosexual male, I point to myself as *suspect*, paradoxically located as one who can draw on the cultural capital of the master signifiers circulated by the Discourse of the University. This plurality of signifiers acts as a way to support the economy of the Phallus within my writing and teaching through the continual approbation and disapprobation of S_1 ("the Truth").[3] As a heterosexual, middle-aged male who moves within the communities of the academy and public schools, I remain privileged as a member of the "chattering classes."[4]

What follows argues that media literacy education using artifacts of popular culture cannot be undertaken without acknowledging how desire is always at work within the network of looks and gazes present within the classroom. These desires are activated in a variety of ways and erupt in moments that remind us that no one individual holds the Phallus. Thus, teaching needs to be open to its own opposites: to de-suture its own master signifiers to de-objectify the objects of knowledge.[5]

My work with students viewing *Supermodels in the Rainforest* (Astral Video Productions 1994) takes up Lacan's (1988) recognition that if images are "our animal weakness,"(Žižek 1994, 88), then, a central problem in teaching media studies has to be about the teacher's paradoxical relationship of desire with the specular images that invigorate and mediate our (im)possible relationship with the Real. In particular, the following discussion explores the two forms of the split subject or separation I encounter in the Symbolic register: hysteria and obsession. I argue that teaching, occupying a place in between the Discourse of the University and the Discourse of the Master, invariably locates the subject within the tension between *having not enough pleasure* (hysteria) and *too much pleasure* (obsession). Lured as I am by the video, I realize that "you can refuse what you despise but you can also refuse what you like too much" (Soler 1996, 253). In scenes from the video, I will argue that both myself and my students are caught in what Žižek (1996) calls *la traversée du fantasme.* (117). From Žižek, I will argue that working with *Supermodels in the Rainforest* was, for me, a question of learning how to "gain the minimum of distance toward the phantasmatic frame that organizes one's enjoyment" and then to momentarily "suspend its efficiency" (Ibid.). From Žižek I draw the impulse to suggest that my attraction to and enjoyment of *Supermodels in the Rainforest* is not the enemy. Obviously, my libidinal investment in the video is one that is lured all the way down. The point is not to get rid of *jouissance* as Žižek argues, but to "unhook" *jouissance* from the phantasmatic frames which support its presence in my affect. Such an act of "unhooking" will offer a new way of seeing the phantasm as an "undecidability" that remains part of my inertia and momentum as a teacher. According to jagodzinski (1996, 30), Lacan was both his own analysand and analyst.

To write and teach in a language that produces "double writing" is a ploy that I undertake with some trepidation. Rather than being someone who is *supposed to know* (the position of the teacher in the Discourse of the University where the teacher invokes the students to learn more and more), or as someone who has the power over what is kept secret (the master holding S_1), I read myself as the neurotic o(su)ffering the symptoms of hysteria and obsession. These symptoms are emblematic of the neurotic defending against an incompatible idea.[6]

In what follows I describe my work with the video in a high school classroom not as an effort to mediate or negotiate a coherent, rational "teacher identity" back into the classroom. Rather, I take up the (pre)text that Žižek (1994) draws from Lacan that "the only truly ethical stance is to assume fully the impossible task of symbolizing the Real, inclusive of its necessary failure"(p. 200). In this context, I offer a description of an empty set—what may be a ridiculous pretext for showing what desire is; more desire. "Desire is desire for a desire" (p. 211). Then, my savage (w)rites against the Discourse of the University.

The first segment of the video features the international model Frederique van der Wahl, known principally for her role in *Victoria's Secret* catalogs and more currently her line of fragrances. Framed against the backdrop of the Costa Rican rainforest, Frederique's allure, for me, is configured around the snare of vision and sound. Following is an excerpt from a monologue she delivers halfway through her portion of the video.

What is happening to the rainforest is really terrible, is really disastrous, for example in certain places. I mean hearing about certain places I can't name because of the government guards behind me where 80 to 90% will be gone in a few years because of capitalism and certain issues that are not that important . . . it will affect everything in our world today . . . I think people should fight for this cause.

A diegesis is constructed around the rhyming effects of music track, narration, and the pastoral foreground. Here we are in the realm of what was.

Soon we will be confronted with the disaster of the cutting down of the rainforest. Frederique's reference to the off-camera "government guards" introduces an extradiegetic element to the scene. Here is an evoked off-screen presence that is a stand-in for the Big Other, the monster that threatens "the immaculate dream."

The polysemic quality of the video is further evident in this excerpt when one considers the dialogic play of narration utterance, music, and location. The fusion of narration, the Duran Duran song, and the background rainforest shots act to construct "spatial and temporal indicators . . . fused into one carefully thought-out, concrete whole," that build a sense of interconnectedness of time and space, or what Bakhtin called "chronotopes" (Bakhtin 1984, 84).

In the dialogic construction along axes of meaning, the *Supermodels* video plays these axes: nature-technology, intruder-native, and sensual-mechanicized. As Richard Middleton (1995) has done in his reading of gender construction and agency in the group Eurythmics' hit recordings, one can see in the *Supermodels* video the dialogic play between audience subjectivity, the interactive voices (the diegetic and extradiegetic narration) set against music background and the visual settings.

In this sequence the transition from shot to shot is saturated with the mediations of the Duran Duran lyrics from the song "Come Undone" that circulate around the Imaginary invocations of an "immaculate dream made breath and skin" and the invocation to fight for the rainforest. On first brush there is a haunting, enigmatic quilting of a rhetorical question for me: who is the subject of this "immaculate dream made breath and skin"? My response is to be overcome with active anaclitic desire, wanting to possess the image of Frederique while I rationalize "she is just an image."

But *she* is *an Other* that remains (for me) the object that is left outside the image. I struggle here for what Lacan would signal as the *point de capiton*, a signifier that will button down my desire for her (Bracher 1993, 29). As the Duran Duran song plays on I want to be *the One* for Frederique, *the One* who will be there when she "comes undone." Such a desire is the passive anaclitic form of Symbolic Order desire (to be the bearer of the master signifiers that the Other wants). I can feel the music and video work on me as I see myself being the one for the Other. Then I snap back. *Jouissance* fades.

I draw on Žižek's (1994) reading of my desire to be both *the One* for Frederique, the obsessional neurotic and the hysteric. "The obsessional neurotic wants to prevent, by means of compulsive rituals, the Other's desire from emerging in its radical heterogeneity, as incommensurable with what he thinks he is for himself" (p. 177). For the obsessional neurotic, the catastrophe is that everything depends on him. For the hysteric the catastrophe is that nothing depends on him. Perhaps this is where the subliminity of the video clip of Frederique slides for me; as a traumatic crossing in-between the voided Imaginary possibilities of being the *no-thing* and *every-thing* for Frederique. I am denied any possibility of the subliminity of "love." She cannot fall in love with me since I am nothing more than myself—a fan who looks from afar. She remains "uncomed and done"—a cruel reversal of my desire.[7]

This scene also raises the issue of the role of the voice in *Supermodels in the Rainforest*. As Mary Ann Doane suggests, the voice in cinema acts, as Lacan calls it, as the "invocatory drive" (*la pulsion invocatrice*) (Stam et al. 1992, 60). The voice remains infrequently used throughout the film. Indeed, except for Frederique's commentaries, a secondary narrator provides the bulk of the narrative text. A metadiegetic level is thus inserted in-between the primal models and the modernist impulse to "document" the facts. The voice-overs provide numerous statistics and punctuate the dance scenes with the Discourse of the University. Throughout, the video struggles to maintain fluidity between the voice-overs of the models and the project of educating the viewer. Bakhtin would frame this tension as being between the "centripetal" forces of the video as a documentary/travel log and the "centrifugal forces" (Bakhtin 1986) of the enigmatic bathing-suit shots and music. As one female student remarked, "This is pretty weird stuff here—striptease Greenpeace."

Without the secondary narration and the metonymy of the river as a means of transportation, the video would be less evocative. I draw on Fiske's (1996) metaphor of culture as a river of discourses. Within the flow of competing representations and events there is continuity and disjuncture as well as undercurrents and dominant flows.

Currents that had been flowing together can be separated, and one turned on the other, producing conflict out of the calmness. There are deep, powerful currents carrying meanings of race, gender, and sexuality, of class and age: These intermix in different proportions and bubble up to the surface as discursive "topics," such as "family values" or "abortion" . . . and these discursive "topics" swirl into each other—each is muddied with the silt of the others, none can flow in unsullied purity or isolation. (p. 7)

Reading Fiske's metaphor into the *Supermodels* video might seem over-determined given the preeminence in the video of the river scenes that run through the program. The lengthy dance scenes, juxtaposed against the scenes of devastation, were incongruous and difficult for the students to balance.

Consider Darja Lingenberg's (one of the models) explanation of the project as not some "normal bathing suit calendar . . . it is going to be beautiful and it is for a purpose." As the camera fades out from her sitting on the beach, a fade—it takes the viewer to her dancing on the beach at sunset, and then to her writhing around in a boat dressed in a body suit, complete with *faux* snake scale designs.

Mary Ann Doane (1991, 209–248) raises Freud's evocation of the torrid dark continent of Africa as a metaphor for female sexuality in the patriarchal code of imperial conquest and exploration. For me this is a reading of the video that reminds that there is virtually no reference made to the specific location of the video shoot. We are only obliquely told, in the credits and advertising material that accompanies the video, that it is shot in the Costa Rican rainforest. For Doane, a journey to "torrid zones" represents, for the West, a journey without maps or referents. Indeed, I would draw from Doane's claim that hot zones are the realm of the Imaginary— places where all things are possible in the mind of modernity.[8] As Pile and Thrift (1995, 90–91) argue, the imagination of the West is not configured around "the construction of the self around some arrogantly figured Other. Some blank hot zone of darkness"; rather, it is construed around "the cold hard facts" of a world where precision is necessary for survival and colonization.

THE RAINFOREST AS A STAIN IN THE REAL

Environmentalism is a symptom of an impossible demand we place on the world that remains as Other to us. Yet when we ask the world what it wants of us, the world's ambivalence remains beguiling. When countries such as Costa Rica attempt to create "nature preserves" these efforts are undermined by the hysteric hordes of tourists who travel to the parks to capture their beauty before they disappear. Consider Costa Rica's Manuel Antonio Park, a 1,700-acre reserve that was established in the mid-1980s (Ronter 1997). Now, with over 600 visitors a day, the ecology of the park is threatened. On the perimeter of the park there are over 100 hotels and bed-and-breakfast establishments. A marine reserve adjoining the park now attracts sports fishermen who pay $800 a day to catch a tuna. Casinos and luxury hotels are now in the works. The entire country is now seen as a leader in environmental protection—a media construct that has brought over 800,000 visitors a year and contributed $700 million to the Costa Rican economy in 1996. Tourism is now the country's main source of income. Can "eco-adventures" be the answer to Costa Rica's future? Searching for that pristine promise of untouched wilderness has rendered the 27 other Costa Rican parks a desired destination for increasing numbers of well-intentioned people who, by their very presence, destroy the future they want to preserve. Indeed, monkeys are attacking tourists in an effort to get their food. Park authorities developed plans to manage the monkey population in an effort to contain the problem. Tragedy is a master that enjoys its own reason.

There is ludic ironic justice in that even the monkeys are fighting back: a piece of the Real described by one of my students as the irony of "guerrilla-monkeys" fighting back. Lacan reminds us that only in the Imaginary is *contra-diction* possible. Can "guerrilla monkeys" become a

Figure 9.1
Cross-Reading the Discursive Fields of Bakhtin and Lacan

Type of Discourse (Bakhtin)	Authoritative	Internally persuasive	Idiolect	Discourse of madness (autolect)
Social Effects	CENTRIPETAL	Consensus	Dissensus	CENTRIFUGAL
Visual Economy	Invisible (the gaze)	Transparency (the look)	Uncanny	Grotesque
Source	The Big Other (the Father of Enjoyment)	Interpellated subjects	Feminine undecidability	Absolute otherness (does not lack)
Lacanian Register	Veiled Phallus	Symbolic	Imaginary	Real
Exemplar from *Supermodels*	The gaze (scopophlia: operation of the camera)	Frederique's monologue	Dance sequences, Mr. Dumma's alterity	Interview with rainforest guide

possibility that gives the hysteric some hope? Saving the rainforest has become a discursive "media event." As Fiske (1994) reminds us, "media events are sites of maximum visibility and maximum turbulence" where clarity is difficult if not impossible" (p. 7). Or, as Žižek (1994) indicates of the impossibility of communication: There is simultaneously not enough and too much communication in a world where contact is seen as a "by-product" of the late capitalist project to reveal the phantasmatic quality of real life (p. 210).

In the virtual "forest of desires" of *Supermodels in the Rainforest*, my students and I were in the confluence of discursive currents where desires are signified in relation to each others' "monstrous distortions" (ibid.). Following Bakhtin (1986), I import the construal of meaning in the Symbolic "structured in difference." *Supermodels* works as a polysemic text in its capacity to play not only along the dialogic axes of *natural-technology, preservation-destruction*, but more importantly in its ability to create the phantasm of presence by keeping the transcendental Phallus moving between the types of discourse that Bakhtin sees as generating a text "structured in difference." Given the wide range of responses from my students, it is evident that powerful eddies and undercurrents work through this polysemic text.

Figure 9.1 illustrates how the video works to create the discursive effects of drawing together centripetal trajectories or discursive currents of *madness* with *idiolect, internally persuasive*, and *authoritative* discourses. Further, student comments about the film will illustrate how our work with *Supermodels* moved across these discursive registers.

AUTHORITATIVE DISCOURSE

Both male and female students remarked that the film was "way too cheesy" and "an obvious ploy to make money, not save the rainforest." As one student asked rhetorically, "Can they expect a few bucks made from the video to make any difference?" Consistently, students turned against the authoritative discourse of the video and rejected its call to help the rainforest. "So I like nice breasts and send some jerk money for the video. What's he gonna do with the money—bribe government officials?" The students' comments raised the issue of context and location alluded to earlier. The video seems to be shot in a generic rainforest, located in no country in particular.

INTERNALLY PERSUASIVE

Students reacted very little to the statements made by the models, but more so to the "factoids" provided by the narrator. Students expressed dismay and frustration with the voiced-over text that made the situation "seem so hopeless," in one student's view. Another asked, "Fight for the rainforest? What is that supposed to mean?" Students were persuaded by the statistical evidence provided but consistently found the shots of rainforest destruction "made them sad." I was struck by several students' comments that the "statistics made me sad, the pictures made me angry."

IDIOLECT

Students were quite bewildered by the dance sequences and posed calendar shots. One female student commented that the video was nothing more than a "*Babewatch* in a jungle movie." Others saw the dancing as a "good way to hold people's attention." The dancing continued to disrupt students' reading of the video. "Just when I thought they were making a point some babe would pop up and prance around," complained one female student. Not surprisingly, what remained a recurring student comment was that the cameras seemed to spend more time on the models than on "the problem." What remains problematic throughout the video is that the possessing gaze of the male subject is never dismantled. Despite the claims by a few students that the dancing was "really art," few others were convinced.

DISCOURSE OF MADNESS

As the students remarked, there were moments in the film when "it all came together," and others that seemed "just plain bizarre." Several students remarked that the rainforest guide (Mr. Dumma) seemed "fake, like he was trying to be a native," while others said "he was too real to be faking." When Mr. Dumma says, "You can fool me in the city, I don't respect no man in the jungle," several students thought this was "silly macho stuff."

Many students said the dance sequences were totally "out of place" and "grotesque." Consider one female student's sarcastic comment, "Like I would go into a village of poor people and dance around in a two-hundred-dollar swimsuit . . . right?" The linkage between the dance performances and what they signified were widely variant among the students. It is problematic to suggest then that the dances as signifiers were quilted with the signified through the Phallus to create a presence of artistic creation or scopic pleasure for students.

For Lacan (1977), the *copula* created between the signifier and signified is the Phallus. The Phallus is the *is*, or being attributed to a thing (Oliver 1995, 75). If that is the case, then Fiske is right in asserting that the operation of the gaze is not something that exists in a vacuum, that in all discursive activity a river of meanings runs through representational ploys.[9]

INVIGORATING THE PLURALITY OF THE PHALLUS: TEXTUAL POACHING

While many students found the *Supermodels* video problematic, "textual poaching" offered fruitful techniques for students to reactivate the images in the video and "adapt these materials and weave them back into their everyday lives" (Jenkins 1992, 40). The steps that I suggested for students were drawn from Jenkins' strategies of "scribbling in the margins" where students write themselves into the text through recontextualizations, cross-overs, and other textual reworkings (pp. 162–177). *Recontextualization* involves writing in missing scenes or vignettes to extend the possibility of the action or characters carrying on outside of the offered text. One example was a student who described a story of one of the supermodels traveling to their community to "save our stinky sad little town from the pulp mill." Several students saw connections between the rainforest issue and the logging practices of the local pulp mill that holds a lease the size of Scotland.

Cross-overs were the most commonly used strategy by students. Loosely defined, cross-overs involve locating the characters in another story or context. Initially, I thought the students would find this the most difficult, but soon it became apparent that this strategy would be the most enjoyable for many of them. By putting the supermodels into circulation in other texts, primarily advertisements, students found ways to locate the underlying commercialization of the video. As several students remarked, "the message of the video is beauty sells, so why not make this really obvious?" Of the class of 24 students, 14 chose this approach (12 females, 2 males).

For Fiske (1987), tactics within the contradictory pleasures of the "carnivalesque" is the way that ideology works through the *signifieds* and *subjectivity* to mediate meanings produced in culture. What quickly became apparent in the students' work was their capacity and interest for reworking the *Supermodel* motif with intersections from other locations in print media such as advertisements for cosmetics and "beauty products." Female students engaged these opportunities more than male students. Several students echoed the comment by one student, Jamie, that "these are women that work hard at being seen a certain way. I like doing that sometimes too but I know in the end it is just a game. So why not have some fun with this?" Jamie's ad, "Don't Cry for me Costa Rica" was, as she explained, "something that popped out at me when I saw an ad for Maybelline eye shadow." Although Jamie found the video "rather crazy," she thought "the message was really good." She explained her use of the Maybelline product in her ad, "so even though I use this stuff, I realize it is just as much fun as parading around in a video like this." In late capitalism, the subject is neither the coherent cherub of reason nor the devil child of chaos, but perhaps an amalgam of the two.[10]

Two male students produced rather clever "cross-over" responses. "Extinction is forever, your beauty isn't . . . Be a Revlon Girl" was Mark's attempt to "show how trivial the whole thing is—being a supermodel and makeup and stuff." His explanation to the class raised some eyebrows and a few questions from female students like Laurie. She challenged him, "Why do you say everything about makeup is trivial? If there were trucks in this would you be so critical?"[11]

Students engaged the video and the textual poaching opportunities from a multiplicity of locations. Against Ben's effort to "not take things so seriously" was Sandra, who had tears in her eyes when she was explaining her poster to the class. She was especially struck by a billboard she saw in town that advertised Caterpillar Tractors with the slogan, "There are no easy answers, only intelligent solutions." Active in the school's recycling program and the SPCA chapter in the community, Sandra worked several hours on her poster. "When I saw the image of the peasants trying to stop the bulldozer in the video, I knew right then what I was going to do for a poster."

Consider Sandra's comment to the class about her poster:

What really upset me watching the video was how the animals were being hurt too. These animals reminded me of my two cats at home. So I just had to put that image of the monkey in my ad to make this point. Kind of a ghost the way he turned out. I thought that was the best part of how my poster turned out.

There is a quip that "postmodernism is nihilism without tears." I resist such a dismissal of an intellectual impulse that brings students to a location in their own lives where they can see the simultaneity of hope and despair. Sandra's love of animals, which she spoke of in class, reminds me that it is difficult to know which "button" will activate students' affective investments. I am reminded of Carly's playful ironizing of the Duran Duran lyrics to the song "Come Undone" (cited earlier). As Carly explained to the class, "This used to be my favorite song, but now it seems so dumb." Carly rewrote the lyrics in a caustic critique:

> Title: Supermodel Undone
>
> Mine, unbelievable dream made of
> dollars and cents,
> I've been waiting for it. Signed by my own hand.
> Congratulations, I thought were in order.
> (Can't ever keep from going out of the spotlight,
> Can't believe you're taking my contract away.)
>
> Chorus:
> Who do you call, who do you blame, when you don't
> get signed . . .
> Wish I could get lost in a camera filled room,
> everything will be all right if I could just sign a contract now.

Clearly, students like Carly had no difficulty problematizing the participation of the supermodels in this video, although, as one student suggested, "Who are we to judge them? We would do the same . . . make money any way we could." A male student asked, "But how do we know for sure that they did this for money? We should find out before we judge." Generally, the female students saw the issue of "being paid" as irrelevant. "The real issue is what kind of message this is sending to people," complained a student in frustration.

CLOSING IN ON MY TEACHERLY SYMPTOMS

Using polysemic texts such as *Supermodels* allows for what Jay calls for: using the eye as a source of disruptive energy—"*l'oeil, c'est la force*"(Jay 1994, 565). Lacan would ask teachers to invigorate their media practices with these questions: Whose desire and hopes are articulated? Whose are repressed? What is the specular economy that produces such psychic investments? In a small way, textual poaching the *Supermodels* video gave students the opportunity to engage the range of discourses embedded in

Supermodels while making meaning for themselves. What the students produced is not resistance, Fiske (1993) would say, but the "desire to control one's immediate condition" (p. 78).

In recalling Lacan's four discourses of cultural criticism (the Discourses of the University, Analyst, Hysteric, and Master), it is clear that all modes of signification act to valorize and repress different facets of psychic life (knowledge production, ideals, self-division, and *jouissance*) (Bracher 1993, 53). What I have applied so far in my reading of *Supermodels* slides in-between the Discourses of the University and the Analyst, which are all veiled, perhaps, by the master signifiers of cultural criticism and media literacy (I stand again in danger of creating a new Discourse of the Master). Drawing on the analytical tools of the University, I have attempted to construct my analysis around systems of knowledge. The tropes of humanities scholarship and scholarly footnotes are exemplars of this discursive move in this chapter. I stand mindful of Bracher's (1993, 78–80) caution that cultural criticism should produce social change, not simply produce more knowledge. Empowering students and myself to act *more responsibly* was a project caught up in the return of *objet a* as our *jouissance* spilled out from our working with the polysemic text of the *Supermodels* video.

In other ways I have appropriated the Discourse of the Master as I deploy criticisms of eco-tourism as a twisted form of capitalism; as I play the game of cultural critic who just might know how to save the rainforest, remake the world, and protect supermodels from their own destructive tendencies. I remain embroiled in the Discourse of the Hysteric, where I am unable to produce my own master signifiers that help me work through the lures of the *Supermodels* video. I am doubly hystericized by having to present this chapter as a coherent text that might give the master signifier to the Other, to the reader.[12]

Lacan's reading of phenomenology influenced his work as a psychiatrist. Merleau-Ponty reminded him that consciousness is not an object but an attempt to piece together a set of incoherent desires. The "map of I" extends as far as I can reach, but I can only reach as far as I can see. Meaning and apprehension are melded by the act of "mimicry"; we are captured in the image outside of ourselves. This capacity to image-in (imagine) forms the basis for Lacan's *Imaginary* register; the specular relationship the child constructs with the visual field of sensing. My *Ideal Ego* is the place I see for myself (the look), while the *Ego Ideal* is the place from which I look. "The Ego is what puts the Subject aside" (Feldstein 1996, 41).

The hysteric enjoys no reason. The hysterical symptom lies in the dream, in the Imaginary where contradiction is not possible. Thus I am lured, as were some of my students, to the supermodels as they work through the polysemic text of the video in the four discursive registers, as Bakhtin (1984) described earlier.[13]

As I reflect back over the students' comments on the film, I sense the contradictions that drew me to have students critique and work with this video as a potential learning resource. The hysteric "is always absent at the right moment" (Soler 1996, 269). The hysteric refuses or fails the *jouissance* of the Other. This refusal is driven by the hysteric's return in the body, where subjectivity is buried in the unassimilabilities of the Other.[14] To a degree textual poaching allows a movement toward the inassimilable space without lapsing into presence or a belief that "one has got it right."

What of the pedagogical appropriateness of the video in the classroom? Why bring such an incommensurable set of teaching practices forward for scrutiny? The hysteric reminds the obsessive part of me that there is no object (signifier) that is capable of plugging up the (w)hole of desire. As with the look of the subject directed ahead toward the world, the object cause is always behind. While *lack* produces the vector of desire, the object of desire invariably brought through to the individuated subject through castration is imagined to be ahead in the look but is in fact behind in the form of the gaze. *Objet a* is the equivalency of castration, where the subject of speech is the object that is posed for the subject, but one that is refused. For me, the *Supermodels* video presents the "cruel symptoms" I have, as both the hysteric and obsessive, caught in the fact that desire cannot make the lack disappear (Soler 1996, 257).

> For that which I am doing, I do not understand; for I am not practicing what I would like to do, but I am doing the very thing I hate. But if I do the very thing I do not wish to do, I agree with the Law, confessing that is the good. (Romans, 8: 15–16)

So the Master speaks.

> For I know that nothing good dwells in me, that is, in my flesh; for the wishing is present in me, but the doing of the good is not. For the good that I wish, I do not do; but I practice the very evil that I do not wish. (Romans, 8: 18–20)

So the lured eye(I) speaks.

There can be no refusal for desire. *Supermodels in the Rainforest* is a palimpsest of my *excess* and *gratuity* (the response to the Father) of an ego and a world that is guilty of burning in its guilt. We live in the gaze of the Big Other that resulted from the trauma we experience from the loss of innocence.[15] "The world on the brink of disaster" gestures toward the plenitude of the Real. We have been evicted, chased from the Garden of Eden, out to the unmapped torrid zones of the rainforest from where the *Thing* will come at us.

For my students and I, there is no point in trying to save *Nature*, since *Nature's jouissance* is unmappable. Perhaps all we have is our own *jouiss-*

ance. Social studies, and the Discourse of the University that it is scaffolded around, cannot save the world. Perhaps all we are able to do is live through the trouble of doing so. For many students, the rational arguments do not motivate them to act.[16] I too, at times, am overwhelmed by my own imbecility. What, if anything, do I know of the *global warming, ecology*, and *the future*. These signifiers and my own neurotic attachments to them seem to be an endless stream in the social studies curricula. *History* and *the future* are signifiers that are hard to swallow.

Anxiety is anticipation that does not know its object. Perhaps that is why both my students and I are overwhelmed at times. Every generation tries to dream the next. If a lifetime is the thickness of a page, then time would be an encyclopedia 70 miles thick (David Harrington of *The Kronos Quartet*, in Winn 1997, 103).

I remain a thin remnant touched by the Real. One of my student's parents was a geologist who had just returned from Costa Rica. He was promoting a World Wildlife Fund project to rehabilitate deforested land and protect virgin forests by turning the areas into parkland. To promote the project he brought in slides and some mounted insects to show the students. A particularly exotic insect captivated several students. One student, who was usually quite quiet, could not contain his enthusiasm as he blurted out, "This shit is much too weird." That single little bug (a piece of *objet a*) enthralled the class much more so than did the *Supermodels* video.

Both that one little bug and a single page of the encyclopedia stretch beyond our ability to read "all of knowledge." They are metonyms for where our agency and possibilities for social change appear. Even if we could teach students all of the knowledge we had in the Symbolic, they would still lack. Yet, a single leaf carries with it a piece of the Real that invigorated and brought hope to the class. The class did take part in a campaign to save the Costa Rican rainforest. Despite the concerns raised earlier about the impact of tourism on Costa Rica, the students remained committed to a major fund-raising project. As one student suggested, "We need to start somewhere—this beats the alternative—letting everything fall apart." The class did raise $600 and was able to "purchase" several hundred acres of park reserve.

Perhaps this project, this one little act, was a response to the Duran Duran lyric:

> Who do you need, who do you love
> When you come undone?

It is axiomatic, in cultural criticism informed by psychoanalysis, that the central project for the teacher is working through the chiasma of desires that flow within conflicting symbolic representations and imaginary possibilities of a world that seems increasingly unassimilable. Media literacy as a pedagogical project lives in a nexus of time where teachers and teaching are either "too early or too late," where "consciousness is premature or after the fact" (Foster 1996, 207). The *subject of the present* and the *present of the subject* are genealogies that are co-emergent in my subjectivity and, as such, the Real remains radically inaccessible. Recall the supermodel Darja Lingenberg's demand "to be beautiful for a purpose." Her symptom resonates with my students and me: We want to learn for a purpose. In-between *desire* (amid the paradoxical forms of late capitalism) and *prohibition* (my forbidden erotic attachments to video) emerged our *jouissance*.

NOTES

1. Canada has had a strong academic tradition of media critique from universities such as McGill and York that has been slow to move into the public schools. See Will Straw (1993). Through magazines such as *Border/Lines*, *Adbusters*, and *Fuse*, media literacy has been further advanced. More recently, the Media Awareness Network (http://www.media-awareness.ca/) has provided teachers with a powerfully rich array of strategies for incorporating media literacy into their teaching.

2. This award-winning documentary features Sabrina Barnett, Nicole Breach, Leilani Bishop, Brooke Boisse, Tasha Moto Cunha, Darja Lingenberg, Rebecca Romijn, Brenda Schad, and Frederique van der Wahl.

3. The operational imperative of the Discourse of the University is to foreclose the chance that students can ever know "the Truth" (S_1 in Lacan's frame).

4. I owe the designation "chattering classes" to Stephen Lewis, who reminded teachers in a speech several years ago that academic communities in Canada have increasingly privileged "studying" as opposed to "acting" on issues of social injustice.

5. Again from Žižek, as cited in Peter Osborne (1996), the Phallus can be used to open the field of plurality. As I address the desires present in the classroom, I do so as an aesthetic gesture that invokes a de-suturing of the teacher as master.

6. Soler (1996, 249). In writing all of this I realize the real eyes of the superego are still looking. The story I am telling no longer makes sense. In Lacanian terms, "I no longer have a coherent self to make sense of" (see Žižek, 1994, 77). My embarrassment in writing about these "teacherly" justifications for ordering the video and showing it to my students is a self-erasure, a falling away from an "extimate body" that uses a name to locate "myself" in the Discourse of the University (as a concerned "academic" studying the environment).

7. A friend once jokingly reminded me that my infatuation with Frederique was "twisted because she doesn't even know you—how can you be so attracted to her?" But surely my friend missed the point: My attraction to her was based on the impossibility of ever getting to know her "radical heterogeneity."

8. Doane contrasts this to the cold Alpine and northern climates where without a map one dies.

9. I cannot help but wonder if the Phallus fails in the video precisely because it cannot conceal itself. As Jacques Lacan (1977, 288) reminds us, the Phallus is

most effective when it is veiled. As long as the video contained its authoritative discourse behind the diegetic narration and the visual registry of the rainforest panoramas, students found the video "quite interesting and fun to watch." But as the dance sequences and interviews with "natives" continued, students generally could not invest in the discourses of the idiolect and madness.

10. Fiske proposed a threading of pleasure through the fabric of cultural meaning-making. In late capitalism, *leisure displaces labor, consumption displaces production*, and *commodities* become the instruments of leisure (see McLaren, 1995).

11. Laurie made her poster as a cross-over to a Gillette Sensor Excel advertisement, showing the supermodels shaving their legs in the river with piranhas close by. The ad read, "A cut that won't ever bleed," gesturing to the safety of the razor with the voracious fish nearby. She had some trouble explaining her intention to the class. "Are you for or against the video?" students asked. She claimed that "my ad is just making fun of the whole deal, you know."

12. In *Seminar III*, Lacan argues that all human knowledge is tied to paranoia, a helpful caution when engaged in teaching. All seeking is hiding; all hiding is seeking. The *fort/da* game returns the gaze as a love object. So here I am given the task of reading Lacan within "the dialectic of jealousy" to get things right, which is the "primordial manifestation of communication" (Lacan 1993). What follows is a shuttling back and forth in ways evoked by Lacan. "When we see ourselves we see only a look. We do not get nearer to what we are. The mirror image is back to front," as cited in Sarup (1989, 14–15).

13. I am an obsessive, drawn as I am to write these lines and register my complaint within the Symbolic code of the analyst's discourse that I have appropriated; that is, the difference between seeing me as a hysteric or an obsessive. Both are neurotic symptoms of the same cause. The hysteric plays out his refuge in the Imaginary, the obsessive in the Symbolic. Slips of the tongue, dreams, and other processes that live close to the unconscious are for the hysteric. The hysteric is constantly unsatisfied since there are no signifiers for his *jouissance*. The obsessive sees his desires as impossible; he is lost in thought and tries to be the master of his desire through too much thinking. The hysteric, on the other hand, talks too much (see Soler 1996, 263–266). I remain obsessed by my own inability to finish what I have started. This is the problem for the obsessive "who plugs the lack with signifiers" (ibid., 270). The mirror of this page reminds me that I am the reflexive split between my (narcissistic) vision and the (in)capacity of my grasp to shape the objects of the world into that image. The word, my text, is never adequate for the thing: a demand, a repetition, a look, that can never (over)come what it aims at. What I look at is not there.

14. I follow Levinas's (1987) ethical call to acknowledge the radical alterity of the other.

15. The Big Other, the Symbolic Order, has no ultimate signifier that guarantees its own consistency (Žižek 1994, 172). Perhaps this is no more apparent when teachers like myself present students with the apocalyptic possibility that "Nature will be destroyed by man." Do I present myself as a new master: as one who holds the "agalma, the secret treasure" that will unlock the Real (i.e., "the future that is not to be.")? The phrase "the end of life as we know it" was a common refrain in social studies classrooms in the 1980s, given the threat of nuclear annihilation

invoked by Reagan's hysterical Star Wars defense shield. It has become the (obsessive) project of critics ("who think too much") of the plan to point out that a defense shield will technically not work. These activities maybe miss the point. A Star Wars defense shield is a project of the hysteric—the point is maybe that it does not matter that it will fail. In circulating both threats (the environmental and nuclear) in the classroom, students are robbed of *jouissance*. A possible recovery of *jouissance* is gestured in the remark by one of my students: "I believe we will eventually destroy ourselves, but recycling makes me feel good. You know, it is sort of like when I was a kid: I was a lot happier when I believed in Nature and Santa Claus." As sad as it was for me to hear this comment, it is instructive. "Thinking too much" is a symptom of the obsessive academic that my students often resist in me. As one student asked me, "Do you ever have a good time—when you are not worrying about how screwed up the whole world is?" Here we see "*jouis-sense*, enjoy-meant: the moment at which sheer self-consuming enjoyment" of doing something eclipses the repressed knowledge that the master signifiers of environmental discourse are void of content (Žižek 1994, 154).

16. As one of my students suggested, "All this environmental scare stuff doesn't make sense. If we are so stupid then why are we smart enough to know we are so stupid?"

REFERENCES

Bakhtin, Mikhail. 1984. *The Dialogic Imagination, Four Essays by M. Bakhtin*, trans. C. Emerson and M. Holquist. Austin: University of Texas Press.
———. 1986. *Speech Genres and Other Late Essays*, trans. Vern W. McGree. Austin: University of Texas Press.
Bracher, Mark. 1993. *Lacan, Discourse, and Social Change*. Ithaca, N.Y.: Cornell University Press.
Doane, Mary Anne. 1991. *Dark Continents: Epistemologies of Racial and Sexual Difference in Psychoanalysis and the Cinema*. London: Routledge.
Feldstein, Richard. 1996. Subject of the Gaze for Another Gaze. In *Lacan, Politics, Aesthetics*, ed. Willy Apollon and Richard Feldstein (pp. 45–61). Albany, N.Y.: SUNY Press.
Fiske, John. 1987. *Television Culture*. London: Methuen.
———. 1993. *Power Plays/Power Works*. London: Routledge.
———. 1994. *Media Matters: Everyday Culture and Political Change*. Minneapolis: University of Minnesota Press.
———. 1996. *Media Matters*. Minneapolis: University of Minnesota Press.
Foster, Hal. 1996. *The Return of the Real*. Cambridge, Mass.: MIT Press.
Grossberg, Lawrence. 1992. *We Gotta Get Out of This Place*. New York: Routledge.
Haysom, Ian, 1997. Coffee Craze Isn't for the Birds: Ecological Troubles Go Up Along with Demand. *Edmonton Journal* (February 17), A1, A7.
jagodzinski, jan. 1996. *The Anamorphic I/i*. Edmonton: Duvall House Publishing.
Jay, Martin. 1994. *Downcast Eyes: The Denigration of Vision in Twentieth Century French Thought*. Berkeley: University of California Press.
Jenkins, Henry. 1992. *Textual Poaching*. London: Routledge.

Kellner, Douglas. 1995. *Media Culture: Cultural Studies, Identity and Politics between the Modern and the Postmodern*. New York: Routledge.

Lacan, Jacques. 1977. *Écrits: A Selection*, trans. A. Sheridan. London: Tavistock.

———. 1988. *The Seminars of Jacques Lacan: Book II, The Ego to Freud's Theory and in the Techniques of Psychoanalysis, 1954–1955*, ed. Jacques-Alain Miller, trans. Sylvania Tomaselli. Cambridge: Cambridge University Press.

———. 1993. *The Seminars of Jacques Lacan: Book III, The Psychoses, 1955–1956*, ed. Jacques-Alain Miller. New York: Norton.

Levinas, Emmanuel. 1987. There Is: Existence without Existents. In *The Levinas Reader*, trans. Alphonso Lingis (pp. 29–36). New York: Norton.

McLaren, Peter. 1995. *Critical Pedagogy and Predatory Culture*. New York: Routledge.

Middleton, Richard. 1995. Authorship, Gender and the Construction of Meaning in the Eurythmics' Hit Recordings. *Cultural Studies* 3: 465–485.

Oliver, Kelly. 1995. *Womanizing Nietzsche*. New York: Routledge.

Osborne, Peter, ed. 1996. *A Critical Sense: Interviews with Intellectuals*. New York: Routledge.

Pile, Steve and Thrift, Nigel, eds. 1995. *Mapping the Subject*. London: Routledge.

Ronter, Larry. 1997. The Spoils of Eco-tourism. *Edmonton Journal* (January 5), E7.

Sarup, Madan. 1989. *An Introductory Guide to Poststructuralism and Postmodernism*. Athens: University of Georgia Press.

Soler, Colette. 1996. Hysteria and Obsession. In *Reading Seminars I and II: Lacan's Return to Freud*, eds. Richard Feldstein, Bruce Fink, and Marie Jaanus (pp. 248–282). Albany N.Y.: SUNY Press.

Stam, Robert, Burgoyne, Roberta, and Flitterman-Lewis, Sandy. 1992. *New Vocabularies in Film Semiotics*. London: Routledge.

Straw, Will. 1993. Shifting Boundaries, Lines of Dissent. In *Relocating Cultural Studies: Developments in Theory and Research*, ed. Valda Blundell, John Shepherd, and Ian Taylor (pp. 86–102). New York: Routledge.

Winn, Steven. 1997. *The Kronos Quartet*: Fiddling with the Future. *Utne Reader* (January–February): 102–103.

Žižek, Slavoj. 1994. *The Metastases of Enjoyment: Six Essays on Woman and Causality*. London: Verso.

———. 1996. Gaze and Voice as Love Objects. In *Gaze and Voice as Love Objects*, ed. Renata Salecl and Slavoj Žižek (pp. 90–126). Durham: Duke University Press.

Chapter 10

Cyberspace, Identity, and the Passion for Ignorance

John Lenzi

Critical educational studies often rely on psychoanalytic theory to describe the unconscious links between texts and discourses and individual subjects in the person of teachers, students, and administrators.[1] This is not the approach taken in this chapter. Instead, this chapter proposes a methodology that relies on psychoanalytic theories applied to popular culture, here movies, in order to highlight unconscious fantasies and mechanisms pertinent to education and educational institutions.[2] Specifically, the focus is that popular films about technology, computers, and cyberspace indicate that the penetration of computers and the Internet into our schools and our everyday lives is accompanied by powerful unconscious fantasies concerning the acquisition of knowledge and its effects on personal identity.

Cyberspace, in the guises of the Internet, the World Wide Web, virtual reality, and computer-based training has become commonplace at work, home, and school. Manipulated in the media as a signifier of progress, information-age rationality conceals unconscious signifiers and fantasies about the mastery of knowledge via cyberspace and its effects on people. These fantasies are best illustrated in a still developing genre of popular techno-movies such as *Lawnmower Man, Wild Palms, Strange Days, The Net, Johnny Mnemonic, Virtuosity,* and *The Thirteenth Floor.* These films provide rich and suggestive material for interpreting the fantasy relationship between cyberspace and the individual user's identity. Since these films focus on the kind of knowledge a user acquires in cyberspace, psychoanalytic theories about knowledge and ignorance lend themselves to interpret the contradictory fantasy effects portrayed in them. Both Lacan's theory of ignorance as a transference phenomenon and Bion's theory of knowledge, or K, are two modes of interpretation that will be explored here.

THE PASSION FOR IGNORANCE AND KNOWLEDGE

While the bedrock of psychoanalytic theory is the dynamic unconscious, the bedrock of its method is the analysand's transference to the analyst, where "infantile prototypes re-emerge and are experienced with a strong sensation of immediacy" (Laplanche and Pontalis 1973, 455). Transference has a binary structure since it is both an illusory identification and an illusion in time. That is, the analysand both mistakes one person for another and mistakes the present for the past. The "strong sensation of immediacy" occurs because the transference relationship is saturated with the emotions of love and hate. What Lacan added to the traditional theory of transference has to do with these emotional effects. To the emotions of love and hate he argued that a third emotion was always operative with the other two—ignorance as an affect. Moreover, he maintained that ignorance is the strongest of the three because it provides the underlying structure for both love and hate. For Lacan, love "is a passion that involves ignorance of desire" (Lacan 1998, 4). It is his concept of ignorance of desire that allows us to extend the theory of transference from the relations between people to relations between individuals and institutions and cultural phenomena, such as computer technology and cyberspace, in order to shed light on unconscious fantasies about knowledge. These fantasies are precisely the concerns central to the plot and characters in the techno-movie genre.

Lacan initially thought that ignorance was the fundamental state or attitude of any person who began psychoanalysis (Lacan 1991, 271). However, he did not credit this insight to the practice of psychoanalysis. In the 1950s, Lacan noted that ignorance, love, and hate have been traditionally recognized as the basic triad of human passions, both in Western philosophy starting with the Greeks and in the East where Buddhism made ignorance central to its worldview (Lacan 1977, 94). He argued that psychoanalysis and philosophy highlight ignorance as a passion because both are engaged in a dialectical operation where a person "speaks without knowing, as one who is ignorant," and he traces the history of this dialectical effect from Socrates, to Montaigne, through Hegel and finally Freud (Lacan 1991, 278).

In later years, Lacan systematized how ignorance functioned in the transference with his concept of *le sujet supposé savoir*—the subject supposed to know. Relying still on philosophy, Lacan sets up Plato's *Symposium*[3] as the precursor and model for his concept by noting that Socrates takes the position in the dialog as the one who knows nothing—except he does know something about Eros, or desire. Now Lacan concludes that transference does not originate with the start of analysis, as he thought earlier, but when the analysand begins to attribute to the analyst some special or secret knowledge about him/herself of which she (the analysand) is ignorant of and desires to know (Lacan 1981, 225, 233). His linking of ignorance and desire was vital to his theory, and is in line with the linchpin of his observation that the one thing the human subject can not negate or escape is desire; that is, to not want to desire is to desire not to desire. For the practice of analysis it was a limiting and humbling concept. In essence it meant that any analyst's position in the transference was not based on training or psychoanalytic knowledge, or knowledge of the patient's life history. The transference field of ignorance and desire was solely the product of the dialectical interaction between the two participants and the special knowledge, attributed to the analyst by the patient, was something he too was ignorant of.

Lacan's final elaboration on ignorance of desire remains aligned with Freud's often overlooked view that what is significant about transference dynamics are their illusory and unreal quality (Freud 1915 [1914]). Lacan's concept hinges on the illusion that we set up any Other as an embodiment of a desirable knowledge that we lack and are passionately ignorant of. If we extend this theory to culture at large such as institutions, social groups, or cyberspace, they too can embody that of which we are ignorant of and desire to know. It is precisely this transference relationship that the protagonists in the movies *The Net* and *Johnny Mnemonic* have to cyberspace. Before turning to these two movies, it is important to consider Bion's theory of knowledge that resonates with the unconscious effects of desire and ignorance that Lacan noted.

Bion elaborated a psychoanalytic theory of thinking that attempted to explain both how the ability to think develops in infancy and how it also could be applied to interpretation of psychoanalytic sessions. Starting with some essential concepts in British object relations theory, he constructed his theory of thinking out of the unconscious dynamics of Love, Hate, and Knowledge, or his shorthand L, H, and K.[4] It is his theory of K that is relevant here in order to interpret the unconscious dynamics in the representations of cyberspace. For Bion, K was not an abstract mental phenomenon but was an emotional function linking two people. The developmental prototype of K was the intimate physical and psychological relationship between mother and infant. He formulated this relationship as xKy. This means that x is in a state of getting to know y and y is in a state of becoming known by x. However, he also postulated two other qualities of K. First, he conceptualized that there was also a negative "minus K" where the potential link is stripped of meaning or filled with meaninglessness and results in misunderstanding. Second, based on his work with patients who suffered from thought disorders, he postulated a "no K" state. According to Bion, we fluctuate between these three states of K, including the "no K" state where the complete destruction of the capacity to think annihilates our ability to link with reality. There is a strong similarity between Bion's descriptions of "minus K" and the "no K" states and Lacan's theory of ignorance. For example, if we think of the "no K" state as the presence of an absence (i.e., the absence of thinking), it describes, from a different developmental perspective, ignorance as the lack that fails to link us to an Other or external reality. The "minus K" state is similar to Lacan's, positing that when the analysand imagines that the analyst possesses magical knowledge about him/herself, the analysand misunderstands both who the analyst is and his/her own desire to know. These primitive and deeply unconscious responses to knowledge and ignorance are what the masters of cyberspace in *The Net* and *Johnny Mnemonic* suffer from.

THE PASSION OF CYBERSPACE

When William Gibson (1986) coined the term "cyberspace" in the 1980s, he gave it a semiotic, a social, and a psychological dimension. He called cyberspace a "consensual hallucination" which consisted of an "unthinkable" fusion of electronics, light, words, letters, and other signifiers set in the "nonspace of the mind" (p. 67). Contemporary cultural critics who are "pro-cyberspace" range from those who find in it a new hope for individuals who can, in chat rooms and with the new technology, playfully create pseudo-identities, to those that argue that cyberspace is simply an accurate representation of our postmodern condition.[5] Critics who are "suspicious" of cyberspace, especially in the guise of virtual reality, tend to emphasize the contradictions or rupture between actual bodily propriosensation and psychic life (Heim 1993). For example, the virtual reality user experiences a sense of omnipotence that an outside observer sees as meaningless gestures (Wooley 1992). Žižek's (1997) critique is suspicious of cyberspace, but his synthesis of Hegel, Lacan, and the Frankfurt School and his emphasis on everyday experience sets him apart from the others. I have oversimplified this debate, but note that it is cast in the terms of Marx's earlier critique on the effect machines and mechanized factory labor had on workers' bodies and minds. The alternative being explored in this chapter is to examine cyberspace as an unconscious representation, and popular movies provide a convenient semiotic space for this interpretive work.

When characters in techno-movies form a relationship with technology, and specifically cyberspace, the protagonists are often positioned in a signifying chain of fantasies that are characterized by hallucinations, violence, and the disintegration of personal identity. At the same time, cyberspace as social ideology is represented in these films as the means to save Western culture and democracy from chaos and anarchy. This contradiction between individual incoherence and social coherence highlights unconscious dynamics that may render suspicious the contemporary media's rationalization that the computer and the Internet are signifiers of progress. From a psychoanalytic perspective, we must ask what is the fantasy structure developed in the movies *The Net* and *Johnny Mnemonic*, where cyberspace embodies society's progressive salvation, but renders the heroic experience of the masters of cyberspace as regressive, primitive, and unreal?

The films *The Net* and *Johnny Mnemonic* were both released in 1995 when the press was filled with stories about the World Wide Web, the information superhighway, chat room stalkers, and the virtual classroom. Even though *The Net* is presented as a plausible "real-life" story and *Johnny Mnemonic* is based on William Gibson's futuristic science fiction, there are two striking similarities between the films. First, both films feature protagonists whose primary relationship is with cyberspace and not with another human being. Second, mothers and fathers are significant to the fantasy structure of both protagonists.

The Net is set in the present and the protagonist is an independent computer consultant who works out of her home. Angela Bennett, played by Sandra Bullock, is known and respected for her skill at debugging computer viruses. The plot is driven by her discovery of a virus that one of her clients sends her to debug that has been created by a group of conspirators who intend to extort and dominate all corporate Western democracies by infecting computer systems worldwide. Once the conspirators discover that she has a copy of their program, she is pursued by a seductive assassin while on vacation in a foreign country. More important to note, she lives alone, works constantly on her computer, including ordering food from a Web site, and her free time on the tropical beach where she vacations is initially spent with her laptop.

Angela Bennett's true relationship to cyberspace becomes manifest when the conspirators change her identity in all computer systems worldwide (i.e., they alter her driver's license, credit cards, mortgage, etc.) and they replace her with a double at her workplace, where no one knows what she actually looks like, since she always worked from home. With her new identity in cyberspace, as Ruth Marx, she is seduced and pursued by an assassin named Devlin, and she desperately turns to Champion, her dysfunctional therapist, for rescue. The Hollywood representation of the fight for the survival of Western democracy's computer systems is apparently to be played out by an angel, a devil, a dysfunctional Champion, and Marx.

Since people are either dangerous or ineffectual, it is only when Angela once again gets access to a computer and is reconnected to cyberspace that things turn in her favor. In cyberspace she restores her identity, e-mails the conspirators' virus to the FBI, infects the conspirators' mainframe with a virus, murders the assassin pursuing her, and saves the free world.

Damaged identity and saving Western civilization are also the major themes in *Johnny Mnemonic*. Loosely based on a short story by William Gibson, this film is set in the year 2021. The world portrayed in *Johnny Mnemonic* is the world as it might be had Angela Bennett failed to expose the conspiracy in *The Net*. In *Johnny Mnemonic*, national governments and democracy no longer exist. Global corporate conglomerates control the world in 2021. A resistance movement of computer hackers called Loteks fight a guerrilla war on two fronts from a decayed urban neighborhood. They fight both a cyberspace war by hacking the global Internet and they physically fight for their lives against a global crime syndicate that the corporations have hired for protection. Cyberspace is now an extremely dangerous place. It is contaminated with deadly "black ice viruses" that make it totally unsafe for important or confidential data. Now, the only way the corporate conglomerates can safely move data around the world is by hiring elite couriers who have "wet-wired" silicon memory drives implanted in their brains. Johnny, played by Keanu Reeves, is one of the elite data couriers.

After Johnny lies about the disk capacity of his drive implant he receives a massive download of data in Beijing and is instructed to deliver it to Newark. Killers immediately pursue Johnny, like Angela. He slowly discovers that the data which has so dangerously overloaded his brain implant was stolen from a pharmaceutical conglomerate. The firm has kept the cure for Attenuated Nerve Syndrome, a plague that has infected half of the world's population, a secret in order to maintain profit margins from its drug treatments. Eventually, Johnny, like Angela, is connected to cyberspace with the help of the revolutionary Loteks, downloads the cure, and cyberspace and global consumer society are once again made safe for the future.

CYBERSPACE IS SUPPOSED TO KNOW

Both central characters are isolated, lonely individuals who are masters of cyberspace. However, as the stories progress it is cyberspace itself that posseses the magical knowledge or power that they lack. Stated plainly, people are useless to both Angela and Johnny. The passion of ignorance, or "no K" state, destroys their ability to link to other people through love and hate. Instead they become empty containers who can only link to the unthinkable hallucination of cyberspace. Although Johnny has a female bodyguard and Angela has a psychiatrist, both characters only come alive when they are online. In fact, they both demand the same thing from the people around them and it is oddly enough expressed by a similar line in both films—"I need a computer." We can now ask, what is it that they unconsciously lack, or more accurately, what desire are they ignorant of and how will it be signified in these films? The conscious plot answers that cyberspace signifies the prosthesis of our instrumental reason so that their desire to save society can be interpreted as logical and heroic. That is, cyberspace signifies both their individual mastery of technology and their heroic autonomy from the violent and dystopic society portrayed in both movies. However, this conscious reasoning does not explain why their desire for cyberspace is also embedded in a fantasy structure that implicates their father, mother, and a fragmentary personal identity.

First, in Angela and Johnny's world there are no fathers. The opening sequence of *The Net* highlights this chilling absence by showing a father's suicide after he assures his young son from his cell phone that the boy will have unlimited access to video games. When Angela speaks of her own father, she dismisses him by saying, "he just transferred out one day." Later, her psychiatrist suggests that her dilemma is connected to her father's disappearance, but she vehemently denies this. In *Johnny Mnemonic*, there is no reference to a father. The notion of paternity is completely negated and is further signified by the fact that Johnny does not know his last name. This non-representation of the father indicates a primitive unconscious structure that pre-dates the presence of the father. The presence of the mother becomes vital to these primitive fantasies about non-existent fathers, but the two characters' internal representation of their mothers is also problematic.

As the film reveals retroactively, Johnny has no memory of his mother. The real reason he wants to download the pharmaceutical company's data from his brain implant is so he can recover his childhood memories that had to be deleted in order to install the implant. The specific memory that he eventually recovers at the end of the film is of his mother at his seventh birthday party. There is also another maternal image that appears to Johnny in cyberspace. This cyber-maternal imago literally haunts the pharmaceutical company's mainframe computer. It turns out to be the cyber-ghost of the murdered CEO of the company and Johnny's secret ally in cyberspace. The signifiers of damaged memory, a non-existent mother, or a ghostly mother are oddly concretized in *The Net*. However, in this movie, it is Angela's mother's memory that is damaged. Angela's mother is institutionalized in an idyllic hospital, suffering from Alzheimer's disease. While Johnny has no memory of his mother, Angela's mother has no memory of her. In an unconscious twist on the classical Hollywood ending of boy-gets-girl, both characters are "restored" to damaged images of mother.

Non-existent paternity and the fantasy of damaged and ghostly mother are the unconscious underpinnings of Angela's loss of identity in cyberspace and Johnny's multiple identities in cyberspace. When Angela's identity is altered in cyberspace she begins to question who she is. When Johnny is asked about parents, home, or his last name he has no memory of them. Angela restores her original identity by overcoming her double in cyberspace while Johnny's victory in cyberspace is accomplished by literally doubling himself in order to evade the viruses that pursue the cyber-Johnny.

Both characters rely on the knowledge of cyberspace to restore and heal their fragmented identities. If we interpret that the desire of their selfhood lies in cyberspace, it is because for Angela and Johnny there is primitive unconscious desire that they are without human parents. So, what is the magical knowledge that they attribute to the computer and that cyberspace is supposed to know? It is the ignorance of a primitive and dangerous desire for a world where fathers are non-existent and mothers are ghosts. As Bion's theory predicts, "no K" does not link to the real world but it leads to the paranoid-psychotic fantasies that plague Johnny and Angela. They live in a world where one doubts who one is and doppelgangers and mirror reflections are as real as one's self. Lacan did not consider this, but perhaps these are the dangers that come when the transference of ignorance of desire is projected onto something inhuman like cyberspace. However, we cannot blame Johnny and Angela if we consider how society and social relationships are represented in both films. The society of the present and the future is portrayed as violent and dysfunctional. In *The Net*, the man trying to murder Angela bluntly asks: "Look around. Do you think things are working?" In *Johnny Mnemonic*, the cities are dying and half the population is infected by a plague. In both films, political demonstrations are used as background sequences and if this was not enough to signify society as dangerous, both movies have scenes set in hospitals where people are murdered—not healed. People are just too dangerous to project onto them the magical knowledge of the Other who is supposed to know. Cyberspace, the non-human space of the mind, will have to suffice.

THE RETURN OF CYBERSPACE

The ghostly mother, the non-existent father, duplicate and fragmented identity, disease, and dystopia—this is the signifying chain of fantasies that both characters download into their cyberspace transference of terminal ignorance. From a psychoanalytic perspective, the heroism of these cybermasters is suspect since their passion for ignorance about who they are links them to cyberspace, but its effects are what Bion described as "no K." Knowledge does not link them to reality. From a critical perspective, the perennial Hollywood happy ending is unsettling. Cyberspace may be a dangerous consensual hallucination, but it's better than dysfunctional social relations with diseased or incompetent human beings. Hollywood's cyberspace, made safe for consumers, promises a timeless transference of our desire to preserve the illusion that there is an Other who possesses a knowledge about ourselves that we are ignorant of. The conclusion we can draw from these movies is that cyberspace, as an instrument of education and reason, comes with primitive unconscious fantasies about knowledge and ignorance reified as lack. Computers continue to be rationalized as value-neutral extensions of knowledge and mastery, but this ideology ignores the sociocultural fantasies that people bring to their interactions with technology (Broughton 1985). Angela and Johnny do not so much follow the Delphic oracle's advice to "know thyself" in cyberspace as they make cyberspace safe for the consumer ideology of lack and ignorance of desire. At the same time, as individuals, an omnipotent and primitive fantasy is preserved where mothers and fathers are annihilated and the self disintegrates. It is not that cyberspace is the substitute representation of the parents, but it becomes a representation of the non-existence of the parents.[6]

The application of psychoanalysis to representations of technology in popular culture will become more important as the virtualization of social relations proceeds. What psychoanalytic theory offers is the ability to interpret the individual and collective fantasies that will accompany this transition, and popular movies are an excellent source for the dramatic play of these fantasies. As Haraway argues in her cultural analyses, there is less and less difference these days between science fiction and social relations (Haraway 1991). The link between a psychoanalysis of popular culture and the ideology of progress, education, and technical reason may show a way to transform the destructive manifestations of the unconscious (Broughton 1995, 272).

NOTES

1. For an overview of critical educational theory and psychoanalysis, see Appel (1996).

2. My experience with the methodology of using psychoanalysis to interpret popular movies I owe to my work with two mentors. I was a member of Dr. John Broughton's research group on popular films for two years, and I worked with Dr. Joseph Simo at his Agora Seminars on "cinemiotics."

3. There is an entire cottage industry debating psychoanalytic originality or lack thereof. This may be a straw man argument, considering how much psychoanalysts have borrowed and referenced from philosophy. For example, consider this "Lacanian" quote central to Plato's *Symposium*: "If you reflect for a moment, you will see that it isn't merely probable but absolutely certain that one desires what one lacks, or rather that one does not desire what one does not lack." See Plato (1986, 76).

4. For the full scope of Bion's theory of thinking, see Bion (1959, 1962, 1984).

5. For pro-arguments concerning the rebirth of the individual in cyberspace, see Leary (1991). For arguments grounded in postmodern theories of subjectivity, see Turkle (1995).

6. For more on the representation of the non-existence of the object, see Green (1986, 277–296).

REFERENCES

Appel, Stephen. 1996. *Positioning Subjects: Psychoanalysis and Critical Educational Studies.* Westport, Conn.: Bergin & Garvey.

Bion, Wilfred. 1959. Attacks on Linking. *International Journal of Psychoanalysis* 40: 308–315.

———. 1962. A Theory of Linking. *International Journal of Psychoanalysis* 43: 306–310.

———. 1984. *Learning from Experience.* London: H. Karnac Books.

Broughton, John. 1985. The Surrender of Control: Computer Literacy as Political

Socialization of the Child. In *The Computer in the School*, ed. D. Sloan (pp. 102–122). New York: Teachers College Press.

———. 1995. The Bomb in the Bathroom: Anality in Hi-Tech Warfare. In *Trends and Issues in Theoretical Psychology*, ed. I. Lubek, R. Hezewijk, G. Pheterson, and C. Tolman (pp. 270–276). New York: Springer.

Freud, Sigmund. 1915 (1914). Observations on Transference-Love. In *The Standard Edition of the Complete Works of Sigmund Freud*, ed. James Strachey (vol. 12, pp. 157–171). London: Hogarth, 1953–1974.

Gibson, William. 1986. *Neuromancer*. London: Grafton Books.

Green, André. 1986. Potential Space in Psychoanalysis: The Object in the Setting. In André Green, *On Private Madness* (pp. 277–296). Madison, Conn.: International Universities Press.

Haraway, Donna. 1991. *Simians, Cyborgs and Women: The Re-Invention of Nature*. London: Free Association.

Heim, Michael. 1993. *The Metaphysics of Virtual Reality*. Oxford: Oxford University Press.

Lacan, Jacques. 1977. *Écrits: A Selection*, trans. Alan Sheridan. New York: Norton.

———. 1981. *The Four Fundamental Concepts of Psychoanalysis*, ed. Jacques Alain-Miller, trans. Alan Sheridan. New York: Norton.

———. 1991. *The Seminar of Jacques Lacan: Book I, Freud's Papers on Technique, 1953–1954*, ed. Jacques Alain-Miller, trans. with notes by John Forrester. New York: Norton.

———. 1998. *The Seminar of Jacques Lacan. Book XX, Encore: On Feminine Sexuality, the Limits of Love and Knowledge, 1972–1973*, ed. Jacques Alain-Miller, trans. Bruce Fink. New York: Norton.

Laplanche, Jean, and Pontalis, J.-B. 1973. *The Language of Psycho-Analysis*. New York: Norton.

Leary, Timothy. 1991. The Cyberpunk: The Individual as Reality Plot. In *Storming the Reality Studio*, ed. L. McCaffery. Durham, N.C.: Duke University Press.

Plato. 1986. *The Symposium*, trans. W. Hamilton. Harmondsworth: Penguin Books.

Turkle, Sherry. 1995. *Life on the Screen: Identity in the Age of the Internet*. New York: Simon & Schuster.

Wooley, Benjamin. 1992. *Virtual Worlds: A Journey in Hype and Hyperreality*. Oxford: Oxford University Press.

Žižek, Slavoj. 1997. Cyberspace, or, the Unbearable Closure of Being. In Slavoj Žižek, *The Plague of Fantasies*. London: Verso.

Part VI

A Strange(r) Conclusion

Chapter 11

Assessing Lacan's Teaching Within Historical Intellectual Achievements; Or, "Was Lacan a Scientific Educator?"

Harry Garfinkle

PART I: THE ALGORITHMIZATION OF PRODUCTION

To some, yesterday is a long past. To others, yesterday is the journalist's "who did what, where, when, with whom, with what?"—all the facts fit to print. To me yesterday is my experience, my memory, my recall, my recognition, and my empathy with all that happened to me and my brothers and sisters in all of my previous historical incarnations the world over, for I am everyman/woman. Having stated my bias, the problematic that I intend to explore takes the form of two questions:

1. What contribution does Jacques Lacan's psychoanalytic practice make to technological productivity?
2. At what paradigm of science were Jacques Lacan's psychoanalytic teachings foundationally based?

In order to interrelate my two key questions, I have constructed a number of tables, which I hope will telescope the extensive historical detail that I need as background to my evaluation of Lacan's achievement. My technological history goes back to ca. 900–1200, to the civilizational social formations that Western historians have generally designated as "Feudalism." This was the era when, in Western Europe, the algorithmization of production first took place. I have consequently identified the shifts in this process by a table of "algoregm" shifts, schematically a lifetime, or 75 years long. Table 11.1 details these advances in technological progress.

Most of the world's productive work is covered by Table 11.1. The technicians of yesteryear have since attended Mechanics Institutes and gone on

Table 11.1
Technological Progress in the Scope of Western European History

---

In the era of feudalism (900–1200)—clerical and knightly estates dominant
Algoregm 1 (900–975)—animal power technology
Algoregm 2 (975–1050)—wind power technology
Algoregm 3 (1050–1125)—water power technology
Algoregm 4 (1125–1200)—navigational technology

In the era of patrimonialism (1200–1500)—royal absolutism dominant
Algoregm 5 (1200–1275)—prime mover technology
Algoregm 6 (1275–1350)—town public works technology
Algoregm 7 (1350–1425)—movable type technology
Algoregm 8 (1425–1500)—time measured work technology

In the era of capitalism (1500–1800)—urban haute bourgeoisie dominant
Algoregm 9 (1500–1575)—mechanical technology, Leonardo da Vinci
Algoregm 10 (1575–1650)—dynamic technology, Galileo Galilei
Algoregm 11 (1650–1725)—cybernetic technology, Thomas Savery
Algoregm 12 (1725–1800)—organic technology, Jethro Tull

In the era of ecumenism (1800–2100)—global agglomeral capital dominant
Algoregm 13 (1800–1875)—mass production technology, Eli Whitney
Algoregm 14 (1875–1950)—quality control technology, Leon Trotsky
Algoregm 15 (1950–2025)—design control technology, Stuart Davis
Algoregm 16 (2025–2100)—nano control technology, ?

---

to become the engineers of today. The reader can, therefore, decide for himself/herself what answer to give to my first question, "What contribution does Lacan's psychoanalytic practice make to technological productivity?" The answer may be "none at all," or it may fall somewhere on the scale that Table 11.1 represents. This leads me to a subsidiary, follow-up question: "If a worker without a university education were to have attended all of Lacan's Seminars, and read all of the *Écrits* and signed up for Lacanian analysis, what benefits would have accrued to him or her?" Even in the world's advanced industrial countries, only about 5 to 10 percent of the population reach the level of university education that would have qualified them to participate in his line, at his level, of learning. Is psychoanalysis then, forgetting for the moment its cost, for the workers of the world? "*Cui bono?*" is still the issue.

Question 2: "At what paradigm of science were Jacques Lacan's psycho-

Table 11.2
Paradigm Shifts in Historical Perspective

In the era of patrimonialism (1200–1500)—royal absolutism dominant—characterized by orthopsychology

Paradigm 1 (1200–1275)—The epistemology of co-ordinance Averroist—clerical

Paradigm 2 (1275–1350)—The epistemology of congruence Erastian—royal

Paradigm 3 (1350–1425)—The epistemology of concurrence Urban—guild

Paradigm 4 (1425–1500)—The epistemology of consonance Academic—paideia

In the era of capitalism (1500–1800) national haute-bourgeoisie dominant—characterized by metapsychology

Paradigm 5 (1500–1575)—The epistemology of correspondence—Empiriological

Paradigm 6 (1575–1650)—The epistemology of corroborance—Phenomenological

Paradigm 7 (1650–1725)—The epistemology of constrisance—Semiological

Paradigm 8 (1725–1800)—The epistemology of consonance—Historiological

In the era of ecumenism (1800–2100) global agglomeral capital dominant—characterized by parapsychology

Paradigm 9 (1800–1875)—The epistemology of transculturation—Ecological

Paradigm 10 (1875–1950)—The epistemology of enconscientation—Anthropological

Paradigm 11 (1950–2025)—The epistemology of conscientization—Nomological

Paradigm 12 (2025–2100)—The epistemology of reconstitution—Ecumenical

---

Note: The term "enconscientization" refers to Paulo Freire's (1970) Portuguese term *conscientizacao* (translated as "conscientization") to indicate an earlier recognition that conscience is a cultural creation.

analytic teachings foundationally based?" I begin my discussion of this question in the thirteenth century, because this is when scientific method, in the paradigmatic sense that Thomas Kuhn (1962) introduced, in *The Structure of Scientific Revolutions*, received its first criterial comparative treatment. Table 11.2 thus skips from Plato and Aristotle to the paradigmatic sequence that developed in Europe after the twelfth century.

PART II: PARADIGMATIC SHIFTS IN HISTORY

Looking at Table 11.2, it is not immediately clear where, on this spectrum, Lacan's foundational form of scientific method would fall. In my philosophy classes at Columbia University, neither my Logical Positivist nor my Wittgensteinian professors would grant Freudian psychoanalysis full scientific status. At best, they grudgingly admitted, it was a proto-science, trying to qualify. Lacan would face the same hurdles of acceptance. However, since these teachers did not periodize the paradigmatic changes in scientific method historically, and they continued to use the model they had adduced for the physical/natural sciences as the appropriate one for judging the scientific criteria of the social/humanist studies, I have put their judgments aside. I have also accepted the scientific status of the *Geistes-wissenschaften*, as promoted by the various German schools of philosophy, especially the rationale promoted by Wilhelm Windelband (1848–1915), the first leader of the Heidelberg School of Neo-Kantianism, to the effect that David Hume's fact-value separation doesn't hold up, and that problems of epistemology rest on judgments of axiology (value theory). I disagree with him, however, in his claim that the physical sciences are "nomothetic" (based on the laws of nature) while the cultural sciences are "ideographic" (based on the form of the particular individual). I would make the case, instead, that all of the sciences are Bayesian/statistical in nature, and that the oecoumene/the noosphere, in its biospheric and geospheric context, is the holon/the universe of discourse for all of the sciences dealing with the behavior, endeavor, and praxis of the genus Homo.

Unpacking Lacan's paradigmatic standing now entails examining the criteria that characterized each epistemological shift in scientific method, and then establishing that he transcended these criteria. Thus, Jacques Lacan was, in his childhood, subject to his parents' Roman Catholic observance. Can a case be made that he outgrew its authoritarian bearing and came around to an Averroist (Averroës, 1124–1196, "epistemology of co-ordinance,") which entailed the separation of church authority and secular rationality, as Paradigm 1 (1206–1275) required and, similarily, Paradigm 2 (1275–1350)? France, when he was growing up, was ostensibly republican, but it was under a constitution greatly influenced by its authoritarian Napoleonic Code antecedents. The question can therefore be posed: "How much of the conformity orientation of his childhood familiarization stuck to him?" Ditto with Paradigm 3 (1350–1425). In class terms, his parents were petty-bourgeois merchants. Once more, the question arises, "How much of the competitive authoritarian ethics of the capitalist trader remained in his bones?" Then, with regard to Paradigm 4 (1425–1500), the lingering effects of the Concordat that Napoleon had signed with the Pope, restoring elementary education to clerical auspices, remained. Lacan's parents had the right to enroll him in a parochial school program, which they did. They sent him to St. Stanislas, operated by the Marist Brothers. There, his further socialization could not exclude subjection to continuing pedagogical authoritarianism. Being coldly analytical means examining the "as the bough is bent" argument. Lacan, in his adult life, went on to disown authoritarian indoctrination, but given the enduring power of familial enculturation and community and school acculturation, how much of his childhood and youthful ensconscientation remained residual in his interpersonal values and social relations? Those who liked him and followed him willingly said, "He had charisma!" Those who left him, like Luce Irigaray, said, "He didn't leave you enough space to be your own person."

The next four paradigm shifts (P5–8/1500–1800) were all under the aegis of capitalist science. In their day, they passed for objectivity. However, in the light of the examination of their foundations by the Frankfurt School, they constitute an ideological orientation. The values of the British Enlightenment, the French Illumination, and the German *Erklärung*, which the current postmodernist deconstructionists are at pains to calumniate, are not so pristine. So, what of modernism do we salvage?

I propose to abide by the comments that Martin Buber made in response to this critique. In 1947, I was enrolled at the Hebrew University in a reading course with him. Our theme was "a good man/woman in his/her time." We examined the morality of the three fathers (Abraham, Isaac, and Jacob) and the four mothers (Sarah, Rebeckah, Leah, and Rachel) as well as Noah and Job, of whom the Hebrew Scriptures make the *obiter dictum* "X" was a good man/woman in his/her time. Thus, all the kings of Israel and Judah were also rated in terms of whether they did good in the eyes of monotheistic Jahweh. And, in China, too, there are classical documents wherein the Emperors are rated as good or bad. Buber drew my attention to Aristotle's and Xenophanes' treatment of this issue. He made the point that, in each age, most people adhere to the conventions and customs of their in-group; and that, in both Greek and Latin, the mores are the basis of the prevailing morals. The philosophers, however, as men and women of sophia/wisdom wanted something more. Aristotle consequently introduced the notion of "transcultural ethics"; the Stoics introduced the measure of goodness in terms of how one treated the "Oikoumene" (the humanly inhabited Earth/Gaia). Epicurus measured goodness in terms of how men and women treated each other in the Garden/ashram that they shared, and Cicero introduced the norm of "humanitas" as the criterion for goodness judgments. More recently, the Jesuit Father Malcolm Hay (1960), in his book *The Foot of Pride*, raised the question, "Who is fit to be declared a saint?" He made the point that services to the Roman Catholic cause weren't enough; that anyone who killed Jews, Moslems, Pagans, or non-Catholic Christians should not be so honored; for example, someone like "Saint" Dominic, who took part in the slaughter of the Albigensians, should lose his halo.

Thus, I approach the notion of "sciencehood in their day" as my basis for judging the worthiness of the exemplars that have received "honorable mention" in the history of science textbooks. For example, Leonardo da Vinci (1452–1519), Nicolas Copernicus (1473–1543) and Andreas Vesalius (1514–1564) are all recognized as contributors to the advancement of science in its Paradigm 5 (1500–1575) mode. They all exemplified the logos of experience (empiriology), and the works they left us are replete with the data of commensuration, denumeration, and ponderation. They measured, reckoned, and weighed things accurately and left with the reputation for objectivity, since whatever they did could be replicated by any other competent scientist. Charcot, as an earlier Brodmann, made a point of identifying the parts of the brain that he was dealing with, so that any other neurologist could replicate his probings. Neither Freud nor Lacan were that specific. At that paradigmatic level, flair was not appreciated. The "epistemology of correspondence" required representational matching of phenomena perceptually, cognitively, conceptually, pictorially, and linguistically. That was how "facts" could be established. Teaching reading by flash cards, showing a picture on one side and its common denotative name on the other side, continues this tradition, as does common journalistic training, wherein the reporter has to ascertain the factual "Who did what, where, when, with whom, with what?" details for the story to be printed.

At the Paradigm 6 (1575–1650) level, the "scientific revolution" ostensibly occurred. William Gilbert (1544–1603), Francis Bacon (1561–1626), Galileo Galilei (1564–1642), Johann Kepler (1571–1630), William Harvey (1578–1657), and Jan van Helmont (1580–1644), among others, gave science its inductive, experimental hypothetication turn; together with Rene Descartes' (1596–1650) universal methodical doubt, the clear and distinct formulation of testing procedures and ideas, the establishment of the analytical geometry parameters of events, and the move to identify the human subject doing the objective investigations (the significance of his "cogito, ergo sum" declaration). What was to become "psychology" thereby attained a twofold formulation: Brain/cognition and mind/cogitation were both recognized as psychic phenomena.

In all, the "epistemology of corroborance" was ushered in. Pierre Fermat's (1601–1665) and Blaise Pascal's (1623–1662) notions of probability, abetted, a little later, by Hermann Conring's (1606–1682) development of statistics; John Graunt's (1620–1674) studies of actuarial demographics; and William Petty's (1623–1687) "Political Arithmetic" national wealth accounting methods all came together to shift the foundations of science from "facts" to "warrants." Robert Boyle (1627–1691), with his 1661 publication of "The Sceptical Chemist," then transformed alchemy into chemistry, and, by his declaration that chemical changes belonged to a different order of being than physical changes, he laid the foundation for general systems thinking. With each subsequent paradigm shift, a new level of reality was incorporated into the general ontological system. Boyle is also credited with having originated the motto of the British Royal Society, founded in 1663: *"Nullius in verba"* (nothing by mere authority).

It is hard to recognize Lacan's psychoanalytic work as meeting the criteria of the scientific work of Paradigm 6 (1575–1650). His language, especially after 1964, is so full of his own connotational allusions that its replication testing experimentally, in the name of corroborance, is virtually ruled out. His claims to honoring Descartes' "cogito" can only be granted if we recognize that his is an ideographic, idiosyncratic version of the original. Mladen Dolar's (1998) treatment of the "Cogito as the Subject of the Unconscious" bears little relation to what Descartes wrote in his "Discourse on Method" (1637) or Antoine Amauld's (1612–1694) "The Art of Thinking" (1662), or Baruch Spinoza's "Principles of Cartesian Philosophy" (1663). Most of the other pieces in Slavoj Žižek's (1998) *Sic* 2 reader *Cogito and the Unconscious* are interesting as literary constructions, but they are short on empirical or experimental evidence at the Paradigm 6 (1575–1650) level in morphology and physiology; at the Paradigm 7 (1650–1725) level in neurology; at the Paradigm 8 (1725–1800) level in embryology; at the Paradigm 9 (1800–1875) level in evolutionary biology; at the Paradigm 10 (1875–1950) level in ecological anthropology; and at the Paradigm 11 (1950–2025) level in terra formation and emancipatory conscientization.

However, if a claim is to be made for Lacan as a scientist, it is probably at the Paradigm 7 (1650–1725) level. I have designated what was considered reliable knowledge in this period as the "epistemology of construisance," using a term with a French root to get across the notion that theoretical construals and semiotic constructions came into their own at this time. Joao Poinsot (1580–1664), writing in Spain, in Latin, in his *Tractatus de Signis* (Treatise on Signs) (1640), had dealt with the semiological side of thought, alongside its empiriological, phenomenological, and logical dimensions. He was, however, still working in the scholastic vein, and his work was not widely known. It was, therefore, John Locke (1632–1704), for his "Essay on Human Understanding" (1690), who received the recognition for his vernacular/modern treatment of this subject.

Locke started empiriologically, with the mind as a *tabula rasa*, to explain "semiosis," which entailed building up a structure of experience through assigning sign relations to the things of nature and the things of experience. These gave rise, in turn, to practical and speculative understanding. Upon this foundation, phenomenological reflection (à la Descartes) on the role of signs adopted in rendering experience meaningful gave us the theory of semiotics (*signa in actu signato*). In the United States, C. S. Peirce (1839–1914), with his discussion of "semiosis," developed these ideas further, while in the Soviet Union, L. S. Vygotskii (1896–1934) produced a historical materialist, dialectical treatment of the relationship between thought and language. Lacan does not indicate any familiarity with the American or Russian studies; instead, his sources were the French Structural linguistics "Course in General Linguistics" (1913) of Ferdinand de Saussure (1857–1913); the French Structural anthropology of Claude Lévi-Strauss (1908–   ); and the middle term between them, the structural linguistics writings of Roman Jacobson (1896–1982) on metaphor and metonymy.

Lacan's originality, as expressed in "The Language of the Self" (1968), lay in relating the Structuralist concern with language to the unconscious in man. For Lacan, language was the tool by which one was able to reach the unconscious, and he held that the unconscious itself was "precisely structured as a language." The book also contains a number of what would appear to be anti-humanist, postmodern types of pronouncements. Lacan questioned the importance of human individuality and advocated the "decentering" of man. He questioned Descartes' and Pascal's claim that man was a thinking reed. Contrary to Spinoza, Lacan, in some places, even seemed to hold that the apparent subject does not advance to a "self" who can go from being the subject that reflects on experience of the world out there to also reflect on his subjective representations. The "subject," instead, in the passive voice, was thought. This seems to be in line with the self-regulating governor technology of the 1650–1725 period (e.g., Thomas Savery's (1650–1715) work on the steam engine) that the engineers of the day were trying to master. Lacan's main emphasis on the unconscious as structured like a language can perhaps make sense in the context of today's fifth-generation computers, in which are incorporated the artificial intelligence wiring that is required to enable them to function as translating machines, metaphorically as cybernisms.

In the Paradigm 7 (1650–1725) context, Francis Grisson (then Professor of Physics at Cambridge University) introduced the evidence for the excitability of nerve or muscle tissue and sought experimentally to demonstrate how nerve fibers could act as vital forces, and like electrical wire, produce and carry energy. He further explored how the property of sensitivity was directly related to the presence of nerves in interaction/communication. By these explorations, he opened up the possibility that neurology could be integrated with physiology and morphology to account for hitherto unexplained aspects of human behavior. The triadic system was also introduced in this period as a feature of Paradigm 7 (1650–1725) science. To physics and chemistry, Niels Stenson (1638–1686) (in Latin, Nicolaus Steno) added geology. His linkage was crystallography. He also explained fossils as neither "deceiving products of the devil . . ." nor "practice creations of God" before the flood, but ordinary ancient animals that, in death, had been petrified.

In the range of changed ways of thinking, John Evelyn is also to be remembered. Although he is better known as an essayist and diarist, he was, at the same time, the author of the first scientific monograph published by the British Royal Society, entitled "Sylva, the Care of Forest Trees" (1663). He drew on his father's experience as a forester to introduce the notion of "habitat preservation," and to urge on the British aristocracy the practice of forest "conservation and regeneration." His recommendations mainly fell on deaf ears, and England's forests were cut down apace. His ecological notions were, however, picked up in France, where Colbert, the chief minister to Louis XIV, passed France's first Forestry Act (1669), and, at Nancy, established Europe's first Forestry School to train foresters to implement Evelyn's regenerative forest practices. Lacan does not seem to have incorporated an ecological dimension such as "habitat protection" in his work. At the Paradigm 8 (1725–1800) level, Count Buflon introduced the ecological framework of the "biome." At the Paradigm 9 (1800–1875) level, Kurt Mobius introduced the ecological framework of the "biocenose." At the Paradigm 10 (1875–1950) level, V. I. Vernadsky (1863–1945) and Teilhard de Chardin (1881–1955) introduced the ecological framework of the "biosphere" as grounded in the "geosphere" and hosting the "noosphere." At the Paradigm 11 (1950–2025) level, the global ecological, emancipatory work of James Lovelock and Lynn Margulis nomologically directs the further course of terra formation and ensures that Gaia, the human home base, is not to be allowed to run down by fossil fuel burning, industrial global warming, ozone layer breaching, and so on. An ecological awareness does not appear to have had any residual effect in Lacan's psychoanalytic efforts.

Spinoza (1633–1677) contributed the term "conatus" to psychology/philosophy, and Lewis's large *Latin Dictionary* (1996) gives "effort, exertion, struggle, endeavour" as denotative synonyms, followed by about half a column of classical Latin usages by Cicero, Plautus, Quintilian, and so on. Dr. J. D. Bierens de Haan has, furthermore, made a study (in Dutch) of Spinoza's uses of the word "conatus" in his "Ethics" (*Conatus in suo esse perseverandi*). In none of these references is "conatus" translated as "desire," which is the sense inherent in Lacan's usage. Lacan has thus, once again, gone beyond the demands of historicist precision to claim the "Alice in Wonderland" right to make a word mean whatever he wants it to mean, namely, the sexual connotation suitable to his Freudian version of psychoanalysis.

This matter is of some import, for Lacan, in his youth, was a devotee of Spinoza, but in the end, he did not adhere to Spinoza's intended emphasis. Most critical, I would say, is his failure to recognize that Spinoza treated the term "conatus" in an axiological manner, not just in an epistemological sense. In the same sense, it appears to me that Montaigne treated his reflective and skeptical essays as expressing value, not just meaning, and Descartes regarded the "clear and distinct ideas" which withstood the test of universal doubt as normative expressions of "truth." The "real," the "true," the "good," and later, J. J. Winckelmann's (1717–1768) "the beautiful" were all brought together in Immanuel Kant's (1724–1804) three "Critiques"—"The Critique of Pure Reason," (1781, on epistemology); "The Critique of Practical Reason" (1788, on ethics), and "The Critique of Judgment" (1790, on aesthetics). This meant that by the time that Paradigm 8 (1725–1800) science was being developed, the combination of productive industrial technology; the integration of physics, chemistry, and geology; the interaction in medical biology of the morphological, physio-logical, and neurological components of the body; the formulation of cog-nitional, cogitational, and conational psychology; the constitutionalization of religious liberty, political liberty, and economic liberty in jurisprudence; and the harmonization of the real, the good, the true, and the beautiful in philosophy had been incorporated into the sociological and personological matrix of capitalism's progressive side. Epistemology had been transformed into axiology, and the paragons of humanity began to be recognized in characterological or ideal-type terms; for example, Denis Diderot's (1713–1784) idealized biography of "Rameau's Nephew" (written 1761, pub-lished 1805).

Paradigm 8 (1725–1800) science then, via Kant's and Laplace's (1749–1827) "Nebular Hypothesis," added "cosmology" to the general systems roster of physics, chemistry, and geology. And Kasper Wolff (1734–1794), as a *Wunderkind* of 25, in 1759 published a book that laid the foundation for the addition of embryology to the morphological work of Vesalius, the physiological work of Harvey, and the neurological work of Glisson. He even illustrated the epigenesis of a developing animal/chick/human, and showed how undifferentiated tissue gave rise to specialized organs. Then, nothing much happened in this field until 1817, when Christian Pander (1794–1865) published a paper on the three layers that were formed and became specialized in the early development of the embryo. That paper was, in turn, read by Karl von Baer (1792–1876), who, in time, became the leading authority on the subject; and, in the 1830s published a two-volume textbook on embryology that became a standard text in teaching hospitals.

Psychology, too, underwent a vital transformation at the Paradigm 8 (1725–1800) level. This is not so evident when viewed piecemeal, but over the four paradigm shifts of the 1500–1800 centuries, a metapsychology was forged. In the Paradigm 5 (1500–1575) period, the more active beginnings of capitalism were registered in the psyche of some individuals in the form of a shift from behaviour to endeavor, and from awareness to conscious-ness. The phenomena of the world became more accurately and objectively delineated and recognized as distinct objects of experience/perception/cog-nition. At the Paradigm 6 (1575–1650) level, systematic scholars/method-ical doubters, like Descartes, identified the human subject as the one who was doing the knowing-act. Phenomenology was added to empiriology, reflective-consciousness to attentive consciousness, and cogitation to cog-nition. Then at the Paradigm 7 (1650–1725) level, the work of Spinoza and Leibniz kicked in, and conation, the ethical preservation of striving for a higher good, became recognized in the form of "the self-conscious self" that could know the brain world, the mind world, and the symbolized value world. Finally, at the Paradigm 8 (1725–1800) level, we can recognize that the "self," in creative, polymath, artistic, scientific, social, and civil involvements and personifications like Goethe and Mme. de Stael, became a *Mensch*—a whole person, a characterological human being, not just an epistemological knower. The Lunar Society of Birmingham tried to become such a coterie of whole persons. The radical utilitarians around William Godwin and Mary Wollstonecraft also tried to constitute such a sodality. At their ideal best, the men and women of the Enlightenment, the Illumination, and the *Erklärung* tried to create the bequest that we call "Modernity." They should not be shortchanged.

PART III: PARADIGM SHIFTS SINCE 1800—THE ECUMENIST PERSPECTIVE

And yet, there is a nagging flaw in all of the eight pre-1800 paradigmatic formulations. Ontologically, they all represent closed system models of reality. Epistemologically, they miss the point behind the line from the poet Rainer Maria Rilke (1875–1926), "In the depths all becomes law." They all miss the role of the "unconscious." And, axiologically, they are not ecumenical in their scope. Paradigms 9–12 (1800–2100) consequently each uncover an area of blindness glossed over in the first eight paradigm shifts. Once it is realized that the picture of reality that comes from a paradigmatic formulation depends on the theory of knowledge that renders it "sound/ elegant/charming/beautiful/sublime," we have to accept a principle of "uncertainty" as governing whatever we try to pass off as solid/certain/ material/concrete. This is a point fully recognized by Nobel Laureate Ilya Prigogine (1997) when he entitled his most recent book *The End of Certainty*. From Paradigm 9 (1800–1875) on, epistemology rests on heuristics, not axiomatics. And epistemology in turn is dependent on the value theory, the axiological justification, that selects it. Put crassly, in Paradigms 9–12 (1800–2100) scientists are on the side of the protesters at the Berlin Wall, the protesters at Greenham Common, the protesters at Clayoquot Forest, the protesters at Seattle, the protesters at the ring fence in Quebec City, and the protesters at every subsequent gathering of the capitalist elite rulers of the world's commanding heights. For, as the poet Charles Baudelaire (1821–1867) put it, *"il faut epater les bourgeois"* (down with the bourgeoisie).

Paradigm 9 (1800–1875) science, therefore, eschews the fact/value separation which graced the first eight paradigm shifts and takes the side of the insufficiently beloved. At this paradigmatic level, Karl Marx (1818–1883), Friedrich Engels (1820–1895), and Clara Zetkin (1857–1933), as socialists/communists; and Mikhail Bakunin (1814–1876), Peter Kropotkin (1842–1921), and Emma Goldman (1869–1940), as anarchists; are on the side of the angels, and the corporate capitalists are "the enemies of the people." Axiology is all about ending the exploitation of the workers of the world. It is all about restoring the "surplus value" which has been forcibly expropriated and "legitimately" appropriated from the working classes of the world. Paradigms 1–8 (1200–1800) scholars were *class-blind* in their provenience; Paradigms 9–12 (1800–2100) scientists would carry on the struggle to right this wrong.

The same point is made at the Paradigm 10 (1875–1950) level. V. I. Lenin (1870–1924) called this phase of capitalism "imperialism." At gatherings such as the Berlin Congress (1878), the colonialist carving up of the world was completed and the cartellization of the globe proceeded apace. Even when political independence was nominally granted, the forced expropriation and "legitimated" appropriation of "unequal exchange value" continued. Paradigms 1–8 (1200–1800) scholars were *race-blind* in their concerns. Paradigms 9–12 (1800–2100) scientists would carry on the struggle to right this wrong.

Once more, at the Paradigm 11 (1950–2025) level, an emancipatory movement has arisen to right a long-standing injustice—the patriarchal domestication and exploitation of women and those who, like them, are marginalized. Conscientized women, like Simone de Beauvoir (1908–), published profound analyses on the status of women (e.g., *The Second Sex*, 1954) and organized a feminist movement designed to get back the forcibly expropriated and "legitimately" appropriated "unpaid labor value" produced by women. Since Lenin's days, there has been a further development of capitalism, with the transnational conglomerate taking the place of the international cartel. I have called this phase of capitalism "agglomerism." There is still a glass ceiling; there is still inequity in the pay scales that women earn, and there is still gender blindness, even among many at the Paradigms 9 and 10 (1800–1950) levels of science. A photograph taken of the 34 heads of state attending the Quebec City FTAA gathering in April 2001 at the Summit of the Americas showed the world 33 men and one woman. It speaks eloquently to this subject.

Finally, Paradigm 12 (2025–2100) science can, at this time, only be a projection into the future. However, since we are dealing with injustices affecting more than half of humanity, it is possible to identify at least one more category of wrong to be righted. This is in the area of ecology. The continued concentration of global industrial and finance capitalists through mergers and consortia of power brokers may result in a further stage of capitalist development, in the direction which I have called "avaleurism." More and more of the resources of the world are being swallowed up by profiteers who are forcibly expropriating the people who now earn their livelihood from them, and more and more of humanity's productive usufruct is being "legitimately" appropriated through the legal subterfuge of patent rights legislation. The humanly occupied oikoumene of the Stoics, which James Lovelock and Lynn Margulis have personified as the goddess of the Earth, Gaia's realm, is being subjugated to serve the interests of freebooter free riders who have the money, capital, and manipulative media means to make the public believe that this is the best of all possible worlds. And who is there to say "nay" to them? At present only a thin number of environmentalists/Greens/ global ecologists are to be found who have been conscientized to the point where they are ready to commit themselves to the deconstruction of the prevailing social and cultural institutional arrangements, and reconstitute them on global ethical, aesthetic, and spiritual foundations.

Leon Trotsky was once asked, "Suppose you achieve communism, and there are no more hungry people, and there are no more poor people, and there are no more oppressed people, what will you struggle for then? His answer was: "The world is, however, also inhabited by hungry for love people, by poor in spirit people, by longing for friendship people, and by oppressed for hope people. When communism is achieved, I shall commit myself to the struggle for the second aesthetic Renaissance, for beautiful, comradely feeling is a rare treasure in this world."

A Paradigm 9 (1800–1875) epistemology and characterology would, in my terms, have to move from an individualistic capitalist foundation to a communal/ecumenical ecologist foundation. Darwin's and Wallace's co-evolutionary biological theories of natural selection also incorporated the human processes of social and sexual selection. Haeckel, in Germany, pointed up the ecological aspects of evolution, and Mobius, in Australia, placed Evelyn's habitats and Buffon's biomes into the context of the bio-cenose, as evolution's ontological framework. Marx and Engels then supplied the basis of the Paradigm 9 (1800–1875) epistemological advance by eliciting the criteria for the transformation of capitalism into socialism/communism. Fourier, Bakunin, and Kropotkin formulated an analogous communalism/anarchism emancipatory approach. Marx's notion of the "mode of production," defined ecologically as dealing with the social relations of reproduction and the socioeconomic relations of production is the basis for my neologism "commodiance." If we treat capitalism and socialism/communism/communalism/anarchism as modes of civilization, then the new kind of knowledge required is the how-to of changing one mode into another. An epistemology of "commodiance" then can teach us how to disestablish/deconstruct the institutions of capitalism and dialectically reestablish/reconstruct/reconstitute the mode of civilization that is emancipatory for workers in that it does not expropriate by force or appropriate legally the "surplus value" of their labor. The progressive technological, epistemological, and characterological elements of the capitalist mode of civilization are to be retained, while its exploitive, retrogressive elements are to be superceded. This is part of the sense of Hegel's notion of *Aufhebung* as a key factor within the process of dialectical transformational intelligence. In formal terms, the existing conditions form the thesis, the sublation of their restrictive elements form the negative dialectic, and their supercession by progressive elements form the positive dialectic, which, put into action as the antithesis to the present thesis, will result in the new modal synthesis—the radical, root-altering, emancipatory new mode of civilization.

The question at issue in this study is, however, whether preparation for, and membership in, Freud's IPA (International Psychoanalytical Association) French section is an emancipatory engagement. Similarly, was Lacan's teaching at the ENS (*École Normale supérieure*) and the EFP (*École freudienne de Paris*) productive of an emancipatory mentality? And again, was Lacan, done over by his son-in-law Jacques Alain-Miller's ECF (*École de la Cause freudienne*), engaged in an emancipatory project? Finally, we come to the generic question: How are the 20 or so Freudian-Lacanian French psychoanalytical offshoot groups to be evaluated? The answer, unfortunately, is beyond my ken. It would require an insider's familiarity to offer an evaluation and an assessment.

Meanwhile, capitalism in the period between 1800 and 1875 developed into a corporatist and colonialist mode of civilization and Marx and Bakunin formed the oppositional First (Communist) International. Effectiveness at the Paradigm 9 (1800–1875) level of application then required embeddedness in a characterology and, to point up the social dimension, a praxiology of involvement in the disestablishment of corporate-colonialist capitalism and its replacement by a more democratic and equitable mode of civilization.

Having established the emancipatory axiological parameters of Paradigms 9–12 (1800–2100) science, it is now possible to go back and fill in their epistemological and ontological innovatory components. At the Paradigm 9 (1800–1875) level, in addition to the technological aides serving as prosthetic sense and body extenders, the "unconscious" is probably the leading potential source of new knowledge. I doubt that any great discovery or invention is ever a one-person achievement, but, as an exercise in metonymy, I regard F.W.J. von Schelling (1775–1854) as the prime contributor to the "unconscious" at the Paradigm 9 (1800–1875) level, Sigmund Freud (1856–1940) at the Paradigm 10 (1875–1950) level, and Jacques Lacan (1901–1981) at the Paradigm 11(1950–2025) level. A few speculative projections at the Paradigm 12 (2025–2100) level will complete this section.

In contrast to the Paradigms 5–8 (1500–1800) metaconscious psychological development from empiriological, to phenomenological, to semiological to historiological consciousness, I see the Paradigms 9–12 (1800–2100) development as a continuous opening up of the field of paraconscious psychology. Schelling put the unconscious into scientific thought within a fifth-level general systems theory, namely, the addition of a naturalistic biology as influencing the previous cosmology/geology/chemistry-physics constellation. Then at the Paradigm 10 (1875–1950) level, Freud, through the influence of the evolutionary anthropology of Edward Tylor, added anthropology as a sixth-level general system constituent. I would credit Ilya Prigogine and David Bohm, with their pre/beyond/*ur* Big Bang speculations as formulating the need for another dimension at the Paradigm 11 (1950–2025) level, and for having consequently introduced a seventh-level general system theory. At the Paradigm 12 (2025–2100) level there will then probably be a neo-Buddhist teleonomic eightfold path addition. The sequence at the unconscious level is likely to be from a transculturation conscience psychology to an enconscientation conscience psychology to a conscientization conscience psychology to a reconstitution conscience psychology. Freud's second toponymic triad, his id/ego/superego sequence, is the source of the trajectory that I am formulating. He said, "Where id was, ego shall be." I am adding, "Where ego was, in Paradigms 3–8 (1500–1800) science, there superego/conscience shall be, in Paradigms 9–12 (1800–2100) science. This puts epistemology into its proper axiological foundations.

Finally, I come to the ontologocal characteristics of Paradigms 9–12 (1800–2100) science. At the Paradigm 9 (1800–1875) level the great innovation was the open system theory of evolution that Charles Darwin (1809–1882) and Alfred Wallace (1823–1913) independently hypothetcated. They recognized the course of natural selection, sexual selection, and social selection; the ongoing processes of adaptation, acclination, and assimilation have since been introduced as ancillary, causative, formative aspects of the way the world works. Marx linked biological evolution and historiological revolution together by positing changes in the mode of civilization as being due to the combination of changes in the pattern of social reproduction, on the basis of natural sexual and social selection and changes in the mode of production on the basis of cultural selection. I have designated the learning of how to reconstitute a mode of civilization as "commodiance."

The ontology of Paradigm 10 (1875–1950) science was modified within the context of revolutionary changes in cosmology (e.g., Einstein's (1879–1955) work on the Theory of Relativity and Quantum Theory and Max Planck's (1857–1947) work on Quantum Theory and Black Body Radiation). V. I. Vernadsky (1963–1945) then linked the astronomer's planetary geosphere with the biologist's biosphere and the anthropologist's noosphere into a general systems ecosphere, the conservation and regeneration of which would be empowering. I have designated the learning of how to regenerate an ecosphere as "compuissance."

The ontology of Paradigm 11 (1950–2025) science was due to further developments in cosmology, biology, and anthropology and their better teleonomic integration. The emergence of the environmentalist movement, and especially its eco-feminist segment, has helped to conscientize more and more people to commit themselves to enhancing and protecting the web of life, of which humanity is one link in the great chain of being. I have

Table 11.3
Paradigms of Science Criteria Before and After 1800

Paradigmatic Criteria 1500–1800 (P5–P8)	Paradigmatic Criteria 1800–2100 (P9–P12)
1. Closed system models	Open system models
2. Natural science models for social sciences	Social science models for natural sciences
3. Individual or unitary collective perspectives	Social or polyvalent collective perspectives
4. Characterological axiological values	Praxiological axiological values
5. Ideological universals and essences	Special interests vantage points identified
6. Enlightenment/Illumination/ Erklärung constructs	Deconstruction of Enlightenment/ Illumination/Erklärung constructs
7. Class interests biases ignored	Class interests biases challenged (P9— 1800)
8. Race interests biases ignored	Race interests biases challenged (P10— 1875)
9. Gender interests biases ignored	Gender interests biases challenged (P11—1950)
10. Gaian interests biases ignored	Gaian interests biases challenged (P12—2025)
11. Metapsychological foundations	Meta- and parapsychological foundations
12. Personal liberal/progressive objectives	Social radical/emancipatory engagements
13. Fact-theory-value separation	Fact-theory-value concomitance
14. Four or less levels of interaction	5 to 8 levels in General Systems Theory
15. Absolutes, certitudes, positivities claimed	Relativities, uncertainties, heuristics abound

designated the learning of how to secure the linked interdependence of geosphere, biosphere, and noosphere as "convivience."

Last, projecting the possible characterization of reality/ontology in the context of Paradigm 12 (2025–2100) science, I can foresee or, at least, hope that a critical number of people will have been transculturalized, enconscientized, and conscientized to such an extent that they would be able, in the course of their comprehension of what is desirable and possible, to forge a commodiant, compuissant, and convivient characterological, ecumenical, auto-emancipatory, sociocultural movement. What I envisage is a successor to the various international attempts at reconstituting our present exploitative mode of civilization. I commit myself to the actualization of the "First Oikoumenal."

Finally, in review I offer as my conclusion Table 11.3. Ideally, this table should be followed by applying these criteria to Freudian psychoanalysis, Lacanian psychoanalysis, and to post-Lacanian psychoanalysis. Regrettably, the scope allowed for this study precludes this kind of treatment. I have been told that, worldwide, there are now about 10,000 Lacanian and post-Lacanian psychoanalysts about, but that they are split among more than 20 factions. This bit of data alone, if reliable, would make categorization difficult. I shall, therefore, conclude by leaving it to the reader to determine which of the post-1800 criteria of science are to be credited to the extant corpus of the works of Jacques Lacan (1901–1981), since his register, barring undiscovered treasures, is now complete.

REFERENCES

Dolar, Mladen. 1998. Cogito As the Subject of the Unconscious. In *Cogito and the Unconscious*, ed. Slavoj Žižek (pp. 11–40). Durham, N.C.: Duke University Press.

Freire, Paulo. 1970. *Pedagogy of the Oppressed*, trans. Myra Bergman Ramo. New York: Herder and Herder.

Hay, Malcolm. 1960. *The Foot of Pride*. Boston: Beacon Press.

Kuhn, Thomas B. 1962. *The Structure of Scientific Revolutions*. Chicago: University of Chicago Press.

Lewis, Charlton P. 1996. *A Latin Dictionary*. Oxford: Clarendon Press.

Prigogine, Ilya. 1997. *The End of Certainty: Time, Chaos, and the New Laws of Nature* (In collaboration with Isabelle Stengers). New York: Free Press.

Žižek, Slavoj, ed. 1998. *Cogito and the Unconscious*. Durham, N.C.: Duke University Press.

Index

About the Contributors

Marshall Alcorn is Associate Professor of English, Humanities, and the Program in the Human Sciences at George Washington University. He teaches theories of subjectivity, literary theory, and writing. His most recent book is *Changing the Subject in English Class: Discourse and the Constructions of Desire*. His essays have appeared in *PMLA*, *College English*, *Rhetoric Review*, and *Conradiana*.

Douglas Sadao Aoki is an Associate Professor in the Department of Sociology at the University of Alberta. He has published in a range of social theory and educational journals, including *Theory, Culture & Society*, *Harvard Educational Review*, *Body & Society*, *Cinema Journal*, and *Journal of Historical Sociology*. His principal research interests are psychoanalysis of culture, the social theory of the body, and teaching theory.

Mark Bracher is Professor of English and the director of the Center for the Psychoanalysis of Culture and Society at Kent State University. He is founder and editor of the award-winning journal *JPCS: Journal for the Psychoanalysis of Culture & Society*; author of *Lacan, Discourse, and Social Change: A Psychoanalytic Cultural Criticism*; and coeditor of *Lacanian Theory of Discourse: Subject, Structure, Society*. His most recent book is *The Writing Cure: Psychoanalysis, Composition, and the Aims of Education*.

Derek Briton is an Assistant Professor at Athabasca University, Canada's Open University. His research focuses on the psychoanalysis of society and culture, particularly the implication of Lacanian psychoanalysis in pedagogy. He is the author of *The Modern Practice of Adult Education: A Postmodern Critique* and *Reading Lacan with Education: Applications, Implications, Possibilities*, as well as numerous book chapters and journal articles.

Kirstin Campbell is a Lecturer in the Department of Sociology at Goldsmiths College, University of London. She has published articles on psychoanalysis, social theory, and feminism, including most recently in *Angelaki* on Jacques Lacan's theory of language and in the *International Journal of Sexuality and Gender Studies* on Judith Butler's use of psychoanalysis. Her forthcoming book focuses on Lacanian and feminist theories of knowledge, and she is also working on a study of Foucault and Lacan's theories of subjectivity.

J. C. Couture works in professional development with the Alberta Teachers' Association. His dissertation, *The Gift of Failure: Teacher Commitment in a Postmodern Classroom*, examined the intensification of teachers' work from a Lacanian standpoint. He has published extensively on the impact of technology and high-stakes testing on school life. His most recent publication, "Teachers' Work in the Global Culture of Performance" (with Liying Cheng), appeared in the *Alberta Journal of Educational Research*.

Harry Garfinkle is Professor Emeritus, Department of Educational Foundations, University of Alberta. He received his Doctorate of Educational Philosophy in 1950 and was a Visiting Fellow in the Department of Anthropology at Cornell University. He "retired" in 1988 after 38 years of teaching. He has been very active in the Green Party of Alberta and continues to voraciously read and develop his vision of an "oicoumenal consciousness" and establishing its base.

Gustavo Guerra is Assistant Professor of Humanities at Olivet College. He has previously published in *Style*, *Papers on Language and Literature*, *New Vico Studies*, and *Journal for the Psychoanalysis of Culture and Society*. His current work centers on pragmatism, psychoanalysis, and cultural theory. He is also editing a book on the work of Slavoj Žižek.

jan jagodzinski is a Professor in the Department of Secondary Education at the University of Alberta in Edmonton, Alberta, Canada, where he teaches visual art education and curricular issues as they relate to postmodern concerns of gender politics, cultural studies, and the media (film and television). He is a founding member and editor of the *Journal of Social Theory in Art Education*, past president of *Media, Culture and Curriculum* (Special Interest Group of the American Educational Research Asssociation), and author of *The Anamorphic I/i*, as well as *Postmodern Dilemmas:*

Outrageous Essays in Art & Art Education and *Pun(k) Deconstruction: Experifigural Writings in Art & Art Education.*

John Lenzi is a doctoral student at Teachers College, Columbia University. He is also University Registrar. Independently trained as a psychoanalyst, his academic interests include the psychoanalysis of education, identity development, and the critical analysis of popular culture and technology. He is also the Director of the Relationships Lab and Vice-President of the Martin and Mirash Ivanaj Foundation, both located in New York City.

Robert Samuels is an Assistant Professor at the University of California, Santa Barbara. He is very active in the Society for the Psychoanalysis of Culture and Society. Many of his articles have appeared in *JPCS: Journal for the Psychoanalysis of Culture & Society.* His book credits include *Between Philosophy and Psychoanalysis: Lacan's Reconstruction of Freud* and *Hitchcock's Bi-Textuality: Lacan, Feminisms, and Queer Theory.* He is currently engaged in a project concerning the Holocaust.

Betty-Anne Schlender completed her doctoral work in the Department of Secondary Education at the University of Alberta. She is an English teacher with over 20 years of experience in the classroom who has presented papers at various conferences (AERA, CSSE, Westcast, APCS) in the areas of psychoanalysis and reading and psychoanalysis and teacher education.